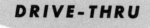

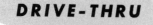

DRIVE-THRU

DREAMS

A Journey Through
the Heart of America's
Fast-Food Kingdom

ADAM
CHANDLER

FLATIRON
BOOKS
NEW YORK

www.flatironbooks.com

Designed by Jonathan Bennett

Library of Congress Cataloging-in-Publication Data

Names: Chandler, Adam, author.
Title: Drive-thru dreams : a journey through the heart of America's fast-food
    kingdom / Adam Chandler.
Description: First edition. | New York : Flatiron Books, [2019]
Identifiers: LCCN 2019002978 | ISBN 9781250090720 (hardcover) |
    ISBN 9781250090737 (ebook)
Subjects: LCSH: Fast food restaurants—United States. | United States—Social life
    and customs.
Classification: LCC TX945.3 .C45 2019
LC record available at https://lccn.loc.gov/2019002978

Our books may be purchased in bulk for promotional, educational, or business use. Please contact your local bookseller or the Macmillan Corporate and Premium Sales Department at 1-800-221-7945, extension 5442, or by email at MacmillanSpecialMarkets@macmillan.com.

First Edition: June 2019

10 9 8 7 6 5 4 3 2 1

For Mom, the first and best storyteller

CONTENTS

They could not tarry, and also,
they had not made provisions
for themselves.
—EXODUS 12:39

You paths worn in the
irregular hollows by the roadsides!
I believe you are latent with
unseen existences, you are
so dear to me.

—WALT WHITMAN

McDonald's is my favorite
restaurant.

—KANYE WEST

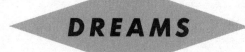

DRIVE-THRU

DREAMS

Nowhere special. I always wanted to go there.
—THE WACO KID

In the summer of 2012, bright yellow flyers were posted around Bethel, a remote town of six thousand unsuspecting souls on the bush of western Alaska, with some life-changing news: In a few short weeks, a brand-new Taco Bell would host its grand opening, just in time for the Fourth of July. In a historically dry town with one paved road, one measly Subway shop, and virtually no public transportation, the announcement was met with ecstasy and jubilation. Word whipped around town as quickly and enthusiastically as a subarctic breeze.

Tragically for the folks of Bethel, the news was fake. The signs directed anyone interested in working at the landmark Taco Bell to-be to call a number listed on the flyer. The number belonged to a local resident who was apparently embroiled in a seven-layer feud with a diabolical hoaxer. The besieged victim had to break the news dozens of times over: There would be no Taco Bell for the Fourth of July in Bethel, Alaska.

As swiftly as the joy had spread, dejection and low spirits followed. "That's right. Officially, Bethel is *not* getting a Taco

Bell," went one local radio broadcast after a flood of calls. "I repeat: Bethel is *not* getting a Taco Bell." The hoax meant that the nearest Cheesy Gordita Crunch would remain a four-hundred-mile trek by plane to Anchorage. "We got excited because we don't have any fast-food chains out here, and the idea of Taco Bell coming in?" the despondent director for the local Chamber of Commerce told the *Los Angeles Times*. "And they were going to be here for the Fourth of July?"

Bethel is impossibly isolated, only accessible by either air or sea. So, when news of the cruel hoax reached Taco Bell headquarters in Irvine, California, the company had no choice but to respond by dispatching a military helicopter to airlift a branded taco truck to Bethel right as the town's Independence Day celebrations were getting underway. "Operation Alaska" included the dramatic transport of 950 pounds of beef, 500 pounds of sour cream, 300 pounds of tomatoes, 300 pounds of lettuce, and 150 pounds of cheddar cheese, followed by the assembly and goodwill distribution of ten thousand Doritos Locos Tacos to an exhilarated crowd. "If we can feed people in Afghanistan and Iraq, we can feed people in Bethel," said Taco Bell's then-CEO, Greg Creed, adding to the semi-subtle militarism of the pre–Independence Day taco airlift.

Given Bethel's size and remoteness, the opening of a permanent Taco Bell outpost was never viable. But on a cloudy, fifty-five-degree summer afternoon in a tundra town in western Alaska, the company conspired to create a brief and surreal sense of belonging through an unlikely combination of spectacle and preprepared food.*

---

* The marketing genius of Operation Alaska actually has a similarly jingoistic historical precedent. Back at the 1968 Winter Olympics, McDonald's responded to convenient

Of course, the story of Operation Alaska would be adapted into a touching national Taco Bell commercial. The ad had it all. Disappointment and then euphoria, the minor fall and the major lift. It features Bethel's mayor along with some of the townsfolk glumly recounting their dashed hopes for tacos amid some choice B-roll of Alaskan wildflowers and a GONE MUSHING sign. Then, we see the redemptive image of a helicopter landing, its rotors whirring, with a taco truck swaying below like a serum for desolation. A happy, disbelieving crowd amasses and telegenic children blissfully chow into one of the brand's newest and most fabled products, the Doritos Locos Taco. And just like that, America's birthday had been saved.

There are no inherited rites in America, but if one were to come close, it would involve mainlining sodium beneath the comforting fluorescence of an anonymous fast-food dining room or beneath the dome light of a car. We do it because fast food is quick and cheap and portable. We do it because we have fond memories of wearing paper crowns at birthday parties, of Happy Meals and Frosties and road trips, and of bygone moments of innocence and intimacy with friends or parents or siblings. We do it because a slightly damp $12 turkey wrap is not a suitable salve for airport stress. We do it because the food is what we want—a little soft and gross and perfect, nestled in colorful wrapping and flimsy little boxes like presents from our first loves. And we do it because the places are familiar to us. It's under McDonald's Golden Arches, for example, a sign more recognizable worldwide than the Christian cross, that about

---

reports of homesickness among US athletes by airlifting a cache of hamburgers into Grenoble, France.

1 percent of the entire world's population breaks bread on any given day.

Simply put, nothing else does what fast food does as well as fast food does it. There is no other place, not libraries or gyms or the collective houses of worship, that 80 percent of Americans frequent at least monthly. And there are virtually no other enterprises that 96 percent of Americans annually embrace. Not even the internet comes close to attracting that much loyalty or participation. On a descending spectrum of American certainty, it goes something like death, premarital sex, fast food, and income taxes. The United States is and remains a fast-food nation.

From its creation to its dominance, fast food is who and where we've been. You can trace most of twentieth-century America through fast food. It cannot be isolated from the entrepreneurial mania of the 1920s Machine Age, the trauma of the Great Depression, the hubris and swagger of the postwar economic boom, the building of the interstate highway system, and the national preoccupations with time and work and individual destiny. The evolution of fast food tracks with the American faith in processed food as well as its disillusion. That evolution also showcases the powerful effect of women entering the labor force. The contemporary story of the country's immigrant strivings, of its loneliness and failures, of its sluggish embrace of different cultures, of its international charisma, and of its regional identities can be distilled through fast food. The landscapes of the South would be incomplete without Chick-fil-A, Cook Out, and Bojangles'. In-N-Out and Del Taco are as Californian as Pollo Tropical is Floridian as Sonic is heartland as Dairy Queen is small-town. The Midwest isn't the Midwest without Culver's, Steak 'n Shake, and Maid-Rite, and the Lone Star State would certainly be dimmer and duller without Whataburger. And if there's any redemption to be found on the New Jersey Turnpike, it's at a Roy Rogers.

The United States is singularly geared to love fast food and not just because the agricultural system is rigged to support it. Far more than anywhere else in the world, Americans drive cars with automatic transmissions on some of the straightest highways ever built. Somewhere, someone is on one of those roads right now. The sun might be out, Steely Dan might be on the radio, and the driver almost certainly has no idea that the very last fries just out of reach at the bottom of a paper bag are linked to Thomas Jefferson, the self-styled gastronome and principal author of the independence decree who first introduced the United States to fried potatoes after serving as the minister to France. "Potatoes deep-fried while raw, in small cuttings, served in the French manner," he requested of White House chef Honoré Julien before a dinner party. "This is the day of the expanding man," the song might go. "That shape is my shade."

In the midst of the ongoing national cleaving over American dining habits, the fast-food industry lives and draws power from its ubiquity and mass appeal. Critics frequently accuse McDonald's and its ilk of being monoliths that throw around their influential purchasing and marketing power to public harm. And while these gripes certainly have their merits, the secret to fast food's success has been its adaptability and its careful study and reflection of American desires and the national order—literal, figurative, and culinary. These oddities and contradictions are a lot of what this book is about.

In the summer of 2015, I first set out to investigate how the industry intersects with American life in a way that makes it such a beloved and resilient institution. I started by driving straight up the gut of the country from the Gulf of Mexico to the Great Lakes, America's two unheralded coasts. As a result this book is a study of fast-food history, not just chronologically, but ethnographically as well. We already know why fast food is bad. But the conditions that made fast food possible are just as important as understanding why its popularity endures, particularly in this atmosphere of discord and high friction.

At its most essential, food is what unites us. The cultural canvas may keep shrinking, but it's hard to imagine Thanksgiving without turkey or the Super Bowl without buffalo wings. And, damn, it feels good to light off fireworks on the Fourth of July and demolish a Big Mac every once in a while.

THE NATIONAL MEAL

Proud Wichita! vain Wichita / cast the first stone!
—ALLEN GINSBERG

One day not long ago, a man named Pete Saari picked up his phone and cold-dialed 1-800-THE-CRAVE, the toll-free number for White Castle's headquarters in Columbus, Ohio. Saari, the CEO of a 3-D printing company based in Eden Prairie, Minnesota, had been commissioned to create a personalized urn to host the eternal remains of Mel Burrows, a fifty-seven-year-old mother and motorcycle enthusiast who had lived in New Jersey. The concept for the urn included a replica of a White Castle slider—the fast-food chain's iconic and diminutive onion and bepickled hamburger. The slider would be nestled inside a rendering of a branded White Castle paper holster that would be set atop a model of a typical White Castle store, perching above the regal-looking decorative crenellated walls. To head off any potential legal catastrophes, Saari needed to get some permissions from White Castle.

The request eventually channeled its way up from the hotline to Jamie Richardson, the company's vice president, whose two decades at White Castle have not diminished his boyish, irrepressible devotion to the code of "the crave." "Literally, you hear some of these things and you can't dream it up," Richardson explained of Saari's proposal. "The first thought is, 'Is that real?'"

It turned out to be very real indeed. Richardson, after calling Saari back, ran the request over to White Castle's general counsel, who approved it right away. "We did not go through three weeks of wringing our hands and asking, 'Oh, does that send the right message? Will people think we're saying that fast food causes early demise? Think of the jokes,'" Richardson said. "No, we said, 'This is about celebrating someone's life.'"

It seems fair to say that, given the choice, many people would rather go directly to hell for eternity than spend their corporeal afterlife in the confines of a White Castle–themed urn. However, when Mel Burrows was diagnosed with her terminal illness, the burger joint became an unexpected fixture in her life. Following Mel's treatments, her sister Stacey would sneak her out of the hospital and, in the perfect act of sororal mischief, the two would steal away to the nearby White Castle. This intimate convention would include conversation and the ceremonial eating of sliders—objects that are themselves physically designed to be tiny reprieves from the world. The motto of their outings until Mel's death became "Let's treat ourselves," which would eventually be featured in large script on the memorial urn produced by Saari. "It might seem a bit silly to some people, but White Castle provided a sense of normalcy during Mel's treatments," her sister explained. "And that was a true gift."

Millions of people eat hamburgers each day, most of the

time for much less significant reasons than did Mel and Stacey, but the experiences of these millions are all improbably linked to White Castle and a fry cook named Walt Anderson. And the story of fast food itself also begins with White Castle, in Wichita, Kansas.

Wichita is an unsung, uniquely American city that should hold Mount Rushmore–esque significance in the national imagination. It's the city that gave the world Cessna and Boeing, the Koch brothers, Hattie McDaniel, James Reeb, and Barack Obama's mother, Ann Dunham. Hank Ketcham, the creator of *Dennis the Menace*, lived his life on the West Coast but set his comic strip about anodyne mischief in Wichita because it embodies a wholesome American idyll, the place for Jack White to disappear, one of the few US cities where the water isn't fluoridated and where it's illegal to serve cherry pie à la mode on a Sunday.

But none of that is why Wichita truly deserves prime billing in our collective whimsy. Wichita effectively endowed the United States with its secular wafer—the hamburger. Americans might think of the burger as a national birthright, but a century ago, the only thing less popular than ground beef in the United States was the Irish. In 1906, Upton Sinclair published *The Jungle*, a novel about the trials of an immigrant worker, partially set in the waste-filled animal stockyards of Chicago. That might not sound like a page-turner, but as your high school English teacher probably told you, the book was a crucial catalyst for the reforms and regulations of the Progressive Era. Sinclair's lurid and all-but-unprintable descriptions of factories with spoiling meat pushed the public to think about food safety and meat and pressured the government to act.* And, as a result, US consumers would be wary of ground beef for many years to come with authorities on food and dining like Duncan Hines warning their readers about the perils of hamburgers in particular well into the 1930s.†

Against this queasy backdrop, in 1916, Walt Anderson first performed the magical, calculated act of crafting tiny ground beef patties and then smashing them flat onto a steaming, onion-laced griddle. Anderson had found meatballs not only stuck to the griddle, but took too long to make; his variation was small, juicy, greasy, quickly made to order, thoroughly cooked through, and came encased in specialty buns instead of bread. They were eventually called sliders; they were delicious, and Anderson sold them cheaply for a nickel a pop at his three-stool hamburger stand in Wichita, buying his first day's provisions of beef and bread on credit and walking away with $3.75 in profits.

What helped Anderson quickly make converts wasn't just his innovative food. To quell the stubborn meta-beefs of the time and to reassure customers that the meat was fresh, Anderson made a public display of grinding fresh meat and then griddling it in a clean cooking space, all in full view of everyone. "Buy 'em by the sack," his slogan implored. Like Thomas Edison crooning "Mary Had a Little Lamb" into his phonograph forty years earlier, Anderson's undersized invention

---

* Sadly for Sinclair, he had wanted the depictions of atrocious working conditions to improve the lives of the working poor and serve as a boon to socialism, but you can't win 'em all. "I aimed at the public's heart, and by accident I hit it in the stomach," Sinclair famously said about his book.
† Ironically enough, the hamburger truly entered the culinary consciousness in the 1920s, around the same time as the hot dog, which, with so many European relatives, encountered fewer impediments to mainstream approval.

would lay the foundation for an entire industry and create the standard for a product that would become synonymous world-wide with the United States.

Though many a grillman from Texas to Wisconsin to Connecticut has passionately claimed authorship of the invention, in many ways Wichita is the most spiritually sound point of origin for the American hamburger and its world-conquering legacy. In the years following the Civil War, the surrounding Great Plains spawned countless national mythologies of noble, rough-hewn cowboys and happy yeomen settling the wild frontier in the name of American progress, Manifest Destiny, intermittent ethnic cleansing, and rugged self-reliance. As we know from westerns, the enduring images of this era are incomplete without their associations to beef; after all, the men heroically gunning up the trails weren't just pioneers, but often mercenaries driving cattle from Texas ranches to Kansas cow towns. From there, the cattle would be shipped north to the very Chicago stockyards that *The Jungle* later decried and then sent east in newly invented refrigerated railroad cars to cheaply feed the growing country as it undertook the Industrial Revolution. Both the meat and the folk tales of heroic exploits undertaken in the Great American Desert were devoured with equal enthusiasm wherever they went.

Following the end of World War I though, new tech-centric fascinations emerged. Industrialization and urbanization reinforced each other across the United States as electricity grew more commonplace, buildings grew taller, and lighting incandesced with greater sophistication. Higher-paying manufacturing jobs brought masses into the cities, which themselves were full of new excitement—burgeoning culture and cheap entertainment, lunchrooms and diners. While out on the farms, mules and horses were being replaced by tractors and steam engines, the smirking sentiments of the famous 1919 vaudeville jam "How Ya Gonna Keep 'Em Down on the Farm (After They've Seen Paree?)" would be confirmed by the 1920 US Census, which showed more Americans living in urban areas than rural ones for the first time ever.

The city of Wichita in particular grew, and Anderson's nickel sliders drew a working-class clientele, often from nearby factories, and his expansion to two more stands would dovetail with a Kansas oil boom that swelled the city's population. Anderson's culinary innovation might have remained a Wichita-specific specialty had he not crossed paths while opening his fourth stand with a real-estate broker named Billy Ingram in 1921. Ingram, a natural-born marketeer in the hyperbolic booster mold of the 1920s, immediately fell in love with Anderson's operation. Ingram became Anderson's partner, personally guaranteeing the loan on the new stand. To combat the persisting stigmas associated with ground beef and gain ground on Wichita's sudden herd of multiplying burger stands, Ingram suggested that the name of the next outpost convey both stateliness and cleanliness: White Castle. (Of course, it helped that the building they found already looked like a small castle.)

In his book *Orange Roofs, Golden Arches*, Philip Langdon credits White Castle with being the first chain to standardize the look and feel of its stores as they opened and blossomed within Kansas and without. White Castles spread to Omaha, Kansas City, St. Louis, and, eventually, Detroit, Chicago, Newark, and New York City. In each store, the walls and interiors were painted and maintained a spotless, sparkling white, and the counters were outfitted in shiny Allegheny metal, later known as stainless steel. A White Castle brochure from 1932 conveys how this credo extended to the customer experience:

> When you sit in a White Castle, remember that you are one of several thousands; you are sitting on the same kind of stool; you are being served on the same kind of counter; the coffee you drink is made in accordance with a certain formula; the hamburger you eat is prepared in exactly the same way over a gas flame of the same intensity; the cups you drink from are identical with thousands of cups that thousands of other people are using at the same moment; the same standard of cleanliness protects your food. . . . Even the men who serve you are guided by standards of precision which have been thought out from beginning to end. They dress alike; they are motivated by the same principles of courtesy.

Today, this patriarchal call for conformity would read like Soviet agitprop or a passage from a dystopian novel. But for consumers that had been scarred by *The Jungle*'s depictions of boil-covered steers and for a country with no uniform health code, the consistency and sameness offered by White Castle signaled virtue and trustworthiness. In the ways that seasonal fare and organic provenance have become largely cosmetic lures nearly a hundred years later, the blueprint of the fast-food industry was set on the premise of predictability and technical precision. And so, decades before McDonald's and the hulking burger chains would arrive on the scene, White Castle offered comfort and reassurance by committing itself to the then-revolutionary task of delivering customers the exact same experience every single time. This extended from the shape and layout of stores across the Plains, the Midwest, and the Northeast down to the size and preparation of the sliders, which were delivered by servers in the same sharp, spotless white uniforms and who conformed to the standards of a rigorous twenty-four-point checklist that included exhortations like "correct bad breath," "have clean shave," and "be prepared to speak pleasantly."

White Castle's neurotic quest to provide identical experiences wasn't just a strategic gambit. It embodied the zeitgeist of the 1920s Machine Age, in which many cherished ideals centered around business and the novelties of technology and efficiency. Even more celebrated than his bigotry was Henry Ford's assembly line, which whet the national appetite for mass-produced products in a decade remembered well for its conspicuous consumption. A Model T cost a prohibitive $825 in 1909. By 1921, aided by the speedier, progressive assembly process, the price had dropped to a more approachable-to-the-masses $310. The country was high on haste, illegal whiskey, efficiency, and the cost-effectiveness of regimented sameness.

White Castle nickel sliders were both *of the people* and innovative, too. Early on, Walt Anderson discovered that shaping his burger patties in tiny squares and mashing them flat with a spatula would allow them to cook quicker and more evenly while locking in flavor. The process also made effective use of every possible inch of the griddle. No less groundbreaking was the choice of a bun, which, unlike bread, absorbed the juiciness of the beef and allowed the center to hold. Like the high axles on a lightweight Tin Lizzie, the specialty bun made the burger portable and sturdy at the very moment the country began to move around for leisure. Between 1915 and 1920, as the hamburger was just starting its journey into the mainstream, the number of cars on American roads jumped from 2.5 million to 9 million. By 1931, 23 million cars would be on the roads. As the country further oriented itself around its cars, a roadside culinary movement fashioned on speed coalesced along with it, but more on that later.

In countless ways, White Castle lowered the drawbridge for American fast food. It had an operations playbook, an assembly-line system, and quickly inspired a shameless slew of regal- and sterile-sounding imitators across the United States—Royal Castle, Blue Castle, Silver Castle, Krystal (as in clear), White Clock, White Tower, White Mana, White Cabin, White Turret, White Fortress, White Rose, White Diamond, and so on and so forth. Led by Ingram, who later bought out Anderson, White Castle would experiment with newspaper coupons and bring facets of its production—from food to construction materials to paper goods—in-house to maintain control and reduce costs. Eventually, in the most basic pursuit of uniformity, the burgers would shift from fresh beef to frozen pucks. But by then, the country would already be hooked.

Ingram also shrewdly understood that to flourish meant luring middle-class families into the ranks of the White Castle faithful, particularly after the Great Depression diminished his working-class clientele. In 1932, around the time Aunt Sammy, the USDA-devised matronly better half of Uncle Sam, was dishing out questionable nutritional advice and recipes to homemakers on the radio five days a week on hundreds of stations across the country, Ingram hired a dynamic saleswoman named Ella Louise Agniel to play "Julia Joyce," a corporate hostess who would preach the gospel of White Castle to the same demographic.

In his 1997 book, *Selling 'Em by the Sack*, David Gerard Hogan details how Joyce, forged partially in the image of General Mills' own fictitious shill, Betty Crocker, would appear at women's groups around the country as a White Castle emissary armed with bags of sliders along with talking points about the nutritional merits of hamburgers and the time and effort they'd save in the kitchen. Inevitably, Joyce would drag her guests to drop in on a nearby White Castle restaurant, where they would marvel at its clean, orderly, and high-tech operation. As Agniel's efforts proved out, she quickly rose to become a trusted voice and high-level figure in the White Castle hierarchy. "By the end of the decade it was not unusual to see businessmen and housewives standing in line next to construction workers, policemen, and taxi drivers," notes Hogan. And so, White Castle managed to sell nearly twice as many burgers in 1937 as it did in 1930.

But as dazzling as all these feats were, White Castle's greatest contribution remains the rise and redemption of the hamburger, which forever changed the country and the world. Prior to World War I, with its bloodthirsty nationalist chanteys, the United States was a physically and spiritually disconnected land. Little, if anything, would qualify as quintessentially *American* in a country where different languages, cuisines, and forms of entertainment held the knit of ethnic enclaves and immigrant communities. Without a drop of legal booze, the gaze was nationalized during the Roaring Twenties and made this tribalism seem provincial. Americans started to see the same films and tuned in to the same radio shows, drove their Model Ts, and lived in cities as a majority for the first time ever. Soon they wanted the same gyrating washing machines and the same electric refrigerators and Radiolas from the same national department stores. They wanted to load their pantries with national brands like Wonder Bread, Cream of Wheat, and Minute tapioca from the very same grocery aisles. And they wanted the hamburger, a thoroughly modern sandwich that came enciphered with humankind's evolutionary longing for fire-cooked meat.

In this climate, passing fashions like cloche hats and flagpole sitting briefly took hold, while other fancies like premarital sex and mah-jongg somehow became more widespread and permanent fixtures in American society. Where a cartoon character such as Betty Boop (1930) reflected the flapperism of the era, J. Wellington Wimpy (1929),* Popeye's financially reckless and burger-obsessed hanger-on, not only embodied the American id, but also offered proof of the hamburger's arrival as the national food—an arrival meticulously and masterfully orchestrated by White Castle and Billy Ingram.

The White Castle slider was, by no means, the first hamburger to appear on a menu or a griddle. Nevertheless, before Anderson and Ingram, the hamburger in all of its scattered iterations was just a weird, peonic meat sando, without ideal, definition, or exemplar, living in a dusty and disconnected network of fiefdoms. And you can't have a kingdom without a castle.

Despite his successes, Billy Ingram had a conservative approach to growth, which meant that White Castle remained (and remains) a privately held, family-owned, slider-sized enterprise. The company would ultimately be overshadowed by bigger, fast-franchising chains. Today, White Castle still operates

---

* The character even served as the namesake of a hamburger chain in the UK.

in many of the same neighborhoods it did in the 1920s, where, even in the land of oversize burgers, the slider retains its cult status.

The company also tells the story of the American devotion to the sacrament of fast food better than even Billy Ingram ever could. Today, the company celebrates its most loyal fans by enshrining them in the Cravers' Hall of Fame. There's the couple from Montana that drove all the way to a White Castle in Chicago for Valentine's Day, then turned around to get home for work the next day. The woman with a castle-themed ankle tattoo in Mt. Pulaski, Illinois, who decorates her home with old store fixtures. The sister of the navy mechanic who smuggled twenty-five frozen sliders in a cooler from Detroit, Michigan, to Holy Loch, Scotland, so that they might be shared among the homesick leathernecks aboard the USS *Simon Lake*. The fastidious Bronx accountant who took a $300 cab ride and a 6:00 A.M. train after a snowstorm imperiled his weekly White Castle ritual of six cheeseburgers and a sack of onion rings. The family of three in Dearborn, Michigan, who, after once forgetting to buy cookies for Santa Claus in time, have since made a tradition of leaving White Castle sliders out on Christmas Eve.

"We get to be a part of people's lives in ways that are really sometimes seemingly small, but in other ways are much, much bigger than the physical nourishment we provide with the food we sell," Richardson told me. "It's about being part of people's good memories and being an oasis and a place where they can just have that moment of respite."

The already unusual tale of Mel Burrows's White Castle urn doesn't end with a company suit granting permission for a design. From there, it morphs into a story of good business begetting good citizenship. According to White Castle executive Jamie Richardson, Pete Saari was so moved by the two sisters' story that he decided to create the urn for free. White Castle would make a $10,000 donation in Burrows's name to the American Cancer Society and induct the sisters into the company's Hall of Fame.

For plenty of good reasons some have eschewed the national model that White Castle created and instead sought out culinary experiences that seem personalized and native to their local enclaves. But with all due respect to tin ceilings, Edison bulbs, and boxed wheatgrass, customs can still be meaningful and intimate even in generic plastic booths beneath generic fiberglass ceiling panels. Fast food offers the access and reliability of both the personal and the banal. "A ritual creates a freedom from anxiety that isn't rote," Richardson said. "It's standardization, but within that standardization there's still an experience that's a little bit unique."

2 THE COLONEL

I fed truck drivers and millionaires all at the same table. . . .
I don't care if I had truck drivers sitting down there and here
come a doctor. I didn't know who he was. I thought everybody
could eat at the same table. I didn't know anything,
only to be friendly. So that was my first restaurant.
—HARLAND SANDERS

It's difficult to imagine a time when the concept of the American Dream didn't exist. While big thinkers such as Thomas Jefferson, Alexis de Tocqueville, Emma Lazarus, Frederick Jackson Turner, Mary Wollstonecraft, and Karl Marx offered different depictions of the idea in one form or another, not until 1931 was the term coined and popularized by historian James Truslow Adams in his book *The Epic of America.** As Adams defined it, the dream centers on what he believed to be a strictly American possibility:

---

* Originally, Adams wanted the book to be titled *The American Dream*, but his editor, thinking it would never sell, overruled him.

The American Dream is that dream of a land in which life should be better and richer and fuller for everyone, with opportunity for each according to ability or achievement. It is a difficult dream for the European upper classes to interpret adequately, and too many of us ourselves have grown weary and mistrustful of it. It is not a dream of motor cars and high wages merely, but a dream of social order in which each man and each woman shall be able to attain to the fullest stature of which they are innately capable, and be recognized by others for what they are, regardless of the fortuitous circumstances of birth or position.

It's easy to trip over the irony that Adams, a wealthy former investment banker living abroad in London, felt so passionately about the promise of America, just as the bite of the Great Depression began to leave the worst of its mark.* But once released into the world, the American Dream became a new romantic and politically charged shorthand for success, prosperity, and upward mobility, dispatched like a bumper sticker every election season as a byword for a land of freedom, heroes, bootstraps, destiny, and opportunity.

Just as Adams's *The Epic of America* was receiving an enthusiastic reception on both sides of the Atlantic, a forty-year-old man named Harland Sanders opened up a new roadside gas station on a rough stretch of Appalachian highway. Sanders was an ill-tempered middle school dropout with a huckster's instincts and showman's virtuosity. But if one per-

---

* To be fair, *The Epic of America* also rails against the idea that bigger means better, decries how financial success became a moral virtue in the United States, and chides Americans for failing to reckon with social dangers such as income inequality.

son ever fully proved Adams's interpretation of the American Dream to be possible, it was Sanders, whose dogged, frustrating trajectory toward "fullest stature" and worldwide fame started at that humble service station in southeastern Kentucky, far from the whirring velocities of the car and hamburger assembly lines.

What's most affecting about the story of Harland Sanders, later known by much of the world as the Colonel, is how unlikely it all was. How Sanders would come to embody the troublesome and elusive concept of the American Dream involves decades of endless scrapping, bad breaks, grueling work, and self-promotion. Because Sanders's story is so mythical and his image so corporatized, it's easy to forget he was even a real person. But not only does his biography trace America's adolescence and fulfill the most classic interpretation of the American Dream, it's also a useful prism through which the history of fast food can be understood.

The four-room shack where Sanders spent his early years sat off a country road three miles east of nowhere Indiana that, in 1890, could have passed for 1790 frontier wilderness. One day when Sanders was still very young, his father, Wilbert, a twenty-nine-year-old butcher with a broken back, came home from work sick with a fever and died hours later. Harland's mother struggled to find work and eventually took a job peeling tomatoes at a canning factory in town, leaving five-year-old Harland to look after his two younger siblings and do the family cooking for days at a time. Little did he know, these privation-born domestic chores would set the path to his becoming the Colonel. Later, in interviews and television ads, Sanders would hark back to the pride he felt in baking a loaf of bread as a seven-year-old child in his kitchen. "So I set my yeast, made the sponge, made the dough, baked off the bread. When I was done I had the prettiest loaf of light bread you ever saw."

From there, the Sanders myth goes—preteen dropout, hired out at ten for farm labor by his mother, stepson to a hostile stepfather, and thirteen-year-old runaway. When Sanders was about sixteen and working as a streetcar conductor in New Albany, Indiana, he lied about his age to join the army ahead of America's second occupation of Cuba. Soon, he was jammed on a ship of mules, retching his meals overboard into the Atlantic. "Being that close to that many mules was bad enough," he later wrote in his 1974 autobiography, "but I had never been near no water bigger than the old swimming hole."

Once Sanders got to Cuba, his commanding officer apparently figured out that Sanders was way too young and sent him back stateside. Sanders returned by way of New Orleans, where his dizzying American odyssey resumed. He took a boat up the Mississippi and rode the rails around the South. Still in his teens, he became a railroader in the golden age of the industry, just before World War I and ahead of the rise of automobiles and airplanes, when railroad engineers were the heroes of the era. Back then, trains accounted for 98 percent of intercity travel in the United States and more than 75 percent of its freight traffic. Working the trains would also account for a 50 percent increase in the vocabulary of young, intemperate Sanders, whose coworkers taught him to cuss with the heat and steam-laced ferocity of the Cannonball Express.

In addition to this newfound eloquence, Sanders displayed flashes of what would make him a great showman in his later years. He was a deft public speaker, exceedingly self-assured, and when he wasn't in a trademark swearing fury, Sanders proved to be charismatic and proficient in the dark art of schmoozing. He successfully argued to save the job of one of his fellow railroad workers, and following his dismissal from the Illinois Central Railroad—apparently, for getting in a fist-fight with an engineer—Sanders decided to study law by correspondence. He took on cases with his trademark force of will and fancied himself the second coming of Clarence Darrow. "He was particularly proud of the time he was able to negotiate better settlements for the mostly black victims of a train wreck, and of his efforts to stop courts from pressuring defendants into settlements," the writer Alan Bellows noted of Sanders's lawyering years. Sanders seemed poised to do well with a career in law; that is, until he got into a courtroom fist-fight with a client over unpaid fees. From there, he went on to build and sell a successful ferryboat operation, went belly-up in a failed lighting-systems venture, and sold insurance, at which he triumphed until fired, as he often was, for his stubbornness, fondness for fisticuffs, or insubordination.

He next served as a secretary for a local Chamber of Commerce before becoming a tire salesman for Michelin just as the Model T made cars fashionable. To help nail his quota, Sanders would make a promotional, sales-generating spectacle of himself, walking around county fairs in Michelin's famous puffy "bib" suits. To demonstrate the brand's superior strength, Sanders would deputize local boys to pump tires alongside competing brands until the latter ones exploded, to the delight of the gathered crowds. By one account, Sanders lost his Michelin job after a bridge collapsed while he was using his Packard to tow the family Model T across it, leaving him badly bloodied and without the transportation that the job required. But by the following week, he had stitched his own scalp back on and hitched a fortuitous ride with an oil executive. Sanders talked his host into letting him manage a gas station and did well by it until a drought and then the Great Depression forced it to close. By then, his reputation as a salesman had gotten around. Soon enough, Sanders got another chance, at that fabled station in Corbin, Kentucky, where he would slowly carve out the makings of a hospitality empire.

Like traffic circles and the rules of soccer, the governing dynamics of the American Dream have always been vague, frustrating, and subjective. By the terms set by James Truslow Adams, Sanders had already achieved the dream simply by the dint of his ambition and his legendary dissatisfaction with the status quo. In *The Epic of America* Adams holds up Kentucky-born Abraham Lincoln as a virtuous exemplar of American success, but not for grandiose achievements like the Emancipation Proclamation or losing his Senate election to Stephen Douglas despite winning the popular vote. "Lincoln was not great because he was born in a log cabin," Adams wrote, "but because he got out of it—that is, because he rose above poverty, ignorance, lack of ambition, shiftlessness of character, contentment with mean things and low aims which kept so many thousands in the huts where they were born."

Since the dawn of the republic, a person's ability to make it in America has often been depicted in the most cold-blooded terms, where success is a simple matter of character and drive rather than luck or fate or inborn social advantage. Adams's assessment isn't so different from a sentiment later expressed in *Hillbilly Elegy*, the influential 2016 memoir by J. D. Vance, about escaping Appalachian poverty. In it, Vance writes, "What separates the successful from the unsuccessful are the expectations that they had for their own lives." In spite of Harland

Sanders's expectations for himself (and the many advantages he held by default), he had no wealth and little stability to show for the first forty grueling years of his life. Like Lincoln, Sanders had escaped the humble shack where he had been born only to end up just over a hundred miles east of Lincoln's log cabin, at the helm of a failing gas station in a troubled corner of Appalachia.

Two of the more spectacular nicknames for Sanders's section of Corbin, Kentucky, were Hell's Half-Acre and the Asshole of Creation. Both names were owed to the ambient poverty as well as its setting near a key intersection between two highways, a corridor where booze runners flaunted Prohibition and deadly violence happened daily. "Bootleggin's, fights, and shootin's was as regular as a rooster's crowing in the mornin'," Sanders once remarked about his surroundings. According to his biographer John Ed Pearce, Sanders kept a pistol under the cash register for safety and a shotgun in the bedroom, which he used to ward off men from killing each other outside his station. To advertise his business, Sanders shrewdly sought out the sides of barns because, he said, "good old boys riding around like to shoot up signboards, but they thought if there might be a cow or mule on the other side of the sign, they wouldn't blast away like they liked to."*

These *complications* notwithstanding, Sanders's service station flourished as travel by car surged in popularity in the

---

* Ironically, Sanders's penchant for strategic advertising drew him into a blood feud with Matt Stewart, an equally hot-tempered rival gas station owner. One day in May of 1931, Sanders got word that Stewart was defacing a sign that had been diverting traffic from his service station to Sanders's. When Sanders set out to confront him with two visiting Shell executives and caught him in the act, Stewart unloaded his pistol on them, killing one of them before Sanders subdued him with a shot to the hip. (Stewart later died in jail under suspicious circumstances.)

1930s. His business became a well-regarded and convenient pit stop for motorists exploring their way down the fledging Dixie Highway, which connected the Midwest to Florida. They would gas up, and Sanders would make a grand production of wiping their windshields and offering free air to build a loyal clientele. Ever the angler, Sanders realized he could further outgun his rivals if he started offering food to this emerging breed of road dogs. "I got to thinking," he later recounted. "One thing I could always do was cook." And so, Sanders started to whip up the staples of his larder on his old Vulcan range—steak, okra, biscuits, chess pie, and Kentucky mock oysters. Often, he would prepare meals for his family, and they would only gather at the table to dine after hungry travelers hadn't appeared to eat dinner first. Increasingly, travelers would linger to grab a bite of country ham or even the homemade fried chicken that their opportunistic host had begun offering.

More and more, these hungry travelers appeared as they drove in on newly built roads, spent nights in newly built motels, and experienced the country in unprecedented ways. In her book *Dixie Highway*, Tammy Ingram outlines how, despite an endless jam of contentious and competing social and political forces, America's first "fully-fledged interstate highway system" helped to efface regional isolation in the United States. Much in the way that technologies such as radio and the rise of the hamburger had nationalized the cultural gaze, the Dixie Highway physically served disparate groups of "tourists, businessmen, farmers, and everyday travelers alike." On the Dixie route through Corbin, Sanders nourished unlikely gatherings of strangers with his vernacular cuisine on a daily basis.

Sanders parlayed his successful reputation as a cook and turned one spare table in a gas station storeroom into an entire café in 1937. But the food at the Sanders Café wasn't the only draw. In his book *Open Road*, Phil Patton details how Sanders, true to form, emphasized the benefit of offering both dinner and a show:

> He told stories about the local moonshiners and tall tales of his days working on the railroad and getting in fights with his bosses.
>
> When the audience was deemed appropriate, he poured over these stories, like gravy over his ham or chicken, a profanity whose color and inventiveness was remembered years later by his listeners. "He had a heart as big as a barrel," said a man who knew him then, "but, Lord, he would cuss a blue streak."

Alas, Sanders's luck didn't quite stick. The café burned down to the ground in 1939, and once again he was forced to start from scratch. But Sanders, who had become a prosperous, self-made man despite the Great Depression, had gotten a taste of the dream.

In 1940, Sanders rebuilt his café, this time with an adjacent seventeen-room motel. The Sanders Court and Café opened on the Fourth of July with red-checked gingham napkins and a country ham breakfast served with biscuits, red-eye gravy, fresh grits, and eggs.* The kitchen had white walls, ceilings, and floors to project cleanliness and was open so customers could peer in and see how well maintained it all was. Sanders even installed a model motel room beside the women's bath-

---

* It appeared listed on the menu as "$1.70—not worth it—but mighty good."

room of the café so that the "lady of the house" could check out how homey the facilities were and perhaps be persuaded to allow her family to stay the night. To signal how modern it was, Sanders had equipped the room with a pay phone.

Around the same time that Harland Sanders's rededicated roadside business flourished, the influential Austrian-American economist Joseph Schumpeter popularized "creative destruction," a theory that he copped in part from Karl Marx. Creative destruction describes the chaos that ensues when a new industry built on a new technology emerges and leaves networks of outdated industries in its wake. Creative destruction is why many people feel a twinge of sadness when looking over their dusty DVD libraries and wistfully chuckle at the sight of fax machines and newspaper classified ads.

To this point, Harland Sanders's life had been wholly shaped by creative destruction. In his younger years, he had worked the railroads, which had replaced horses and canals. In one of Sanders's early business schemes, he created a company that sold acetylene lighting to farmers, but the rapid and widespread adoption of the light bulb and electricity had completely wrecked his investment. Sanders had settled in Corbin, a town developed by the grimy grace of coal and railroads. The primacy of the railway travel would be overtaken by cars, creating a need for tires (which Sanders sold) as well as roadside food, gas, and lodging (which is how Sanders had made a name for himself in southeastern Kentucky).

Had Harland Sanders had the temperament to remain a lawyer or an insurance salesman, he might have enjoyed a much steadier life. But what made Sanders truly great is that he wasn't just a victim of creative destruction, he was an architect of it as well. One oft-scribbled note in the marginalia of American popular culture is that Harland Sanders wasn't a real colonel. That's true insomuch as he never led troops into battle or ordered an illicit Code Red. But the designation itself is real. A Kentucky governor can bestow the title "Kentucky colonel" upon anyone deemed deserving. And in 1935, Ruby Laffoon—Kentucky's tremendously namely governor, who was directly preceded and followed in office by Flem Sampson and Happy Chandler, respectively—commissioned Sanders with the ceremonial honor, supposedly for his exploits as an amateur midwife.*

What separates Sanders from the countless other Kentucky colonels is that he went Method into the role of colonel with a fidelity that makes Daniel Day-Lewis look like kind of a punk. Sanders *became* the Colonel, first in a black suit and then in his trademark white suit, which matched his hair and a goatee that some historians suggest he dyed white. Wherever he went, he would engage in some "coloneling," making strategic small talk and enhancing the Sanders mystique one table, community picnic, Rotary Club meeting, and social outing at a time. Over the years, the Colonel had prospered and extended his reach—in business, branding, and, of course, chicken.

Among his many projects in Corbin, Sanders endlessly tinkered with the perfect way to make chicken. Frying it in a pan took half an hour, too long by any service standard, but especially for a small highway joint with a time-pressed clientele. And so he labored with Bertha, his beloved first pressure cooker, retrofitting her with valves and risking life and limb to

---

* The pious, teetotaling Sanders often ventured into the nearby Appalachian communities to deliver food and babies, help moonshine-besotted locals dry out, and feed orphans ice cream. Sanders would be recommissioned a Kentucky colonel some fifteen years later for his famous chicken.

find a way to fry chicken faster and better. Miraculously, Bertha cut the cook time from thirty minutes down to just nine through a pressure frying method that locked out grease and sealed in juices.* Equally crucial, his chicken came coated in a batter made of a secret blend of herbs and spices that Sanders had refined again and again, mixing ingredients into piles of flour on the concrete floor of his back porch.

The chicken was a revelation; the result was poultry in motion. The Sanders Café flourished, later recommended as "a very good place to stop en route to Cumberland Falls and the Great Smokies" in Duncan Hines's prestigious national guidebook, *Adventures in Good Eating*. Ironically, Sanders's informal exploits in the kitchen had begun strictly as a means to better eke out a living during the Great Depression. "I figured I couldn't do worse than these people running these places around town," he told one biographer. But, unwittingly and in a very American way, Sanders's efforts as a chef, entrepreneur, salesman, and marketing whiz in those lean years laid the groundwork for what would eventually become an international empire. And as the country slowly emerged from the economic catastrophe of the 1930s, unimaginable opportunity revealed itself on the roads ahead.

---

* Like Lincoln, Sanders would also end up with an official patent.

3 SOFT MARKET

Storytellers were nearly extinct, like whooping cranes,
but the D.Q. was at least the right tide pool in which
to observe the few that remained.
—LARRY McMURTRY

On an unremarkable spring night in 2014, Warren Buffett, then the world's third-richest person, did something more or less unremarkable and went to dinner at the Pool Room of the Four Seasons, one of the nicest restaurants in the world and one of the most exclusive landmarks in New York City. To put it mildly, the restaurant is no joke; culinary historians credit the Four Seasons with being one of the first kitchens to lend cultural capital to seasonal dining in the United States. In addition to luxe menus with rotating ingredients, the décor featured seasonal trees, ashtrays, and server uniforms. (In a 1959 issue, the countercultural *Evergreen Review* dubbed it "the most expensive restaurant ever built.") In the decades before it closed in 2016, the Four Seasons stood perhaps singular in its place in New York City lore as the venue for the elite of all industries to go to and be seen; it's where Kissinger, Oprah, and Oscar de la Renta might have had the same server on a given night. And as if that weren't mythology enough, the origin of the term "power lunch" has actually been pinpointed to the restaurant's jackets-required dining room.

On that April evening, according to the tabloids, Buffett ordered a steak. On the restaurant's legendary bill of fare that could have been something like the grilled filet mignon—a premium cut of meat served alongside decadences such as red-wine, shallot confit, miniblocks of Barolo-herb butter, and hillocks of carrot purée.

Earlier in the evening, Buffett had requested a Cherry Coke, which the Four Seasons obviously didn't stock. But when somebody worth over $60 billion orders off menu, you don't refuse. You send one of your staff scurrying across the white marble floor, past the wall with the largest Pablo Picasso canvas in the United States on it, out of the iconic Seagram Building onto Park Avenue, and into the midtown Manhattan night toward the nearest bodega to scrounge one up. Buffett got his Cherry Coke, but when he requested a cup of Dairy Queen soft-serve ice cream after his steak that night, he found himself out of luck. Unlike Buffett's hometown of Omaha, New York City had no DQs yet. The opening of the first branch was still months away. And so, he had to settle for a dessert of chocolate chip cookies. Even the hallowed hospitality artisans of the Four Seasons couldn't make it happen.

There's something inspired and almost cunning about a man who holds the single biggest stake in American Express turning down a portfolio of lavish mousses, fancy soufflés, and brown-butter parsnip cakes to ask for a paper cup of $3 soft serve. But Buffett, who is said to favor breakfasts of Utz Potato

Stix and Coca-Cola, is also a rare kind of billionaire. He dresses like a state senator from rural Maine, drives his own car to work, and eats like an eleven-year-old, the age he was when he purchased his first stocks. That Warren Buffett has only sent one email in his entire life occasionally appears as a clue in crossword puzzles. Simply because he has managed to amass a massive fortune while also retaining a basic filament of gravitas and humanity, he's called colorful and eccentric.

The irresistible pull of the Buffett folklore is part of why his miniature act of culinary defiance became tabloid fodder. But it also has to do with the contrast between the Four Seasons—the enlightened, urbane, modernist cathedral that Americanized fine dining—and Dairy Queen—the lowly, small-town, and déclassé institution. Page Six reported that Buffett's off-menu order "caused a scene." The Four Seasons even humblebragged about its failure to accommodate Buffett's special request on its Facebook page.

Buffett was ten years old when the first Dairy Queen stand opened in 1940 in Joliet, an Illinois town that's perhaps best known for its prison. The origin story of DQ is one of those old-fashioned American tales of aw-shucks innovation: Dairy Queen was born of a dairy farmer's disruptive quest for better ice cream.

"J. F. McCullough (better known to us as 'Grandpa McCullough') was an old time Dairy Man who always had the idea of selling soft ice cream to the public, not knowing too much about the soft cream business or where to start," begins a company minibiography written by Sherman "Sherb" Noble, who would later open the first Dairy Queen with McCullough and his son. In the beginning, the McCulloughs sold hard ice cream from their family farm in the tiny town of Green

River, Illinois. They would churn the product and, when it was about twenty-three degrees cold, pour it into large containers. Next, they would deep-freeze the ice cream at subzero temperatures so it could easily be shipped off to shops, where it would be served at around zero degrees. But having sampled the ice cream in a warmer state, the McCulloughs were convinced that it tasted better that way. What they lacked was the advanced technology to build a batch freezer that would make a semi-frozen enterprise commercially possible.

Before plunging into an extravagant investment (especially in the late 1930s), the McCulloughs conducted a little market research. The duo called on Noble, a friend and client of theirs, who agreed to offer their soft serve at his store in Kankakee, Illinois, on an August afternoon. All you can eat for a dime. "The reaction was very good, we served over sixteen hundred servings in two hours," Noble recounted. "We had ice cream all up and down the block, even had them eating ice cream in the corner tavern down the street, which was very unusual for this place."

The trio fiddled with the butterfat levels and adjusted the serving temperature and found their way into the right kind of freezer. They christened their venture Dairy Queen, reportedly in homage to the cow, which Grandpa McCullough called "the queen of the dairy business." By 1941, when Pearl Harbor came under attack, ten Dairy Queens had sprung up around the Midwest. Shortly thereafter, Sherb Noble, along with millions like him, stepped out of the picture. "In June of 1942 I went into the service for Uncle Sam and did not return until the fall of 1945," he wrote. "From 1945 on you may know the history of Dairy Queen as well as I do."

* * *

These nonchalant final words about the early, prefatory days of Dairy Queen are more profound than perhaps Noble meant them to be. The prewar years tend to conjure up swing music, jitterbugs, and Bette Davis. But the country that began to emerge from the Great Depression was more shambling and rough around the edges than perhaps collective memory serves.

Few universal truths ever apply to an entire national experience, but on a broad, overwhelming level, the Depression cast a heavy pall over American life that carried through the late 1930s. The humiliation of hunger and rickets and pellagra, the worn-out clothes and Hoovervilles and relief lines, had all sent shamed citizens into a painful extended hiding. While the United States never hit 25 percent unemployment again, as it had in 1933, the so-called Roosevelt Recession of 1937–38 all but wiped away the fragile gains of the recovery.

In 1940, only about half of US homes had indoor plumbing and less than a quarter of the population had a high school degree. The precariousness of daily life had left communities riven by division and suspicion; demagogues advocating for communism, isolationism, socialism, anti-Semitic populism, dog-eat-dog free-market anarchy, and fascism found easy popularity. Segregation still held, and the immigration restrictions of the 1920s, along with the tattered economy of the 1930s, which had caused many newer arrivals to leave, had left the country less ethnically diverse than before. Moreover, the shine of opportunity that had drawn millions from rural areas into the developing cities had also halted.

But slowly, conditions stabilized. The droughts ended and the dust—figurative and literal—settled. In 1938, after decades of worker-rights wrangling, the Fair Labor Standards Act went into law, steered by Labor Secretary Frances Perkins, America's first female cabinet member. The legislation installed progressive and then-controversial mandates such as a minimum wage, a forty-four-hour workweek, and regulations that kept six-year-olds from having to work in textile mills and coal mines.*

With expanded leisure hours, a more standard five-day workweek, and, eventually, single-digit unemployment, Americans started to find the time and means to reemerge from hiding. They went on Sunday drives, whiled away hours in soda shops, and saw movies at drive-ins as they sprung up. And they went for ice cream at places like Dairy Queen, which represented a simple, inexpensive, and decadent invitation to live in public once again.

Though small slider joints had popped up in the cities and diners had started to line the roadsides for travelers and tourists, Americans still overwhelmingly ate their meals at home. In 1940—by culture, necessity, or both—only 15 percent of the average American budget was set aside to dine out.† Dairy Queen, born of Midwestern pastureland ingenuity, reflected this dynamic. Its offerings started with soft-serve ice cream in 1940 and only grew by malts, milkshakes, and banana splits in its first several years. These offerings provided an ideal, and cheap, respite from a culture of home dining; not until nearly twenty years after DQ's founding would savory lunch and dinner items be added to the equation.

---

* At the time, the National Association of Manufactures suggested that the act "constitutes a step in the direction of communism, bolshevism, fascism, and Nazism."

† As Tracie McMillan observed in *The American Way of Eating*, that figure would nearly double to 28 percent by 1975 as incomes surged after World War II and more women entered the workforce.

As a result, the early decades of fast food were dominated by ice cream and beverage stands in small towns and the suburbs. Until the end of 1965, the big-name chains we know today—McDonald's, along with Burger King and Kentucky Fried Chicken—were still just getting off the ground, cumulatively hosting fewer than two thousand locations. By that time, the United States would be dotted with seventy-five hundred outlets of franchises such as A&W, Tastee-Freez, and most famously Dairy Queen.

For these reasons Dairy Queen will probably always be associated with soft serve, idle hours, small-town communal innocence, and wholesome Americana. In a beautiful 2010 ode to the brand, the writer Michael Parks posited that a settlement needed to have a Dairy Queen to truly qualify as an American small town. Anything less relegated it to just a blur on a highway. And soft-serve ice cream, he added, was a key social mechanism. "Soft serve requires a machine. A machine, in turn, requires a store," he wrote. "Not quite solid, and made largely of air, soft serve can't survive a freezer. You can't buy soft serve in a carton. Every cone requires an excursion into the world."

Something poignant churns here. In his Texas-themed semiautobiography, *Walter Benjamin at the Dairy Queen*, the writer Larry McMurtry of *Lonesome Dove* fame regards the arrival of Dairy Queen stores in the late 1960s as an antiserum for a West Texas desert climate that wasn't just physically parched, but socially arid:

> What I remember clearly is that before the Dairy Queens appeared the people of the small towns had no place to meet and talk; and so they didn't meet or talk, which meant that much local lore or incident remained private

and ceased to be exchanged, debated, and stored as local lore. . . .

The Dairy Queens, by providing a comfortable setting that made possible hundreds of small, informal local forums, revived, for a time, the potential for storytelling.

McMurtry recounts sitting with his Dr Pepper and lime and marveling as "all day the little groups in the Dairy Queen formed and re-formed, like drifting clouds." There were cowboys and roughnecks, "men of all crafts and women of all dispositions," the early-rising oilmen and the late-rising courthouse crowd, and the idle gossipers. "These Dairy Queens combined the functions of tavern, café, and general store; they were simple local roadhouses where both rambling men and stay-at-homes could meet."

There's a real and true romantic sentiment in the notion (or self-styled delusion) of America as rugged, unspoiled by pretentious wants, and unscarred by ugly history. As the railroads effaced the plains and cars brought more and more people out of isolation, the small town replaced the frontier as the avatar of down-home American virtue. Somewhere along the way, Dairy Queen became enmeshed in that Rockwellian tapestry. A humble pit stop founded in a small Midwestern town on Route 66 with ice cream and our cherished national values on the menu board.

Now if that all sounds a bit ridiculous, tune your radio dial to a country-music station, where DQ gets name-checked in song lyrics nearly as often as dusty roads, tailgates, starry nights, and dashboard lights. This is certainly helped by the fact that *Dairy Queen* offers some country-ready rhyming options. Here's a sampling of how the chain has been paired in country songs over the years: *front porch swing* (George Strait, Craig Morgan), *seventeen* (Alan Jackson, Trace Adkins, Pat Green), *Jean / Sara Jean* (John Waite / Joey + Rory), *Lake Lurlene* (Michelle Malone), *gasoline* (Rick Trevino), *I ever seen* (Ty England), and *state champs '63* (Brett Eldredge). Of course, more than just its rhyming versatility, this also has to do with what Dairy Queen represents.

For example, Randy Travis's toe-tapper "No Reason to Change" drops this jangly couplet: "Been a whole lot of times when times were lean / A big night out was the Dairy Queen."* And though she's never sung about it, Martina McBride, the so-called Celine Dion of Country, actually left the family farm at sixteen to work at a Dairy Queen in Hutchinson, Kansas, along her way to stardom. However, the brightest blue ribbon for the most hickory-smoked Dairy Queen tribute goes to Neal McCoy's "Last of a Dying Breed," a three-minute love letter to small-town goodness that unleashes several awe-inspiring fusillades of country clichés. In the money verse, McCoy mentions hay balers, overalls, farmer tans, and the VFW hall before shouting out "the fruit-stand sellers, town-square dwellers / Who gather at the Dairy Queen at dawn."

The meaning behind these references fits seamlessly within a musical genre that's obsessed with American mythology, defiant, relatable authenticity, and a bygone, sun-faded way of life. Country is beset by clichés because the clichés have the grit of ordinary truth. As the writer Leslie Jamison once argued, "Clichés lend structure and ritual and glue" and serve as "the subterranean passageways connecting one life to an-

---

* One possible locale for such a big night out would be the Dairy Queen on Garth Brooks Boulevard in Yukon, Oklahoma.

other. They obstruct alibis of complexity and exceptionality, various versions of the notion 'It's different for me.'" Indeed, McCoy's image of small-town workers meeting up at a Dairy Queen at dawn is real and based on something true to life about the way people gather.*

This is at least partially why the backlash against fast food—the official, longest-lasting fuel of the American everyday—has such an elitist chill to it. In many places, fast-food restaurants serve as low-stakes venues for low-stakes congregation. It's what Larry McMurtry saw. And it's also what Warren Buffett saw when he decided to purchase Dairy Queen in 1998. "I've been running a quality check for decades," Buffett said. "I like to buy things I understand. And I understand why people come to Dairy Queen, why I come to Dairy Queen. When I buy . . . that I'm making a bet that ten, twenty, fifty, one hundred years from now people will be doing the same thing. And so far it has worked out that way."

Dairy Queen wouldn't just become a pioneer in the field of soft ice cream. It would also become a pioneer in the field of franchising. All of this speaks to the seductive and petrifying power of American iconography meeting American corporate power. The war effort, with its rationing and limits on nonessential production, kept Dairy Queen from expanding until all the Sherb Nobles returned home. In the ensuing years, Dairy Queen, with the help of a band of merry franchisors, would spring from a handful of stores to nearly fifteen hundred by 1950. Then onward to twenty-six hundred by 1955.

Among the many to notice was a man named Ray Kroc, a

---

* You stay skeptical about these things and then one afternoon you drive past a DQ in the Texas farm country and notice its marquee promoting a happy hour that runs from two in the afternoon until five and realize it's for the locals whose workdays start at sunrise.

struggling paper-cup and milkshake-machine salesman from burbs of Chicago. Kroc became intimately familiar with Dairy Queen's aggressive franchising model, and he would later partner with Harry Sonneborn, a former Tastee-Freez vice president, to steer McDonald's from a roadside stand run by two brothers into a corporate leviathan run by thousands of franchisees and shareholders. But it would be several years before all that. From 1945 on, you may know the history as well as I do.

If a problem cannot be solved, enlarge it.
—DWIGHT D. EISENHOWER

In 1950, four years before Ray Kroc would be struck dumb by the sight of the McDonald brothers' burger outfit in Southern California, Harmon Dobson opened his own first burger joint in Corpus Christi, along the Gulf Coast of Texas. It was nothing special to look at: a small, portable metal stand with a walk-up window. But Dobson, who had spent his career dabbling in diamonds, wildcatting oil rigs, and hawking used cars, compensated for this modest block of black and white with one grandiose offering. Having dealt in the precious and the crude alike, Dobson had created something that was both: a Texas-sized hamburger. A Whataburger.

As we know, the burgers of this era were diminutive by contemporary standards—generally two ounces of beef or less and long sold for a nickel or a dime. Austerity burgers for all economic seasons. (Even diner burgers of the time, which were larger than sliders, were served on four-inch buns, which would now seem quaint and petite.) Dobson served up his heavyweight rebuke with double the beef, double the bread, double the hands required. Just to fulfill this meatly vision, he had to start a side business with a local baker to develop a special pan mold large enough for the specialty five-inch burger buns. What Whataburger would lack in the heartland economy of White Castle, it would make up for in Texan heft. The slider had been born in Wichita as a two-by-two-inch sandwich with onions and a cute slice of pickle for a nickel. A Whataburger came with three slices of tomato, four dill-pickle slices, chopped onions, lettuce, mustard, and ketchup. A quarter-pounder for a quarter.

In its bill of fare and name, Whataburger embodied an aspirational call for the changing landscape of the 1950s. It didn't sound regal and stately or humble and homespun. "What a burger!" represented the radio dial of the national disposition turning from austerity, lima-bean casseroles, and Perry Como to plenitude, meat loaf, and rock 'n' roll.

The early 1950s were an auspicious time to start a business venture, but particularly one featuring oversize burgers. The economy had bounced back from a short postwar recession, inflated prices had fallen, and ground beef was on its way to becoming as cheap as it would ever be in postwar US history. Fears of a traumatic return to the colorlessness of Depression life had been overblown; 1950 would be the last year that all the Academy Award nominees for Best Picture were shot in black and white. The twentieth century was half over, and the American century was just underway and would be coming through in vivid, brilliant Technicolor palettes.

Though the tropes of the simple, rigid, optimistic conservatism of midcentury American life generally tend to inspire either fetish or nausea, for a while there stood good reason for all the mythmaking. The United States had emerged from

World War II suddenly confident, renewed, and energetic. After a decade and a half of economic depression, poverty, and war, the country offered a scoping promise of prosperity for many—though not all. In *American Empire*, historian Joshua Freeman lays out the staggering particulars of America's postwar inheritance. By the war's end, half of the world's manufactured goods were produced in the United States. "By 1947," he notes, "American workers produced 57 percent of the world's steel, 43 percent of its electricity, 62 percent of its oil, and 80 percent of its automobiles." In 1950, the US gross national product was more than triple that of its nearest follower and biggest foe, the Soviet Union.

By 1956, nearly 8 million Americans had used their GI Bill benefits on college degrees or vocational training. And by 1966, 20 percent of the single-family homes built since the war had been financed through GI Bill mortgages. For the next quarter of a century abundance arrived to stay—with high wages, steady productivity gains, and affordable goods. This climate of accelerated development rubbed away at least some of the country's parochial limitations. The preexisting barriers would be replaced with the kind of fabled opportunity that would beget national self-legendizing long after the promises of the era had been weathered by time and broken by hubris, brute force, and corporate lust.

Fittingly, Harmon Dobson's Whataburger stand opened the same day that newspapers around the country reported that all eighty thousand of the remaining volunteer reserves would be mobilized by the Marines for the Korean War. The physical war against the Communists in Korea would be fought with M2 carbines; the ideological battle, however, the containment, would be fought through capitalism. American victories would be brightly strung in industry and innovation and gauged in split-level houses with yards, color televisions, and two-car garages. Out back, on backyard patios, were fired-up grills always covered with burgers, a national emblem of the postwar potluck after years of austerity and meat rationing. After all, nothing better expressed the superiority of the American way than its abundance. Abundance that blended faith with science and freedom and individual destiny with consumerism and hard work. Abundance that armed you against an ideologue in a kitchen debate. Abundance that literally rained down from the sky.

In 1950, a beachgoer strolling the Gulf Coast on a hot August day might have caught a glimpse of a tiny plane up in the ether toting a WHATABURGER banner. Harmon Dobson was in the pilot's seat. He had taught himself how to fly and was now, with his young son, dropping coupons for free burgers from the sky like confetti. "I would sit in the back seat and throw the coupons out," Tom Dobson, now the company's chairman of the board, told me. "That's still just as vivid in my mind as if it was today. He'd fly over town and we wouldn't be very high, maybe a thousand feet, in a little Piper Super Cub, one seat behind the other. He had an air horn on that thing and he'd honk the horn, and whenever he honked the horn, I would throw coupons out the back window all over town. I was probably, maybe six, seven. And then he got in trouble because of the air horn and he was littering. It was very effective advertising. Everybody'd look up and see that air horn and then everyone would talk about it, 'Oh, yeah, that Whataburger man is dropping coupons out of the sky again.'"

Texans, for better and worse, have always cherished a swaggering, size-obsessed, idiosyncratic spirit. This affinity explains everything good or eccentric or colorful in the state from the Alamo to Ann Richards, big hair to Bum Phillips, and Selena to the space program. Not surprisingly, denizens of the Lone Star State were ready to welcome a pricier, Texas-sized burger into the canon. FOLKS, WE PRICED OUR BURGERS TOO LOW AND WE LOST OUR SHIRTS, Dobson painted on a sign after some early success. SORRY, BUT WE GOTTA RAISE THE PRICE TO 30 CENTS. About seventy years after its humble start, Whataburger is (as of 2018) now the country's sixth-largest burger chain in terms of sales and the largest privately held burger company.

Like the hamburger itself, the jumbo-sized burger was an innovation with several disconnected authors in scattered places. One day out in the growing roadside Eden of Southern California, Bob Wian of Bob's Pantry created a double-decker burger as a joke for some regulars who asked for something different. He called the sandwich the Big Boy. But everyone took the Big Mac forerunner quite seriously, and Wian soon renamed his store Bob's Big Boy after the sandwich and started a chain. "A meal in one on a double-deck bun" went one 1950s jingle.

Another notable entry in the big-burger annals belongs to Lovie Yancey. Born in Bastrop, Texas, in 1912, Yancey moved west in the Great Migration that brought millions of black Americans out of the Jim Crow South in the decades after World War I. She opened Mr. Fatburger with her boyfriend in 1947, a three-stool burger stand built in Los Angeles with scrap-metal parts. For five years, Yancey logged long hours behind the counter every single day of the week before splitting from her partner and taking over the entire business. She dropped the extraneous prefix and rechristened the stand Fatburger. Buoyed by Yancey's watchful care and her amply sized burgers, it became a cultural institution. "The name of the store was my idea," Yancey said on a good day in 1985. "I wanted to get across the idea of a big burger with everything on it . . . a meal in itself."

And though these inventions were certainly impressive, no mega-burger makers would be quite as influential as Burger King cofounders James McLamore and David Edgerton. In 1954, they took over Insta-Burger King, a burger outfit based in the suburbs of Miami.

The venture they inherited was a bit of a mess. In a nod to the tech-centric fascinations of the time, the kitchens had been designed to cook burgers in a fully automated, futuristic fashion using a complex network of conveyor belts. In reality, the system stank and malfunctioned constantly. One day, in a pique of rage, Edgerton sank a hatchet into a fritzing conveyor belt, resolving to build something better himself. That invention would be a continuous-chain charbroiler, which would give the burgers their famous backyard taste and created an industry-standard machine.* No longer a true "Insta" operation, the duo simplified the chain's name and labored to find a way to make the whole enterprise work. And then, in 1957, they discovered ground-chuck gold. On a visit to a Burger King franchise in Gainesville, the two happened upon a burger at a shabby drive-in nearby that had become wildly popular among locals. The mammoth burger was served on a five-inch bun with a mess of toppings. Right away, they knew Burger King would carry its own version.

Though both men claimed ownership of the idea, the universe generally credits McLamore with Burger King's history-

---

* Amazingly, Edgerton's creation is still in wide use today.

making variation on the theme. "I suggested that we call our product a *Whopper*," McLamore wrote in his autobiography, "knowing that this would convey imagery of something *big*." Whatever the truth, the Whopper became the ultimate triple threat: Like its quarter-pound brethren, it was much bigger than most other uninspiring burgers *and* it was "flame-broiled," which not only separated it from the legions of griddle burgers, but also fed into an ongoing national cookout craze. Perhaps most consequently, it was the first signature fast-food item to go truly national. Most drive-ins, stands, and diners had hamburgers on offer; Burger King had the Whopper. The Whopper became the franchise's calling card as the monarchy rapidly expanded. Today, the coronation of a new Burger King is almost always accompanied by the unveiling of an all-caps sign: HOME OF THE WHOPPER.

As with the Whataburger before it, consumer willingness to pay a then eye-popping amount (thirty-seven cents) for a Whopper heralded an adaptation to comfort and plenty. "The pressures of prosperity were inexorable, and by the mid-1950s, it became apparent that hamburgers, like cars, had to become bigger if they wanted to compete," the late food writer Josh Ozersky noted in his ode *The Hamburger*. "The Whopper was as inevitable as the hydrogen bomb." The success of the Whopper inspired countless other signature creations, notably the Big Mac and the Quarter Pounder, along with a subsequent riptide of Big Bufords (Checkers/Rally's), Jumbo Jacks (Jack in the Box), Thickburgers (Hardee's/Carl's Jr.), American Colossals (Burgerville), doubles, triples, quads, and innumerable megasized local heroes—the Kodiak Roadrunner (Arctic Roadrunner), the Big Baby (Nicky's the Real McCoy), the Big One (Ward's), the Lotaburger (Blake's), and so on.

But what made the Whopper landmark material wasn't just its size or its specialty preparation or its clever branding. Or that it emblematized the growing appetites of a country that was hurtling forward, headlights on, toward wealth and plenitude. Or even that the Whopper represented the latest dilation of a new, productive, impatient way of life—"a meal in itself," as it would be advertised. In a laden, meaningful way, the Sputnik-sized Whopper signaled comfort that was both excessive and predictable in an age of conformity and militarized expansion, the dangerous indulgences that Eisenhower would famously bemoan in his farewell address.

The 1950s quietly solidified a status quo—of menacing paranoia and various repressions, of arms races, of American troops stationed all over the world, and of a polity in which the two major political parties were so ideologically squished together they often seemed indistinguishable from each other. The entire country, and especially its industries, internalized this sensate state of war, not just because of a real Communist threat, but also because it all came so naturally. Indeed, through the middle half of the decade, the bestselling book in the United States (second only to the Bible, natch) was Dr. Norman Vincent Peale's *Power of Positive Thinking*, which married religion with patriotism and capitalism. By the end of the 1950s, Americans were driving cars with fins and fuzzy dice and buying huge hamburgers using legal tender printed with the newly adopted national motto: IN GOD WE TRUST. For many, it seemed as if there was never a better time to be an American.

5 ARE WE THERE YET?

*I was fifty-two years old, I had diabetes and incipient arthritis.
I had lost my gallbladder and most of my thyroid gland
in earlier campaigns, but I was convinced that
the best was ahead of me.*

—RAY KROC

In 1956, the long-planned expansion of the Interstate System, which had partially been inspired by Eisenhower's marvel at the wide, efficient autobahns of Nazi Germany, was officially funded through the Federal-Aid Highway Act. The building out of the system's nearly forty-seven thousand miles—the biggest public works project in the history of humanity—also reorganized American life into a form that's still recognizable today. Major cities became linked for trade and travel like arteries, bringing food and goods and people quicker and farther than ever before.*

---

* The big roads have also been condemned for paving over paradises, savaging American Main Streets and urban centers, dividing and displacing communities, further segregating cities, encouraging sprawl, and helping to set the country on an unshakable car-centric course.

The highways rose in symbolic and strategic lockstep with the muscular postwar euphoria of US life.* Following the war, the economy boomed. Rationing and austerity were a thing of the past, and beef, steel, gasoline, and credit were cheap. For the first time ever, a majority of Americans became homeowners. Suburbs and babies sprouted up everywhere like weeds and fallout shelters. Women's participation in the workforce steadily grew and prosperity slowly began to democratize.

The big new interstates formalized and made permanent the full-blown (and uniquely American) emergence of car culture that had begun after World War II. Between 1945 and 1950, annual new car sales in the United States surged from about seventy thousand to 6.7 million, and oil surpassed coal as the country's predominant energy source. By 1949, roughly three-quarters of the cars on earth drove on US roads. And by 1957, there would be 55 million cars for 172 million citizens. Miles would become measurements of time, cities would become redefined by their loops and beltways and highway numbers, and mobility became a patriotic expression of freedom. Workers took on new commutes on weekdays, and then on the weekends they would pile their families into cars to discover the country.

Nowhere did this insistent, fast-paced sensibility emerge more formidably than in Southern California—that sun-kissed, casual, most honeyed and climate-controlled realization of modern manifest destiny. Even before the war, Los Angeles alone had nearly a million cars, more than in 80 percent of the states. In just a few short decades, Southern California devel-

---

* By one account, spending on the interstates was credited with increasing annual American productivity by 31 percent in the late 1950s.

oped into a port of call for Tomorrowland, billions in federal and Cold War defense spending, swimming pools and movie stars, massive American migration,* a new and innovative brand of white supremacy, and countless varieties of drive-in businesses, motels, and hotels to accommodate the auto-centric way of life.

Southern California is where, in 1954, Ray Kroc famously first set his intense Vulcan eyes upon one impressive little hamburger stand. After a few tough decades on the road as a paper-cup salesman, Kroc had incorporated milkshake machines into his Lomanesque sojourns, and he had typically been selling one, or maybe two, of his five-spindle Multimixers to clients across the country. But now everywhere he went, Kroc's disconnected affiliation of soda jerks and malt shop operators seemed to be whispering about Dick and Mac McDonald, two brothers who were rumored to be using not one, not two, but eight milkshake machines at their outfit in the sleepy desert town of San Bernardino. The possibility mystified even Kroc, a man who had seen just about every commercial kitchen in America during a career of working odd jobs, playing jazz at speakeasies during Prohibition, and selling kitchen and restaurant supplies. "The mental picture of eight Multimixers churning out forty shakes at one time was just too much to be believed," Kroc wrote in *Grinding It Out*, his mind-blowing autobiography and a seminal monograph about twentieth-century capitalism. Kroc arrived at the McDonald's desert mirage at the western end of Route 66, saw the

---

* Between 1920 and 1940, California's population tripled, and by the early 1960s, the Golden State would supplant New York as the country's most populous state and never look back.

crowds amassed, heard that Multimixer octet playing its scherzo, and was duly delivered.

Kroc quickly understood that the platoon of shake machines was just one part of a total efficiency equation. Dick and Mac McDonald, the sons of a shoe-factory foreman, had struck out for California from New Hampshire to try to make it in the entertainment business and ended up producing a food-service revolution instead. In 1940, the two opened a barbecue drive-in that, like many others of the time, featured a full staff with carhops and an outdoor counter and served about two dozen items, including pulled pork and hamburgers. McDonald's Barbeque did well, yet it caused endless headaches. The carhops made the stand an attractive hangout for teenage boys, who idled endlessly, scared off families, and tended to disappear with the cups and plates and utensils. In 1948, in an audacious turn, the two brothers shut down their profitable shop for three months, meticulously reschemed the basics of their operations by diagramming them on a tennis court, and reopened as a highly efficient enterprise the likes of which the food industry had never before seen. Gone were the conventions of the standard drive-ins of the era with their young carhops in short skirts and majorette boots delivering trays of food to curbs. Instead, their stand had a no-frills, Levittown-inspired assembly-line operation to befit the "age of jet propulsion," as one brother put it, where just nine items were made quickly and well. The Speedee Service System featured two custom-built six-foot-long stainless steel grills, each twice as long as anything available on the market. The Multimixers came with modified paddles that allowed milkshakes to be whipped directly in their paper cups, and a house-commissioned steel lazy Susan facilitated the whirlwind dressing of twenty-four burger buns with condiments. More impressive yet, Dick McDonald had gone undercover as a fake reporter to visit candy companies on a mission to track down a machine that could dispense perfect-sized patties (beef instead of peppermint paste) with the easy pull of a lever.

The burger stand that Kroc ogled in 1954 had dusted the efficient, mechanized Fordism of industrial Midwestern factories with a little Hollywood magic. The food, prepared in a glass-encased visible kitchen that transfixed young onlookers, was kept warm with infrared lights, which worked better than heat lamps. Meals were served in disposable packaging through a window; there were no utensils, no dirty dishes, no malingerers, no delays. In addition to rapid-fire service, McDonald's offered a much more digestible price for a new customer base: members of the burgeoning middle class and their burgeoning families.

"The kids loved coming to the counter," recalled Art Bender, who worked the original McDonald's counter and later became a franchisee. "They would come with two bits in their fists and order a hamburger and a Coke. They could still see Mama in the car, but they also could feel independent. Pretty soon, it sinks in that this is great for the business, this is important." It was also important that a fifteen-cent McDonald's burger cost about half of what an average diner burger did, and as Kroc witnessed firsthand, the stand attracted bigger and more diverse crowds, who lined up, got their orders quickly, and went on their way. (In an echo of White Castle, the first McDonald's neon marquee even bore the motto BUY 'M BY THE BAG.)

National dining habits were among the many norms to be altered by the thundering US economy and car culture. In 1958, just as the new highways were rolling out, the service industry overtook manufacturing as the country's largest economic sector. Dining out, once the exclusive habit of the rich, slowly democratized. "Kroc saw immediately that the prime customers were *families*, young couples, a little unsure of themselves, often with children in tow," David Halberstam noted in his book *The Fifties*. "They were comfortable at McDonald's as they might not have been at a more traditional restaurant. . . . It was an inexpensive, easy night out for the family. In the early days a family of four could eat at McDonald's for about $2.50."

Dick and Mac McDonald were more or less content to stay on their well-oiled colony in San Berdoo, pulling down $100,000 a year in profits off fifteen-cent burgers and buying a new-model Cadillac each year. The relentless Kroc, however, saw an empire of replicas. "When I saw it working that day in 1954, I felt like some latter-day Newton who'd just had an Idaho potato caromed off his skull," he later wrote in his autobiography. "That night in my motel room I did a lot of heavy thinking about what I'd seen during the day. Visions of McDonald's restaurants dotting crossroads all over the country paraded through my brain."

Kroc cajoled the brothers into letting him lead their franchising efforts, and one year later he opened his first McDonald's outpost in Des Plaines, Illinois, near the other end of Mother Road 66, not far from his childhood home. Eventually, as the parties' feuds over control grew more intense, Kroc asked the McDonald brothers, who had no true sense of what the company would become, to name their price; Kroc bought them out by for a cool—perhaps immoral—million dollars each after taxes. Then, Kroc went out with franchise agreements and pursued scrapping entrepreneurs he could enlist to follow the exacting system with beagle-like devotion. In short time, dozens and then hundreds more locations would open their doors.

The company became an unprecedented national success story. Kroc had turned a roadside sapling into a national staple. McDonald's now feeds more people daily in America than the entire population of Australia. Today, there are more than thirty-six thousand McDonald's stores in the world in well over a hundred countries from Argentina to Azerbaijan and in thousands of cities from Chicago, Caracas, Casablanca, and Chişinău to Carmiel, Chengdu, and Canberra. There's a flying-saucer-shaped McDonald's in the deserts of Roswell, New Mexico, and an outpost with a ski-thru window atop a mountain in Lindvallen, Sweden. You can find McDonald's sacred fries in the holy cities of Varanasi, Jerusalem, Vatican City, Mecca, and Medina (Saudi Arabia and Ohio).

Even as the company flourished beyond any possible comprehension, Kroc's manic focus never abated. This is part of why his name still rings out as a titanic paragon of American industry. As he grew in power, Kroc labored to keep a grip on the big plans, while still fussing over the small irritants, an autocrat somewhere on a scale between tin-pot and Pol Pot. After selling Kroc their namesake business in 1961, the McDonald's brothers refused (legally) to hand over the property that held their original McDonald's stand in San Bernardino. In a trademark maneuver, Kroc simply opened a McDonald's across the street and put their stand out of business.

Despite the richness of Harland Sanders's origin story and self-legendizing or Billy Ingram's brilliance as the marketer who delivered White Castle and the hamburger to the American mainstream, it was Ray Kroc who seized the mantle of fast-food messiah and, for a long while, national hero. This had as much to do with his biography and his fanatical, in-born drive for success as his militant business philosophies. Long before Kroc forged the empire that currently employs more people than the entire US armed services, he lied about his age and enlisted to serve as an ambulance driver during World War I. Kroc was fifteen. One of his Red Cross comrades was a fellow perfectionist, high school dropout, and Chicago native named Walt Disney, who had also fibbed about his age and who also went on to establish his own expansive California-born kingdom.* The war ended before Kroc could be dispatched to Europe. Shortly thereafter, he dropped out of high school again, enabling him to spend nearly the rest of his life pursuing the two professional callings that suited his restless disposition: piano playing and selling.

Ray Kroc—whose father had "worried himself to death" over real estate losses in the Great Depression—sported over-size rings, despised unions and MBAs, and admired Barry Goldwater, Boss Daley, and American determinism. The son of an immigrant villager from Bohemia, Kroc had no taste or patience for the bohemian spirit. "We have found out," he wrote, in a 1958 warning to the McDonald brothers about franchisees who deviated from the operational script, "that we cannot trust some people who are nonconformists. We will make conformists out of them in a hurry. . . . You cannot give them an inch. The organization cannot trust the individual." Despite this 1950s-style posturing, Kroc was shrewd enough to capitalize on his franchisees' creativity, which yielded some

---

* Add Ernest Hemingway, another Oak Park–born Red Cross volunteer during World War I, and you get a truly complicated twentieth-century American trinity.

of the company's most successful inventions, from the Big Mac and Egg McMuffin to Ronald McDonald and the Filet-O-Fish.

Kroc was also exacting, fastidious, and cruel. He broke up with his second wife through his lawyer at a party for their fifth anniversary, drank rail whiskey like a prefilleted fish (even after he became obscenely wealthy), and treated business as warfare. "If they were drowning," Kroc once said of his competitors, "I'd stick a hose in their mouth." He later bought the long-suffering San Diego Padres as a retirement project and was nearly boycotted by his players after he berated them over the stadium's public address system in the middle of a game. (This public shaming was, notably enough, met with approval from the crowd.)

Though Kroc was a bully, what separated him from most other bullies was the moral lucidity and meticulous vision that drove his madness and paranoia. In the early days of the company, he would fly over communities in a light plane, scouting potential locations by looking for church steeples and schools. According to legend, Kroc would continue to harangue the managers of various McDonald's stores about their cleanliness until the end of his life. "If you see a man in a three-hundred-dollar suit picking up paper in the parking lot," one old admonition went, "you'd better get out there and help him, because it's Ray Kroc." And rather than dispense new McDonald's franchises solely to his golfing buddies and country-club peers like highballs, Kroc sought out hungry young operators. He wanted success for himself and partners made in his image. He gravitated toward high school dropouts and blue-collar strivers, those with unpretentious minds who could credibly serve their working-class customers, who would also treat the grueling work as a cherished livelihood, and who would stay faithful to one thing—the rigid consistency his system required. And for that, Kroc turned a countless generation of them into millionaires.

Famed chef Jacques Pépin even praised Kroc for understanding American appetites and how they stood in contrast to the traditional habits of the Old World. "Instead of a structured, ritualistic restaurant with codes and routine, he gave them a simple, casual and identifiable restaurant with friendly service, low prices, no waiting and no reservations. The system eulogized the sandwich—no tableware to wash," Pépin wrote in an entry that named Kroc one of *Time*'s most important people of the entire twentieth century.* Pépin concluded with this poignant truth: "One goes to McDonald's to eat, not to dine."

Though he became singularly successful, Ray Kroc was hardly the sole lurking admirer of the McDonald brothers' original operation. The founders of Burger King, Carl's Jr., and Taco Bell, along with countless other would-be entrepreneurs, made their hamburger hajj to San Bernardino and were inspired to try their hands at empire-making after seeing the brothers' model in action. "Our food was exactly the same as McDonald's," an unnamed founder conceded. "If I had looked at McDonald's and saw someone flipping hamburgers while he was hanging by his feet, I would have copied it."

Held together along with figures like Ray Kroc, Harmon Dobson, and Harland Sanders, this class of fast-food founders comprise an impressive, intergenerational consortium of self-

---

* So fabled were Kroc's exploits that *Esquire* named him to a list of fifty twentieth-century contributors to American life in a section reserved for "visionaries," which included Reinhold Niebuhr, Abraham Maslow, and Dr. Martin Luther King, Jr.

made entrepreneurs. Imbued with the Protestant work ethic by which America is still defined and critiqued, they mainly flourished in the wake of an unmatched stretch of national economic fertility. In a way that's telling and now seems heroic, the founders of American fast food also had a lot in common. Overwhelmingly, they came from hardscrabble roots, knew hunger as children, committed to some form of wartime national service, worked countless blue-collar jobs, and generally didn't triumph until well into middle age. They harbored prophetic visions, grand delusions, and Talmudic fixations. Admittedly, most of the ones that succeeded benefited from majority status in race, sex, and religion; they were also relentless enough to endure and overcome endless setbacks.

As we know, Harland Sanders escaped frontier poverty, cleaned ashpans on the North Alabama Railroad, and sold chicken in a roadside gas station in southeastern Kentucky during the Great Depression. Along the way, Sanders would encounter and mentor Wendy's founder Dave Thomas—an orphan and a high school dropout who exorcised his ancient demons by setting up a foundation for foster kids and by getting his GED when he was sixty years old. And that's just the curl of the Frosty. After serving as a navy cook in the Pacific during World War II, Wilber Hardee resisted a call to join the family corn-and-tobacco farm to work as a grill cook and eventually opened his wildly popular hamburger stand, Hardee's. Taco Bell founder Glen Bell, who was also a cook in the Pacific during World War II, rode the rails looking for work, hauled adobe bricks out of an army-surplus truck, and repaired telephones before introducing the taco to much of America. One of Bell's employees, an air force vet named Ed Hackbarth (Del Taco), was the ninth of ten children, whose widowed mother washed clothes and took in boarders to help her family survive the Great Depression. Carl Karcher (Carl's Jr.), an Ohio farm-hand with a middle school education, parlayed a humble hot dog stand into a thousand-unit burger chain after returning from the war. William Rosenberg (Dunkin' Donuts) dropped out of middle school at fourteen, delivered telegrams for West-ern Union, and worked as an electrician for Bethlehem Steel. S. Truett Cathy (Chick-fil-A), one of seven kids, spent part of his teenage years during the Depression in the nation's first public housing project; he later started his Atlanta chain by buying at discount from Delta chicken breasts that had been deemed either too big or too small and frying them into sand-wiches. Al Copeland (Popeyes), another high school dropout, grew up in poverty in 1940s New Orleans, logging time on welfare under his grandmother's care in St. Thomas, another early public housing project in America. "I never forget being poor," Copeland said in his later years. "I know what it is, and I don't want it."

What the founders of American fast food also shared was a recognition of the burgeoning national paradigm—America was (and, in many quarters, continues to be) a young, grow-ing, and hungry country that required fast, cheap sustenance. Family-friendly food that could be eaten on the go, using hands instead of utensils and plates, and served in wrappers that could be tossed out on the way to somewhere else.

In its infancy, the fast-food industry possessed the unique innocence that came from being native to its target audience; from founders and franchisees to cooks and customers, it was an industry of literal moms and pops. Like the Colonel, Edith and Gus Belt sold beer and fried chicken at a gas station in Nor-mal, Illinois, before the Great Depression forced them into their fruitful second act as the burger-meisters of Steak 'n Shake. Esther and Harry Snyder were practically newlyweds when they opened their first In-N-Out franchise in Baldwin Park, California.* But ultimately, like Aerosmith, Johnny Rotten, and organic food, nothing good can remain pure forever. As we'll see, once fast food caught on, it became susceptible to corruption and would be adulterated by the pushes and pulls of American industry. In the early 1960s, the American corporate apparatus—aided by the rise of television and advertising—would take new form and swiftly end the days of innocence.

---

* Though she modestly called In-N-Out the product of her husband's vision, Esther Snyder, one of seven sisters and a former surgical nurse in the navy during World War II, kept the books and peeled the onions in the early days of In-N-Out and eventually served as secretary, treasurer, and president.

A Buddhist monk walks up to a hot dog stand and says,
"Make me one with everything."
—ANCIENT DAD JOKE

Harland Sanders had spent his life laboring to bend a resistant universe to his will. But twenty-five years after first opening his service station in Corbin, Kentucky, the Colonel found himself pressed against the most immovable object yet—the US Interstate Highway System. In the mid-1950s, not long after passing on a handsome offer for his business, he learned that the route of the newly created I-75 would bypass his shop in Corbin and quickly render the Dixie Highway obsolete. Seemingly overnight, Sanders's bustling outfit became a dusty remnant on a forgotten highway, and he closed up another shop, selling it at a loss. He was sixty-five, broke again, and at a crossroads.

After decades of hustle and gristle, Sanders hadn't just reached retirement age, he was nearly at the life expectancy for an American man at the time. He suffered from arthritis and failing eyesight. He had lived a wild life, full of schemes, gambits, and countless fistfights. He was an institution, a well-known pillar of hickory and fury, and a peerless salesman who had invented a product he believed in. He had earned the right to sit back on his porch and get by on his $100 Social Security checks. And for many, that might have been enough. But Harland Sanders wasn't just any salesman and he wasn't just any hustler; Harland Sanders was the Colonel.

A few years before his Corbin operation closed, Sanders had started signing franchise agreements with a scattering of restaurant owners whom he had convinced to sell his increasingly famous chicken. They were small-fry deals accorded by handshakes, a classic Sanders side hustle. He would get a few pennies of passive income for every chicken cooked using his patented method. Untethered from his old base of operations, Sanders—white-haired and two-thirds of a century old—would now (literally) suit up and set out in earnest with a white Cadillac full of pressure cookers, loads of spices, and coolers of chicken, a broken hero on a last-chance poultry drive.

The Colonel steered thousands of miles with his achy hands, dropping in unannounced on places he thought to be worthy of him and his chicken. He would charm his way in and whip up meals for the staff and ownership during dead hours, and if he sensed that a deal was close, he'd often hang around an extra day, sleeping in the back of his car to save money and shaving in public bathrooms and gas stations before plying customers with charm and chicken.

Through this back-roads offensive, Sanders assembled a chicken empire piecemeal, banking on himself and the honor of a disjointed guild of tiny operators across Appalachia, a mix of old friends and associates as well as total strangers. The road made for grueling work, but his proposition was straightforward. Unlike Ray Kroc's rigid, soup-to-nuggets operational regimen, Sanders was simply selling a recipe and the creative repurposing of a Depression-era kitchen gadget. The rest was up to the franchisees. To the Colonel, only the food required martial discipline. And he did not abide defection. One of Sanders's first employees was a sixteen-year-old Kentuckian named Bill Samuels, Jr., who was Sanders's driver and gofer the summer Bill got his license.* Samuels rode around with Sanders, whom he'd later refer to as "the greatest salesman who ever lived," watching him make handshake deals out of the passenger side of the car. After the agreements were made, the two would later double back to make sure proprietors were cooking the chicken properly. It was then that Samuels saw the Colonel's supernatural wrath unleashed upon those who deviated from his standards.

Duly scared straight, Sanders's partners generally fell in line, and most everyone on the program made out well. With logistical support from his second wife, Claudia, who had worked as a waitress at the Sanders Café and who occasionally appeared alongside him in antebellum dress at restaurant openings and who painstakingly mixed and mailed bagged blends of proprietary herbs and spices to remote cookhouses across the Midwest and Appalachia, Sanders cultivated a roster of loyal franchisees that would number into the hundreds. Soon enough, he quit the road. Restaurant operators

---

* Samuels would later guide his own small-beer, Kentucky-born family business, Maker's Mark bourbon, through the whiskey boom with a similar adherence to the Sanders style of stiff-necked devotion. "I'm not talking about craft by making it in a barn, I'm talking about the process of no compromise," Samuels told me at his distillery, a hundred miles northwest of Corbin. "That's the real definition of meaningful craft: no compromise."

now sought him out, and the Colonel's chicken, well, continued to spread its wings.

Kentucky Fried Chicken rose to become, for a time, the largest fast-food operation in the world. By the early 1960s, Sanders had amassed over six hundred franchisees in the United States and Canada, while White Castle remained small and privately held with a few hundred locations, and McDonald's only breached the triple-digit mark in 1959. This feat was achieved not just from Sanders's masochistic exploits on the road or the small-scale word about his famous chicken or his legendary coloneling. No, for once his timing had been just right; Sanders's product and relentless virtuosity as a pitchman made for a perfect combination in the so-called golden ages of both television and advertising. In this effort, Sanders found aid from a few forward-thinking lieutenant colonels.

The first KFC franchisee was a café operator named Pete Harman, a Utahn and fellow teetotaler that Sanders had befriended amid a confederation of drunks at a restaurant convention in Chicago. In 1952, Sanders had paid Harman a visit in Salt Lake City while on the way to attend a conference in Australia where Sanders hoped to be cured of his cursing habit. The conference failed to make a lasting impression, but the fried-chicken dinner Sanders prepared for Harman certainly did. Harman rearranged his entire business around Sanders's exotic fare, which he debuted under the name KENTUCKY FRIED CHICKEN painted on a huge roadside sign.*

Seeing the changing character of the American family dinner and the increasingly mobile and suburban nature of life in the 1950s, Harman conceived the brand's iconic chicken

---

* Harman also came up with the brand's eternal tagline, Finger Lickin' Good.

bucket to bolster his take-out business and to slyly market his expanding businesses. Harman also spread the gospel across local airwaves, shrewdly purchasing a bulk set of unused ad time for cheap. "If there was anything that got Kentucky Fried Chicken off the ground, it was gambling on radio's unsold time," Harman later told Robert Darden in *Secret Recipe*. "We had to change equipment practically every day for two weeks just to cook enough chicken to satisfy demand."

Of course, television would soon conquer the media frontier, beaming alongside the cars and suburbs and heady militarism as hallmarks of the postwar decades. Like roadsters before them, televisions began as luxury items for the wealthy; in 1949, only 2 percent of the country owned a set. By 1962, 90 percent of American households had one. Ahead of his election in 1952, Dwight Eisenhower took acting lessons, and savvy politicians were wise to speak in segment-friendly sound bites. Television created a gold rush in advertising billings ($5.7 billion in 1950 to $12 billion in 1960), and TV commercials supplanted radio spots as the leading advertising medium in the United States by 1954. By the end of the 1950s, *TV Guide* reigned as one of the bestselling periodicals of the entire decade.* Pete Harman capitalized on the medium by inviting local news broadcasts to air stories about his store openings in Utah. With some goading, the Colonel, too, would edge into the shot.

In his improbable seventh act, the Colonel also met a fellow fast-food traveler whose early life rivaled Sanders's in its cinematic deprivation. Abandoned after birth by his unwed mother, Dave Thomas lost his adoptive mother when he was

---

* In 1974, it would famously become the first periodical to sell a billion copies in a year.

five, leaving him and his adoptive father on the go, looking for work, living in trailers and squalid rooming houses. He lied about his age to get a job as a soda jerk at a Walgreens, only to be fired when he was discovered to be twelve instead of sixteen. Thomas ended up in Fort Wayne, Indiana, where he held odd jobs, dropped out of high school to work in restaurants, and stayed behind to live alone in a YMCA at fifteen after his father remarried and moved away. During a stint in the army, Thomas attended Cook and Baker's School and cheffed for a few years in Germany during the Korean War.

Following the Korean War, Dave Thomas returned to his job at the Hobby House restaurant in Fort Wayne, Indiana, where he moved up to head cook. Thomas had married a waitress there and started a family and was struggling to make ends meet. In 1955, he encountered Sanders at the restaurant during one of his famous drop-ins. Thomas tried his best to play it cool. "He introduced himself and asked if I knew him," Thomas later wrote. "I pretended I didn't even though I knew all about him. We sat down over a cup of coffee, and he talked to me like an old friend. I've never met a better salesman. When he left, I had a sense this man was going to change my life."

The two built a relationship and Thomas would later be enlisted by him to turn around four poorly performing Kentucky Fried Chicken stores in Columbus, Ohio, in exchange for a large ownership stake. In a few short years, Thomas pared down the menus, installed an enormous rotating chicken bucket outside the stores, and even started donning the white planter's suit and string tie that had become the Colonel's trademark. In the ultimate pay for play, Thomas exchanged fried chicken for publicity from local radio stations. Whenever possible, Thomas also pushed Sanders to appear more on radio and television and cash in on the novel mystique of Kentucky Fried Chicken in markets beyond the Midwest.

The Colonel was old and prone to fits and couldn't be reasoned with, but he imparted to Thomas the knack of salesmanship and operations and the business of franchising. With his stores flourishing, Thomas eventually sold back his stake to the company, making him a millionaire at thirty-five. Not long after, Thomas opened Wendy's Old Fashioned Hamburgers in Columbus, Ohio, using the nickname and befreckled image of his redheaded, eight-year-old daughter, Melinda Lou, as inspiration. Wendy's restaurants were styled to look like the parlor of a sweet but lonely uncle—bentwood chairs, tabletops covered with old newspaper ads, wood-paneled walls, and Tiffany lamps hanging overhead, and Thomas played the part of that sweet but lonely uncle in a red tie and short-sleeved dress shirt. Over the decades, he appeared in roughly eight hundred television spots (a record for a company founder) in a folksy and almost-introverted demeanor with his old-shoe delivery and big glasses, which were square like his hamburgers because his adoptive grandmother had taught him to "never cut corners." "Popeye wasn't my hero," Thomas once said, "Wimpy was, because he loved hamburgers."

Many of these flourishes could be traced directly back to the Colonel. "He saved me," Thomas later said of Sanders. It was a secular psalm uttered by hundreds of others, farm-road and whistle-stop chefs whose lives and ambitions and properties had been tied up in the perilous work and Sisyphean trials of making a business stick. Then the Colonel appeared in their doorway, looking like a cross between Mark Twain and Santa Claus, with his original recipe.

The media-consuming public took to the Colonel with the

same wonderment that everyone else seemed to. Having finally achieved success in his sixties after so much grief, Sanders next managed unfathomable fame in his seventies, looking the part of a zany, old-fashioned Appalachian chicken genius in commercials, B movies, and on *Lawrence Welk*. He excelled because he had a sharp wit and keenly understood that he was a novelty act, the same spectacle maker who, forty years earlier, had ambled local fairs in a Michelin bib suit. He couldn't be media trained or controlled or ironed flat, but still knew to exaggerate the folksy hayseed in him whenever he went on the air. "He was as much at home in front of a national TV audience as he would have been back in Corbin with a two-dollar dinner customer," his lawyer John Brown, Jr., later said. In other words, the Colonel was a ham who served chicken. He was the perfect embodiment of out-of-time gentility with his black Kentucky string tie, his carved canes, ladled-on accent, and homespun aphorisms, as well as his old-school collection of lapel pins that affiliated him with the Rotarians and the Shriners and the Masons.

Sanders would enter mainstream popular culture at one of those peculiar moments when Americans were susceptible to the dangerous allure of hearkening back—his grandfatherly visage appearing during commercial breaks from news coverage of missile crises and war in Southeast Asia and footage of police dogs, burning draft cards, and fire hoses. Here was the Colonel in black and white, here was his chicken—being demoed on live television and available by the bucket for families to share, brought to you by Geritol and a wink from our simpler agrarian past. Here was the Colonel making his first national guest spot on *What's My Line?* on a Sunday in 1963, six days after John Kennedy's funeral.

Sanders became famous, a bona fide cultural commodity. His archives at the KFC headquarters in Louisville are stocked with pictures of him with everyone from fellow chicken aficionado Alice Cooper to Jerry Lewis and Ginger Rogers. There he is, the onetime 1930s everyman, the gun-toting gas station operator of Hell's Half-Acre, so improbably, posing in Red Square in Moscow, astride a camel in Egypt, smiling beside Dionne Warwick, shaking hands with Henry Kissinger and Zsa Zsa Gabor, receiving the Horatio Alger Award. There he is, in a portrait painted by Norman Rockwell, chief iconographer of Americana in the century of its greatest might. According to KFC, an independent survey in 1976 found him to be the second-most-recognizable celebrity in the world behind his fellow Kentuckian Muhammad Ali.*

That a cook could become world-famous for his or her chicken augured the same thing that all those advertising spends, live demos, quick slogans, and high ratings did: the arrival of American big business in its postwar iteration. Like many other entrepreneurs of his era, after gritting through countless jobs, surviving endless trials, and riding the unforgiving waves of American industry to success, Sanders would be swallowed up by the burgeoning corporate state. In 1964, a coterie of businessmen led by Sanders's lawyer and future Kentucky governor John Y. Brown, Jr., easily convinced the seventy-four-year-old Sanders, who was overwhelmed and overextended by his empire making, to sell the licensing rights to Kentucky Fried Chicken for $2 million.

With the stroke of a pen, Sanders would turn from lifelong

---

* In a national recognition poll from a few years earlier, Sanders trailed only Santa Claus and beat out Richard Nixon.

hustler to a ceremonial figurehead. It would prove to be a terrible deal for Sanders, financially and spiritually. The quaint mom-and-pop phase of Kentucky Fried Chicken—like much of fast food and American industry—was headed the way of heavily standardized, stand-alone stores and franchise agreements instead of handshake deals. National ad campaigns and calculated, bottom-line adjustments to the Colonel's sacred recipes would be imposed. But Sanders didn't know any of that yet. All too fittingly, the Colonel turned the sale into a public pageant. Somehow, he got himself booked on the *Tonight* show, where Sanders appeared before Johnny Carson, alongside a plexiglass coffin said to contain his $2 million in singles.

From his shrewd habituation to the birth of the car culture and his psychotic harnessing of media and marketing power to achieve celebrity to his ultimate fate as a small-fry concern absorbed by corporate powers, the Sanders saga cuts a quick epigraph for the early days of American fast food. And born from nothing and triumphant by dint of his persistence through an undulating sea of setbacks, Sanders was an early prototype of the American Dream. And he would be celebrated so. Following his death in 1980, all flags at state buildings in Kentucky were flown at half-mast, and prior to his funeral, Sanders's body was ordered to lie in state at the state capitol in Frankfort, Kentucky, so that mourners could visit and properly pay homage. John Y. Brown, who had purchased the company from Sanders sixteen years earlier and had since become Kentucky's governor, spoke at the funeral. There among one hundred thousand graves at Cave Hill Cemetery, Brown eulogized Sanders as "not only our founder and our creator, he was our leader . . . a living example that the American Dream still exists."

I had heard for years from our girls that the Big Mac was really something "special," and while I've often credited Mrs. Nixon with making the best hamburgers in the world, we are both convinced that McDonald's runs a close second.
—RICHARD M. NIXON

In 1965, just months after Harland Sanders sold his chicken operation for what would turn out to be giblets on the dollar, Ray Kroc took McDonald's public. The company first offered shares at $22.50 (about $178 in 2018 terms), and by the next day, they were worth $30 ($237), making big shareholders wealthy beyond their greasiest dreams overnight. The McDonald's IPO was one clear sign that fast food had survived its infancy to become a bona fide industrial fixture.* Quick-service chains were now becoming big business, commodities to be traded on the stock market alongside DuPont, General Motors, Boeing, and US Steel. The future shimmered tremulously like

---

* Fitting all too perfectly the theme of innocence lost, three months after McDonald's went corporate, Bob Dylan went electric at the Newport Folk Festival.

a boiling vat of beef tallow, and the already-proliferating fast-food companies would use the same low-cost, highly systematized franchising model to continue their expansion.

As fast food boomed and busier Americans shifted away from dinners at home, food conglomerates took notice. With the corporate powers circling, many fast-food founders either cashed in or cashed out. In the years that followed the McDonald's IPO, Jack in the Box founder Robert Peterson sold his chain to Ralston Purina, United Brands bought A&W drive-ins, Royal Crown nabbed Arby's, PepsiCo grabbed both Pizza Hut and Taco Bell, Burger King became part of Pillsbury, Hardee's was bought by Imasco, and so on.

Other chains weren't so lucky as the fast-food enterprise concentrated its grip on the American suburban landscape. Among the dearly departed are such defunct chains as Pup 'N' Taco, Minnie Pearl Chicken, White Tower, Naugles, Red Barn, and (the *Seinfeld*-famous) Kenny Rogers Roasters. The biggest to fall was the Midwestern chain Burger Chef. The charbroiled-burger outfit, which is widely credited with pioneering both combo meals and kids' meals, grew to become the second-largest chain in the United States by the time it was bought out by General Foods in 1968. But it both expanded too quickly and stumbled under its new corporate minders; Burger Chef, which had over a thousand locations at its peak, would later be sold off to Hardee's before disappearing completely from the terrain by the mid-1990s.*

---

* Culture vultures will recall that the chain was part of a narrative arc in the final season of the hit period drama *Mad Men*. The Burger Chef episodes, which take place in 1969, involve debates among ad agency creatives about whether television campaigns that showcased families with stay-at-home mothers were too antiquated for the time. They chose to recast the fast-food booth with its convenient ease as the new family table,

All of this chaotic, sweeping growth came with collateral damage, and not just in terms of competitors slain or major expansions. The arrival of corporations and food conglomerates would have a direct effect on the food itself as more profitable shortcuts and substitutions were sought. For example, two years after being sold by Harland Sanders, Kentucky Fried Chicken would go public in 1966, and like McDonald's, the stock quickly boomed. Nearly everyone in the company directory, save for Sanders, who was wary of stocks, struck it rich. KFC would be listed on the New York Stock Exchange in 1969, and then, in 1971, just seven years after being purchased from the Colonel for $2 million, Kentucky Fried Chicken would again be sold, for $285 million to booze-and-food giant Heublein. It would then pass through a series of corporate hand-offs and spin-offs. Harland Sanders would become one of Kentucky Fried Chicken's fiercest critics as his scrupulous, time-tested methods met with modifications for mass consumption. "Let's face it, the Colonel's gravy was fantastic, but you had to be a Rhodes Scholar to cook it," one unnamed company executive sighed in 1970. "It involved too much time, it left too much room for human error, and it was too expensive."* Each evolution of a company from a modest, handshake

---

which could be interpreted as a nod to the scaling of suburbia, commuter regimens, and two-income households.

* That Sanders was no longer in charge didn't stop him from arriving at KFC outlets with the patented gravy spoon he carried with him wherever he went and unleashing a torrent of invective upon the purveyor of any product that offended him. Sanders would later be (unsuccessfully) sued for libel by Heublein, after Sanders likened KFC gravy to "sludge" and "wallpaper paste" in an interview with Louisville's *Courier-Journal.* "My God, that gravy is horrible," Sanders fumed. "They buy tap water for fifteen to twenty cents a thousand gallons and then they mix it with flour and starch and end up with pure wallpaper paste. And I know wallpaper paste, by God, because I've seen my mother make it."

Incredibly, the original topic of the interview had been whether a chicken wing constitutes white meat.

business built with sweat equity to an additional column in a corporate holdings ledger dragged it further away from its founding mission, practices, and recipes.

But the incorporation of these adulterations—the powders and artificial flavors, the cheap meat and shelf-stable items—wouldn't be the biggest effect of this new lordship by the suits, shareholders, cost accountants, and profit maximizers. Despite the industry's momentum, there was a real dilemma in Frytown, USA. By the end of the 1960s, the suburban strips, traditional small towns, and highway exits were already bloated with fast-food burgers, hot dogs, fried chicken, tacos, roast beef sandos, seafood, and more. To keep growing, companies started staking out new, fertile terrain. Urban centers became the answer.

The story of fast food's life in American cities runs on a tense political third rail that often passes between trope and urban myth. Modern critics of fast food note the saturation of quick-service chains in city centers, especially when compared to supermarkets and grocers in food deserts, and conclude something unnatural has happened. Others focus on the years of relentless fast-food marketing efforts that have specifically targeted poorer, minority communities within cities and see capitalist conspiracy. But the origins of urban fast food are a bit more complicated. The story begins amid the domestic tumult of the late 1960s.

As we know, in the wake of the postwar boom and the expansion of the interstates, millions of Americans left the cities to settle into newly built suburbs. But as developments go, this one was not terribly equitable. Between 1950 and 1960 alone, the nation's dozen largest cities saw the departure of 3.6 million white citizens and the arrival of 4.5 million nonwhite citizens. The white exodus (and the exclusionary zoning laws and racist subdivision covenants that followed) took crucial jobs, resources, and tax bases out of the cities. The people who remained, many of whom were minorities and the working poor, lost access to quality schools, economic opportunities, and civic services.

In August of 1965, the Watts riots erupted in Los Angeles. The largest and one of the deadliest urban riots of the civil rights era, the six-day fury resulted in dozens of deaths and the damaging or destruction of nearly a thousand businesses and, for many watching at home, brought about the terrifying specter of total revolution. In Watts and around the country, activists were calling not just for jobs, but also for the development of black-owned businesses in urban centers, where black Americans overwhelmingly lived.* At this intersection of race, despair, and capitalism, the interests of fast-food companies, the US government, and the revolution (surreally) converged.

In her book *Supersizing Urban America*, Chin Jou details how, starting in the late 1960s, companies such as McDonald's and Burger King began to aggressively recruit minority owners to open stores in urban areas. These initiatives were undertaken with a mixed bag of motives in mind—companies wanted to gain footholds in new markets, please their shareholders, and avoid the negative publicity that came with ignoring the cause of civil rights.†

---

* According to 1970 census data, over 80 percent of African Americans lived in cities. Meanwhile, a study of the businesses in fifteen black neighborhoods where riots occurred between 1965 and 1967 showed that only about 25 percent of them were black owned.
† In "A McDonald's That Represents the Soul of a People," Nishani Frazier chronicled one episode that motivated fast-food companies to hasten their minority-outreach efforts: A 1969 initiative led by a minister and a rabbi in Cleveland called for a black-owned McDonald's outlet in the city at a time when only a handful of McDonald's outlets around the country were

The potential expansion of fast food into urban centers didn't just make great business sense for growing companies; it was an attractive proposition to would-be entrepreneurs in cities. After all, the fast-food franchises had already boomed in the suburbs. They had cachet and name recognition, along with established popularity with middle-class consumers and banks. Going all the way back to the days of White Castle, the stores and the standardized operations were designed to be easily reproducible. And these weren't the only advantages, particularly in urban areas. "Perhaps the most obvious explanation as to why fast food restaurants tend to outnumber grocery stores in America's inner cities is that fast food is generally more profitable than the grocery business," Jou writes, noting the significant disparities that still exist between the two business models in their profit margins, in addition to the required real estate, onerous leases, and zoning restrictions. The table for urban fast food was now nearly set. McDonald's, Burger King, and their ilk had their expansionist designs. Entrepreneurs in the cities who wanted in on the American dream of business ownership had their ambitions.

Only as race riots fumed across the country did officials belatedly seem to understand that economic opportunity would be a major driver of equality or, in the absence of that, tranquility. "Our nation is moving toward two societies, one black, one white—separate and unequal," went the blistering conclusion of the *Kerner Report*, which had been commissioned by President Lyndon Johnson in 1967 to study the causes of the riots. After the unrest that followed the assassination of Dr. Martin

owned by black franchisees. As support for the campaign quickly grew, the protest morphed into a boycott that forced four McDonald's outlets in Cleveland closed. After the mayor interceded, the stores were sold to black owners or black-led organizations.

Luther King, Jr., in 1968, Johnson directed the Small Business Administration to dispense loans to help businesses create economic opportunities in the cities. Fast-food franchises were seen as good bets to serve as engines for revitalization.

Later that year, with the riots and antiwar protests as the backdrop, Richard Nixon successfully campaigned for president as a "law and order" candidate, casting the counterculture and civil unrest as un-American and a boon to the Communist cause and its recruitment efforts. In response to the domestic upheaval (and, sure, to shore up potential votes for his 1972 reelection campaign), Nixon established the Office of Minority Business Enterprise shortly after taking office. He pledged to issue tens of millions of dollars in government-backed loans for minority entrepreneurs through Commerce Department programs and the Small Business Administration. Nixon couched the philosophy behind these initiatives in that classic American formulation—work and enterprise, specifically "black capitalism," rather than disdainful welfare, would lift Americans, particularly members of disadvantaged minority communities, out of poverty and into the middle class.

In spite of some mismanagement issues and shortfalls in dispersing as many loans to minority entrepreneurs as promised, the federal programs did get results. Thousands upon thousands of government-backed loans were issued, and favoring the perceived soundness of the franchise model, many of them underwrote the spread of new fast-food outlets in different US cities. The availability of these loans were also marketed aggressively by fast-food companies, which established urban-development and minority-outreach departments to help facilitate the process. This arrangement would continue for decades to follow.

And so, unlike Wilco and Lilly Pulitzer apparel, fast food successfully moved beyond the suburbs and highways and took root in American cities. As it grew—according to one tally by business historian Robert Yancy, the number of minority-run fast-food franchises sextupled in just five years from about four hundred in 1969 to over twenty-four hundred in 1974—the industry itself surged to meet its increasingly corporate bottom line. The arrangement wasn't perfect. More than a few minority franchisees would later accuse fast-food chains of redlining as their plans to open stores in new neighborhoods floundered in corporate red tape. Some minority owners were preyed upon in unfavorable business arrangements with white partners, while others claimed they failed to receive the same privileges and general support as white franchisees. In spite of this, expansion created tens of thousands of new jobs in urban areas for decades to come and made what had quickly emerged as a national business phenomenon available to a fuller representation of Americans.

Like the small towns that coalesced around the Dairy Queens in the 1960s West Texas of Larry McMurtry, new urban institutions in American cityscapes were created around fast food. By the late 1960s, for example, McDonald's debuted new store designs that included their fabled, ugly brown mansard roofs and widely incorporated dedicated space as dining rooms for the first time. What had started as an enterprise centered around the needs of fast-moving highway commuters adapted in ways that befitted the dynamics of city life.

That fast food's suburban origins came from prosperity and the exclusive orderliness of the Levittowns, while its urban roots rose out of national disorder, neglect, and economic despair, has a bigger meaning. "The moment when the fast-food industry was beginning to think of the African American market, we were only a few years away from the passage of the Civil Rights Act of 1964," Dr. Marcia Chatelain, a history and African American studies professor at Georgetown University, told *The Washington Post* in 2018. "If we go from a moment in which public accommodation in the restaurant was a site of trauma and racial violence to one in which [the industry is] trying to convince consumers that it is a normal place to go, that there are not any prohibitions against you being there—you can understand why it becomes very appealing and very attractive for people to go to a fast-food restaurant."

From this (imperfect) legacy as well as its inclusiveness, fast food helped secure the loyalty of the neighborhoods it served. One generation after the 1965 Watts Rebellion, riots returned to South Los Angeles following the 1992 acquittal of four LAPD officers in the infamous assault of Rodney King. Despite the six-day upheaval that laid waste to hundreds of black- and minority-owned stores, not one of the five McDonald's in the five-square-mile riot-and-fire zone was defaced or destroyed. Writing for *Time*, Edwin Reingold described the scene following the upheaval: "Within hours after the curfew was lifted, all South Central's Golden Arches were back up and running, feeding fire fighters, police and National Guard troops as well as burned-out citizens. The St. Thomas Aquinas Elementary School, with 300 hungry students and no utilities, called for lunches and got them free—with delivery to boot."

The economics of fast food aren't designed to benefit the surrounding communities much. The food is usually trucked in from centralized prep zones in far-flung places. More often than not, the majority of the money spent at larger chains wends its way out of the community and back to corporate offices and shareholder portfolios. But what fast food does offer is a gathering point for local congregation with a low barrier to access. "Our businesses there are owned by African American entrepreneurs who hired African American managers who hired African American employees who served everybody in the community, whether they be Korean, African American, or Caucasian," Edward Rensi, then the president and CEO of McDonald's USA, said after the riots.

Not long after the events of 1992, Stanford University sociologists set out to interview participants in the riots to figure out why they had chosen to pass over the Golden Arches. Recounting the happenings years later, Chuck Ebeling, the director of corporate communications for McDonald's during the riots, credited the company's small-scale community-outreach efforts like dishing out free coffee and sports equipment. He summed up Stanford's findings about why the rioters left McDonald's alone thusly: "They are one of us."

It's difficult to imagine today's fast-food franchises—the branchlets of multinational corporations, purveyors of deliciously narcotic and obesogenic foodstuffs, frequent practitioners of dubious marketing initiatives, and among the biggest employers of low-wage workers—as credible, organic community centers. But in spite of the rap among its detractors, fast food became a place for uncomplicated assembly in longstanding communities. And initially at least, it offered the germ of opportunity not only for the country's young strivers, but also for its newest arrivals.

8 "YES, IT CAN BE DONE"

*A nation? says Bloom. A nation is the same people
living in the same place.*
—JAMES JOYCE

In the weeks after the Watts riots, Congress passed the Immigration and Nationality Act of 1965, capping off a year of Great Society legislation that included the Voting Rights Act, the Social Security Act, and the Draft Card Mutilation Act. The Hart-Celler Act, which undid the restrictive country-based immigration quotas that had been in place since the early 1920s, unwittingly transformed America's demographic makeup from overwhelmingly white and European to one that was much more ethnically diverse and diffuse. In 1960, roughly seven out of every eight immigrants came to the United States from Europe. Fifty years later, by 2010, about 90 percent of arrivals had emigrated from places other than Europe. This figure included roughly 75 percent of new immigrants who made their way to the United States from Latin America and Asia.*

---

* As Tom Gjelten chronicles in his book *A Nation of Nations*, a late change to the

The passage of the 1965 Immigration Act also dovetailed with the starting point of a fifteen-year period (1965–80) in which two and a half times more Americans would join the workforce than in the previous fifteen years (1950–65). Millions of young boomers and new immigrants were looking for work, and as rates of single-parent homes and divorce rose, more women entered the workplace. These developments, along with the influxes from abroad, would change the character of the country, the nature of its cities, the demography of its workforce, and the diversity of its cuisine.

As a result, American palates grew more adventurous as previously unknown fare entered the mainstream market, a trend that carried into fast food. Within regional American cuisine, the Cajun-themed Popeyes brand took off in the early 1970s and grew into a national chain. A few years later, in 1977, the North Carolina biscuit-and-chicken chain Bojangles' debuted. It was the brainchild of Hardee's franchisee Jack Fulk, who had split off after continually irritating corporate by inventing his own menu items. In 1980, five years after opening its doors in Sinaloa, the Mexican roast-chicken chain El Pollo Loco made its first entrée in the American Southwest and expanded to hundreds of franchises. Around the same time, the immigrant-founded Golden Krust started bringing jerk chicken and Jamaican patties to the masses everywhere from the Bronx and Canada to Florida and Texas, with many of its franchises opened by former nurses from the West Indies seek-

---

legislation to appease more conservative lawmakers shifted the law's focus to absorbing immigrants on the basis of family reunification (mostly meaning Europeans) instead of by their relevant skill sets. This maneuver backfired and the United States went from being 84 percent white in 1965 to 62 percent white in 2015.

ing a way to plug their skills for regimentation into better hours.

As the US population grew and diversified, so did fast food, which mushroomed like a fallout cloud over the Bikini Atoll. Between 1976 and 1986 alone, the number of fast-food restaurants in the United States would triple. In addition to feeding busy, burgeoning masses on the cheap, the industry also served as a channel for assimilation and acculturation among new arrivals. One of those new arrivals was Aslam Khan.

Aslam Khan works out of a nondescript corporate park in Roanoke, Texas, a town that shares its name with that ill-fated immigrant settlement in modern-day North Carolina. That Khan owns nearly three hundred fast-food franchises, including the most outlets of anyone of Church's—America's fourth-largest fried-chicken chain—does not breach the top tier of the most compelling details about him. Aslam Khan is not just a Church's evangelist, he is a guru and an initiator to the cult of the self; he is the Norman Vincent Peale of American striving, the Vince Neil of feel-good optimism. "It took me eighteen years to figure out how to get to the United States and thirteen years to become a millionaire," Khan said in his spacious office on a Thursday afternoon in July 2015.

Khan makes declarations like this in a quietly self-assured manner. His thick Pakistani accent, his effective penchant for self-repetition, and his philosophical turns of phrase all lend Khan a certain magnetism. These qualities are not often found in someone running a self-fashioned fast-food kingdom from a nondescript corporate park in the northern burbs of Dallas. But there Khan sat, neither short nor tall, but physically compact, as if condensed by nature to contain all of his energies.

The next day, Khan would travel to California to drop his son off for his freshman year of college. Like his father, Ibrahim would study business. If Khan felt the woolly twinge of pride and wistfulness that such a milestone moment evokes, it didn't show. To prepare his son for the world, Khan had placed him not in a Church's store, where he might be coddled, but in the store of a competitor, KFC, where his duties included scrubbing the bathroom floors and mopping.

Aslam Khan was born in the northwest hinterlands of Pakistan in a village called Fatehabad. "It's in a mountainous area behind the capital, Islamabad," he began, "and when I was born, there were no roads. There's still no roads. We didn't have running water. There was no electricity. There were no schools, so I used to go four or five miles one way every morning to school. Other kids didn't want to go because we were expected to go through the jungle with monkeys and cheetahs and whatever the rumors were. The kids didn't want to go, but I would pick up and shoot through the jungle to get to the school."

Khan's childhood was intensely deprived. His mother had given birth to nine children and died at thirty-five. He kept a story in his pocket about dancing around a fire to stay warm while she washed his only pair of clothes. "In my mind, I was thinking, 'Why are we so damn poor?' I didn't know anything better, by the way, but I knew this: Normal necessity of life was not available here."

At fourteen, Khan decided to leave home. The nearest high school was twelve miles away, and the family had no money for him to stay at school. His mind made up, he now had to break the news to his father, who begged him to stay and argued that a life's living in Fatehabad would be good enough.

Khan turned away and packed his spare set of clothes. He borrowed five rupees (less than a nickel even today) and left home. Khan walked several miles to the bus stop and bought a three-and-a-half rupee ticket away from his life and family in Fatehabad. "I never went to a city before, that was my first trip ever."

He rode the bus all the way to its final stop, the railway station, where he slept his first night away from home on a bench. The next day, Khan found work washing pots and pans at a bakery, then started at a canteen that would let him work afternoons and evenings while he went to school. He earned $4 a week and slept nights in the back of the store with his coworkers, who were other boys his age. Khan finished high school and got the equivalent of an associate's degree. He ended up in the capital, where, after being rejected from a college, he saw a listing for a coveted job at the US Embassy Club as a waiter and a bartender. Daunted by the long line of fellow applicants, Khan dramatically stretched out of his chair across the desk of his interviewer and said from close up, "I need this job so much I can't afford to miss a single word." The gambit worked and he was hired.

The grounds of the embassy were a berth through which Khan saw the West, learned its diplomatic protocols, and, for eight years, pondered his American Dream. Within a country whose political system was being engulfed by a rigid religious wave, the club was also a cultural oasis. After alcohol was banned in 1977, the US Embassy Club became one of the few gathering places in Pakistan where one could have a drink. The dynamic Khan was at the center of the hospitality, eventually rising to manager. Less than three weeks after Iranian students stormed the American embassy in Tehran, igniting the infamous hostage crisis in 1979, the American embassy in Islamabad was torched. The club moved to a large residence and carried on; Khan remained charismatic and determined. He befriended diplomats, secured the favor of a green card, and eventually flew to America.

The first place Khan walked into for a job in the United States was a Church's district office, where he applied for a manager position. He was immediately rejected. Apparently, references and several years of experience from an embassy club in Pakistan had failed to impress the area manager of a fried-chicken chain in 1980s California. "At the door I stopped at the exit and I said, 'Today is my first day in the United States. Could you kindly tell me where I screwed up so I can prepare for my next job interview?' He said, 'Get the fuck outta here, I don't have the time.'" The manager then tapped his assistant to *show Khan out*. As he left, Khan told himself, "This is the company I'm going to work for and I'm going to teach them civility."

He changed out of his dress clothes, threw on a pair of jeans, and headed to a Church's store, where he applied for a job as a crew member. They started him as a dishwasher at $3.25 an hour. He told himself, "I'll try because I believe that it's not going to take me very long once I get into any system." A few weeks later, his manager pulled him aside and promoted him. Within three months, Khan was a store manager. "I went from there to area manager, marketing manager, marketing director, vice president of operations, chief operating officer," he added, before founding his own company and securing his empire with the purchase of ninety-seven Church's outlets.

But before all that, he did continue to encounter that old manager who had turned him away on his first day in the

States. "He was my boss," Khan explains. "They put me as a manager under him. I did really well under him and then kept on working, kept on working. Now I'm in the office with him, now I'm assisting him. Every Tuesday, he used to meet his boss and so I used to make all of his reports. I said, 'Sir, I have two hours in my time, is there anything I can do for you?' He used to give me all of his dirty work. I said, 'Fine.' I was learning so I did it really well, and each time he would get stuck on a follow-up question he can't answer because I'm the one who's building [the reports]. One day his boss got upset and he said, 'Might as well call Aslam and give him the job because each time I ask you something, you call him.' So I got the job and became his boss. Then every morning he used to pass my office to go to his office and he said, 'Good morning, sir.' I said, 'Get the fuck outta here!'"

Not far from where Khan lived when he first arrived in the States stands the world's oldest-operating McDonald's, in Downey, California. This relic of the drive-in era is just down the road from the birthplace of the Apollo program, which blasted man to the moon.

It's beautiful. Rather than the standard-issue dual arches, the road sign is a towering single golden parabola with an all-caps marquee that reads HAMBURGERS. Perched atop that is a massive neon rendering of the company's first mascot, Speedee, a winking, bow-tied, toque-wearing cartoon waiter. The building, the third-ever McDonald's, was one of the few franchises opened during the reign of the McDonald brothers and still has the company's original red-and-white tile scheme. Minus the Chevy pickup trucks and Priuses outside, it's ready-made fodder for a postcard of a 1950s drive-in: no indoor seating and no drive-thru window—a feature that generates about two-thirds of the business for a typical McDonald's store.* It's also the only McDonald's location where a customer can still get a deep-fried apple pie.

The landmark Downey store isn't just an architectural throwback. Its owner, Ron Piazza, started his improbable-seeming journey to prosperity at just fifteen years old, when he took a dollar-an-hour job on the fryers at McDonald's in the late 1960s. Like Khan, he also traveled the route from shift worker to supervisor to upper management to ownership. Nearly fifty years later, Piazza is an impressive dead ringer for Buddy Garrity and is the owner of ten McDonald's franchises.

The constellations of quick-service companies are steeped in this kind of fries-to-fortunes lore featuring young workers and franchise owners alike. Piazza told me the story of a man he hired as an entry-level employee at fifteen and a half who had worked his way up to upper management after escaping the killing fields in Cambodia. The first thing he'd eaten upon arriving in the United States had been McDonald's, and the rest was history. Piazza numbered off at least four hires who had become owners of their own stores. "Ray Kroc used to pride himself on saying he made more millionaires than anybody else in America."

Piazza's remark sounded a lot like one made by Roland L. Jones, who started as a McDonald's manager in Washington,

---

* Incredibly, after the store was damaged in a 1994 earthquake, company plans to knock down the already-outdated store inspired a public freak-out. That year, the National Trust for Historic Preservation even listed it as one of the country's eleven most endangered historical places, along with the San Francisco Mint, the USS *Constellation* aircraft carrier, a Frank Lloyd Wright estate in Wisconsin, and the entirety of Cape Cod. (Needless to say, the company changed its mind.)

D.C., in 1965 and went on to run three stores. "McDonald's has made more African American millionaires than everyone else," he told the *Los Angeles Times* in 2010. "We are into the second and third generation now of owners." Jones is a particularly notable figure in McDonald's history. A cofounder of the National Black McDonald's Operators Association—an advocacy organization founded in 1972 whose three hundred members now control thirteen hundred franchises in the United States and beyond—Jones was also the company's first black executive, serving as the head of urban operations in the 1970s.

Then there is the story of June Martino, a World War II Women's Army Corps vet, who started as Ray Kroc's bookkeeper in 1948 and rose to become his most trusted lieutenant and one of the most important executives in the company's history. Over twenty years she would serve formally as the company's secretary and treasurer and less formally as a recruiter, franchisee mentor, factotum, corporate peacekeeper, and checker of egos and emotions. Unofficially, she was known as "the vice president of equilibrium." Her contributions were critical to the period in which McDonald's set the framework for its national ascent, and she reaped the spoils accordingly. After the company went public in 1965, Martino's holdings soared in value to $5.3 million (about $40 million in 2018 terms). She would retire a few years later, but not before being named to the McDonald's board of directors for life and becoming the second woman after Queen Elizabeth to be hosted at the New York Stock Exchange's all-male executive dining room.*

---

* Her Majesty has technically owned a few regal McDonald's of her own during her reign. In the early aughts, the Crown Estate bought and eventually sold a retail park in Slough

* * *

Taken together, these stories represent a callback to the gauzy, democratic possibilities outlined by James Truslow Adams and embodied by Harland Sanders and other fast-food founders. They are also central to a national narrative about what it takes to thrive in America: *Work hard, do whatever it takes, and you can come from nothing, advance quickly, triumph spectacularly, fulfill your destiny, buy a Maserati, have a picture taken of you and your friends duck-faced and jumping in tandem on a beach, live the American Dream.* It's a zero-sum system of thought, part of a specifically American doctrine of self-reliance, individual destiny, and cold-blooded optimism with countless adherents, especially in the upper echelons of industry and government.*

Despite the pitfalls of this seductive, blinkered kind of narrative, it's still hard to resist the story of someone who fell in love with America from afar and made good on its promise. A story where triumph is a matter of will instead of a question of statistics. Anything less nicks at the veneer of what America means and what promise its frontier-settling secular religion of optimistic self-reliance truly holds. Part of what makes Aslam Khan so enthralling is that he is a little different from

---

within eyeshot of Windsor Castle that held one set of Golden Arches. In 2015, her massive portfolio grew to include a shopping center in Banbury, which also sports a Mickey D's, with a menu that includes tea and bacon rolls for breakfast, a burger called the Beef and Cheese Feast, and two different veggie burgers.

* A 2014 Pew survey reports that a much higher percentage of Americans hold two specific beliefs about social mobility than citizens of industrialized European countries:

    1. Individual destiny, the idea that your fate is in your own hands (57 percent in the United States versus the European median of 37 percent)

    2. That hard work is crucial to success (73 percent in the United States versus the European median of 35 percent)

others in his position, less inflamed and aggrieved by criticisms of fast-food work, less bothered by the rumors of cheetahs in the jungle. His triumphant odyssey from provincial Pashtun to transcontinental striver to American Dream incarnate has made his faith to be optimism.

And so, if one were bold enough to suggest that the American Dream Khan achieved—dishwasher to millionaire in thirteen years—would be improbable, if not impossible, today, he or she would be treated to the copestone of Khan's bootstraps sermon. "Absolutely not," he started with a wave of the hand. "Most people are denying their ability. Here's what's happening: The capabilities are built, they cannot be bought. If the work ethics are not there, the desires are not there, you can't be anything. I've built my capabilities to be CEO today of five hundred restaurants. Thirty years ago, I didn't know how to run one. I used to think manager was a big cheese. Then I thought, 'Oh, man, can you imagine I've become district manager?' There's a capability built in. You have to be real, you have to know absolutely yourself. What your strengths are, what your weaknesses are, you have to do that discovery. . . . Don't let others tell you, unless you are very ignorant about yourself.

"It can be done, and I'm going to write a book one day called *Yes, It Can Be Done.* I honestly believe there's a great possibility that Americans are becoming complacent. They're looking outward. Why don't you look inward at a country that provided everybody like me and everybody else? There is no country on earth, I promise you—I'm a very well-read man— like the United States. You can be anything you want to be. I don't care about China becoming a superpower, I don't care about Russia or how big they can get, there is no system such as the United States. Everything is here. We're taking it for granted."

Four months later, after decades of stagnant wage growth, the middle class slipped out of the economic majority in the United States for the first time in forty years. And in 2017, Khan would be named the CEO of TGI Fridays.

9 DRIVE-THRU AMERICA

The American street is a piece of highway . . . a straight line that gives itself away immediately. It contains no mystery.
—JEAN-PAUL SARTRE

The cup of coffee that upended the entire cultural equilibrium of the 1990s was purchased by a woman named Stella Liebeck on a Thursday morning in February of 1992. Its meager price of forty-nine cents and eight-ounce serving size were less important than its temperature, a scorching hot 180 degrees. This meant that when the paper cup tumped over into the seventy-nine-year-old widow's lap, she ended up in an Albuquerque hospital for over a week. The lawsuit that would eventually follow in 1994, *Liebeck v. McDonald's*, would result in an epoch-making award, including $2.7 million in punitive damages.

Not surprisingly, news of the seven-figure conclusion to the trial quickly became an item in national and international papers. With each retelling, the facts of the ordeal grew more distorted. Rather than sitting in the passenger seat of her grandson's car, which had been parked in the McDonald's lot at the time of the spill, it was reported that Liebeck had been carelessly driving on the open road while trying to drink scalding coffee. Contrary to some claims, she had also truly suffered—burns covered 16 percent of her body, including 6 percent of the third degree—and her injuries required multiple skin grafts. Though she had only sought to get her medical expenses covered, Stella Liebeck was caricatured as greedy, craven, reckless, and even unpatriotic. When those efforts had failed, a jury had unanimously come up with the colossal award for punitive damages, the rough equivalent of two days of coffee sales for McDonald's.*

Liebeck fast became cannon fodder for hits by late-night television hosts, an easy punch line in monologues and on Top 10 lists. "Now she claims she broke her nose on the sneeze guard at the Sizzler bending over looking at the chickpeas," Jay Leno yukked on the *Tonight* show. Her ordeal would be alluded to in episodes of *Seinfeld* and *Futurama*; Weird Al Yankovic and Toby Keith would refer to it in songs.

The verdict in what came to be known as the "hot coffee lawsuit" had political ramifications, too. Not long after the trial, the case entered heavy rotation as well-funded publicity initiatives for tort reform made use, in ads, of its reputation as perhaps the most recognizable exemplar of lawsuit abuse.† For the remainder of her life and beyond, Liebeck would be linked to the epidemic of "jackpot justice" and the "lawsuit lottery." In prominent op-eds and campaign stump speeches, she was

---

* Unbeknown to most of the public, the total award was later cut $680,000 on appeal before the two parties settled for about half a million dollars.
† According to the 2011 documentary *Hot Coffee*, at least one such campaign was spearheaded by Karl Rove, then an adviser to Texas governor George W. Bush, as Rove also moonlighted as a consultant for companies such as Philip Morris tobacco.

cast as the demon personification of the lost American way, the embodiment of a country whose values had gone soft, molly-coddled, and unrecognizable.

Whether Stella Liebeck was truly entitled to payment from Mc-Donald's for a self-inflicted injury or not, her ordeal divines an entire early-1990s universe. That decade, with its inexplicable exuberance for Weird Al (guilty!) and Leno (not guilty!) and its disdain for litigiousness and assaults on big business, found America on familiar footing—loitering immaturely at the precipice of great opportunity. The old existential Cold War fears of nuclear doom were dissipating with the slow-motion breakup of the Soviet Union. The United States would soon rev toward unparalleled prosperity with frenzied, hypermobile gusto.

By 1990, the American workforce approached unprecedented gender parity with women comprising 47 percent, the result of a steady tick upward from 30 percent across the postwar decades. Though it had seemed revolutionary that about 25 percent of American women with children held jobs following World War II, by 1991 that figure had climbed to 66.8 percent. The continued rise of dual-income households and single-parent homes, along with the divorce rate (which peaked in the early 1980s), helped place convenience at the center of the universe. The nineties were peppered with awe-striking innovations like drive-thru banks and drive-thru dry cleaners and drive-thru photo-processing centers. Fledgling drive-thru businesses came to run the commercial gamut from the practical (pharmacies) to the brilliant and perhaps ill-conceived (liquor stores) to the downright spiritual (chapels). "The working person doesn't have time to come in," the owner of a camera-operated, Chicago-area drive-thru funeral home told *The New York Times* in 1989. "They want to see the body but they don't want to have to wait. I always thought there should be some way they could see the body anytime they want."

The most enduring and widely embraced of these businesses were drive-thru restaurants, which already had cars and the impatient national condition etched into their DNA. Red's Giant Hamburg, a now-defunct Route 66 burger joint in Missouri that opened in 1947, is credited by some with being the first drive-thru in the world. Others suggest the title belongs to Kirby's Pig Stand, a barbecue chain also considered to be the country's first drive-in restaurant. When it opened in 1948, In-N-Out Burger used what it claims was the first two-way speaker in fast food, which is how the drive-thru experience is mostly still conducted today. A few years later, in 1951, Jack in the Box married the McDonald brothers' carhop-free, drive-in model and In-N-Out's limited menu concept and opened as a drive-thru-only operation in San Diego, using a speaker box with a menu board on it a few car lengths behind the pickup window. Jack in the Box's influential drive-thru concept was pilfered with literal fidelity by the iconic California chain Der Wienerschnitzel, which solved concerns about its limited real estate by fashioning a car-sized hole in the middle of restaurants for customers to physically drive through to receive their food.

By the late 1960s, drive-in restaurants had mostly fallen out of favor. Some chains (especially away from car-besotted California) started betting big on indoor seating and dining rooms. However, Wendy's founder Dave Thomas understood that the light at the end of the competitive tunnel was a headlight. "I thought, 'Where is all this business going from the drive-in [restaurant] business? The drive-in used to be real popular, and there are more cars on the road but there are less drive-ins.'" After paring down the menu at Wendy's, Thomas found success with a speedy drive-thru window; bigger franchisors such as Burger King and Kentucky Fried Chicken quickly followed suit with their own.

And so, the drive-thru window, which went mainstream as a bonus amenity in the 1970s, eventually morphed into a necessity for the increasingly frantic way of life in which dining out became a deed born of circumstance more than just luxury. By the late 1980s, nearly 90 percent of Americans were eating at restaurants at least once a week, with 40 percent of them dining out daily. The rapid shift away from eating at home piqued the interest of the Department of Agriculture, which dedicated a study of the phenomenon in 1989. It found that the 34 percent of American food budgets that had been devoted to dining away from home in 1970 had ballooned to nearly 46 percent by 1989. Fast-food and casual-dining chains grabbed a lot of the traffic. In 1989, fast food captured 41 percent of the total amount spent on food outside the home. Three years later, the top two hundred chains reaped more than 50 percent of restaurant sales, besting independent restaurants for the first time ever.

These changes were about more than just familiarity and ubiquity or the convenience of not cooking; they were increasingly about time. It became more and more routine for lunch or dinner to be served in a paper bag and handed through a window to someone in an idling car, where it would be wolfed down on the road or perhaps saved for home (less about half the fries, of course). As the drive-thru lines grew in the 1980s and early '90s, chains schemed up and tested more car-friendly items, designed with dashboard dining in mind. Wendy's introduced pita wraps, KFC invented miniature handheld sandwiches called Chicken Littles, and Taco Bell further embraced the possibilities of the folded tortilla.

A few new arrivals on the fast-food scene also popped up to take the growing need for speed to its logical extreme. Resembling tiny islets in a river of cars, quick-service restaurants like Checkers, Rally's, and Central Park started appearing in the mid-1980s, largely outfitted with double drive-thrus. Customers in cars would often be served out of two windows on opposite sides of the building, a stressful-looking arrangement that all but dared a diner to approach the store by foot. In many cases, there weren't dining rooms anyway, sometimes just a few token outdoor tables for alfresco dining with a small side of car exhaust.

What the double drive-thrus lack in serendipitous community and hospitality, they make up for in velocity and economy. Using mere fractions of the real estate and employees required by bigger fast-food restaurants, these express burger spots have parlayed lower overheads into prices that run about 30 percent less than their competitors'. And with more limited menus, transactions can often be completed in less than a minute. In their impersonal, car-centric character, these bare-bones newcomers in some ways represent a thematic return to the early days of fast food, when the bloated, pricier menus and slow operations of drive-ins and diners seemed primed for disruption. Like a drive-thru itself, time is a flat circle.

Despite the emergence of new entrants and upstarts, the bigger chains reaped the rewards of drive-thru mania. By the late 1980s, the number of McDonald's locations with drive-thrus had grown to seven thousand strong, each with the capacity to serve 144 cars an hour or one every twenty-five seconds. In 1988, for the first time more than 50 percent of McDonald's sales were conducted through the drive-thru window. The primacy of fast food and its drive-thru didn't reveal itself solely through the rogue capture of American food budgets, but also through a new dominance over all meals of the day. And with the help of a handheld specialty item, eating breakfast in America never looked the same again.

Long before the Egg McMuffin became the national breakfast sandwich, it started as a simple culinary mash note. Its creator, a former adman and a McDonald's franchisee named Herb Peterson, loved eggs Benedict. And so he worked away in his Santa Barbara kitchen like a nuclear scientist in Bushehr, seeking breakthrough capacity for an eggs Benedict that would translate to the fast-food world. In the early 1970s, Peterson cracked the code by cooking eggs in a custom-built Teflon ring instead of poaching them, and in a stroke of genius, he replaced hollandaise sauce with a slice of good old, ready-to-melt, goddamn American cheese. The concoction was placed on a toasted English muffin topped with Canadian bacon. Ray Kroc had just finished lunch when he was called upon to sample one; he ate two of them on the spot.

Like its quick-service knockoff, eggs Benedict is an American dish. Culinary historians overwhelmingly trace its creation to Lemuel Benedict, the hungover Wall Street stockbroker who stumbled into the Waldolf-Astoria hotel one morning in 1894 and demanded a breakfast made with bread, poached eggs, pork, and hollandaise. The rest is history. The open-faced creation became an instant standby at the hotel and then beamed out from Fifth Avenue. And from the world's most exclusive mahogany haunts it went out to the greasy Greek diners of Joseph Mitchell, Greenwich Village, and beyond. The Benedict and its countless variations remain a hangover staple for anyone armed with a fork, a knife, and a napkin.

But for those looking for something cheaper and tidier, there is the McMuffin, a more portable analgesic wrapped in its trademark yellow paper. By 1985, the McMuffin comprised 15 percent of the annual company sales. And in 1987, roughly 25 percent of all breakfasts eaten outside American households were served by McDonald's.

With Americans using drive-thrus to eat, bank, be joined in holy matrimony, and pay their respects to the dearly departed, the auto industry rose to match it. It all started with Chrysler, which released the first successful mass-market minivans in 1983—the Dodge Caravan and the Plymouth Voyager. The two praiseworthy, slow-accelerating boxes almost certainly helped save Chrysler* from the doom brought on by the effects of two recessions in the early 1980s and intense new competition from automakers abroad.

Bigger than station wagons and small enough to still fit in garages, minivans became the ultimate family ride: a spacious, affordable, low-to-earth mark of authenticity in fake-looking, fabricated suburbias. After selling an impressive two hundred thousand–plus minivans in their debut year, Chrysler would achieve Peak Minivan in the late 1990s with six hundred thousand of them clunking off lots each year. The Caravan and Voyager were also the first two vehicles since the drive-in era

---

* It would be fair to say that the federal government also helped Chrysler a little bit in this era by floating it a $1.5 billion loan.

to come equipped with cupholders, a profound wink at their domestic nature.

The cupholders in early-model minivans were really just two dorky circular impressions on the center dashboard console. But as the minivan life swung into the mainstream, consumers went as wild for the innovation as they did for Walkmans and Umbro shorts. When Chrysler designers set about redesigning its popular minivans in the late 1980s, they paid special attention to the cupholder, adding a pop-up mechanism that made it more functional for use while driving. "When we began doing the new minivan, we evaluated all the letters that we got," Trevor Creed, a Chrysler interior design chief, told the *Orlando Sentinel* in 1992. "That's when the cupholder thing really began to take off. It was one of those crazy little things that people thought were really neat."

As with most new things, not everyone was smitten. Like the artificial subculture of "minivan and soccer moms," Chrysler's investment in cupholder technology divided industry observers and purists. In 1989, the newfangled scourge of "crannies for drinking cups" was derided as a "future frill" by *U.S. News and World Report*. Chrysler's competitors released their own minivans with their own cupholders, but it would be years before the feature would become a standard in cars built for American markets. Among the more stubborn holdouts were European imports and luxury sports cars. In his book *Small Things Considered*, the writer Henry Petroski marvels at the sophisticated amenities of his mid-1990s Volvo sedan, only to fret at its mostly symbolic cupholder: "In a car that has so many thoughtful design details, like a left-foot rest in a car without a clutch, this was a mystery. Cup holders in automobiles were not part of traditional Swedish culture, however, and Volvo seems only reluctantly to have developed a retrofit for the American car. Whether the company liked it or not, increasingly in the 1990s, American car buyers were expecting something to hold their drinks."

For a while, basic domestic cars delayed getting in on the action, too. Most Ford Probe hatchbacks sported a curved dashboard and no cupholders, including the 1989 model driven by Stella Liebeck's grandson, which left her to balance her ill-fated cup on her seat as she precariously added her customary cream and sugar. One disregarded and sadly ironic grace note of the public disparagement that accompanied Liebeck's saga is that, following the hot-coffee lawsuit, the tide of cupholder adoption turned forever. By the mid-1990s, with a few sporty holdouts, cupholders more or less became a standard feature in American cars.

The busy marriage of minivan mania, dirt-cheap oil, Detroit savvy, and prosperity would pave the way for the rise of the oversize sport-utility vehicle (SUV). The SUV took the necessity-driven, house-on-wheels spirit of the minivan (and flourishing, on-the-go American life) and souped it all up. The SUV remains one of the more enduring emblems of 1990s indulgence, often weirdly coupled with fancy, upmarket coffee in tall cups with sculptured lids and cardboard sleeves.* Built atop truck bases, the SUVs guzzled gas and eroded ozone, aided repressive petrostates, magically *ka-thunked* over curbs. They offered the promise of rugged, off-road capability for a consumer base that would overwhelmingly never go off road. SUVs also

---

* In 1992, the year of Stella Liebeck's accident, the country had fewer than two hundred Starbucks locations.

presented myriad hazards to their owners (fewer safety regulations and high rollover rates) as well as other drivers (high-
set headlights and raised points of collision).

In his book, *High and Mighty*, Keith Bradsher discloses that
internal industry research pegged many SUV drivers as "insecure, vain, self-centered and self-absorbed, who are frequently
nervous about their marriages, and who lack confidence in
their driving skills."* Car companies marketed to these
crowds accordingly, promising adventure and cashing in on the
vehicles' huge profit margins compared to those of smaller
cars. For scolds and grunge rockers, the status-obsessed consumerism that wrought the popularity of Explorers and Expe-
ditions and 4Runners and Navigators could be seen as
shorthand diagnosis for what ailed America in the 1990s.

Strictly by the numbers, the 1990s were largely remembered
as a time of wild affluence. Liebeck's 1992 accident was a tiny
footnote in a year in which the Mall of America debuted and
super size entered the commercial lexicon. From 1992 until
1999, the US economy grew by about 4 percent each year, a
furious, yet-to-be-duplicated rate. For most of the decade, an
average of over 1.5 million jobs were added to the US economy
each year, compared to about half that in the new millennium.
Median household income grew by 10 percent, while rates
of poverty, unemployment, and violence dropped. Stocks
boomed, peace deals were brokered, technology seemed both
manageable and exciting, and the federal government ended
the decade with a surplus.

In truth, the golden gaze of the 1990s shined selectively,
carrying over from a decade contoured by scandalous greed,

---

* Of course, some exceptions apply.

shareholder demands, hostile takeovers, and exploding C-suite salaries. In the 1980s, corporate raiders and executives leaned on financial chicanery rather than innovation to make industries profitable and downsized at the expense of jobs, productivity, and investments in research. As union membership dropped from a quarter of the workforce in 1980 to 16 percent by 1989, worker pay and leverage sank. From 1980 to 1988, the minimum wage, relative to all wages, ebbed from 44 percent to 33 percent. In words and deeds, the American parties enthusiastically bludgeoned the Roosevelt Republic to death and hid the body. The 1990s—its politics anchored to Wall Street and organized money, and its policies fixed on welfare reform and crime bills and trade deals—kept the mayhem going. By several accounts, the twenty-five-year span from 1980 to 2005 saw more than 80 percent of income gains in the United States go to the top 1 percent, while household and credit-card debt soared and Americans became too time-stressed to eat meals at home.

It's almost too perfect that SUVs became the official chariot of the nineties boom times. They channeled the militarism as well as the financial and culinary abundance of 1950s America, but now without the purpose offered by a foe. SUVs weren't just safety hazards; they were isolation chambers, the logical symptoms of an undiagnosed identity crisis for a lone bulky superpower uncertainly throwing its weight around the road. "The S.U.V. boom represents, then, a shift in how we conceive of safety—from active to passive," Malcolm Gladwell wrote of America's unique SUV culture. "In Europe and Japan, people think of a safe car as a nimble car. That's why they build cars like the Jetta and the Camry."

Some posit that the allure of SUVs suggests that Americans

unconsciously believed (perhaps as their institutions were fray-ing around them) that crashes were more inevitable than pre-ventable. And that, in the event of a disaster, heft meant health. "There's this notion that you need to be up high," G. Clotaire Rapaille, a cultural anthropologist and mass-market whisperer, explained of SUVs. "That's a contradiction, because the people who buy these SUVs know at the cortex level that if you are high, there is more chance of a rollover. But at the reptilian level they think that if I am bigger and taller, I'm safer. You feel secure because you are higher and dominate and look down. That you can look down is psychologically a very power-ful notion." According to Rapaille, cupholders served as linch-pins to what soothed our fragile lizard brains: "What was the key element of safety when you were a child? It was that your mother fed you, and there was warm liquid. That's why the cupholders are absolutely crucial for safety. If there is a car that has no cupholder, it is not safe. If I can put my coffee there, if I can have my food, if everything is round, if it's soft, and if I'm high, then I feel safe."

Like fast-food portion sizes and most other runaway com-mercial lunacies, cupholder madness went maximally into the new American millennium. It's now no longer surprising to see cupholders built into grocery carts, pool floats, camping gear, stadium seats, and movie-theater chairs. Not to mention strollers, desks, lawn mowers and industrial cleaners, go-karts and golf carts, poker and mah-jongg tables, couches and reclin-ers. A minivan novelty, built in response to a burgeoning mobile dining habit, forever altered the auto industry, and America's expectation of convenience and comfort. "The catch-phrase in the auto-design community is *McDonaldability*," read a dispatch from the 2004 Chicago Auto Show, "the ability of any vehicle to accommodate standard-size fast-food beverage cups and some of the extras that come with Happy Meals as well."

By 2007, PricewaterhouseCoopers surveys had found that the number of cupholders had come to outstrip fuel efficiency as a priority for the American car buyer, though unprecedented hikes in gas prices in the late aughts would shuffle those priorities and hurt the sales of big cars. But by 2015, the mighty SUVs were booming again, along with a runaway number of cupholders. In late 2017, viral word of the features offered by a new-model Subaru SUV inspired euphoria and disbelief. The 2019 Ascent, pumped as "the biggest Subaru yet," comes equipped with three passenger rows, 260 horsepower, and a staggering nineteen cupholders.

The pathological speed of American life, which may or may not be bolstered by an economic fear of falling behind, seeped further into food culture as the twenty-first century took off. "In 2001, there were 134 food products that featured the word *go* on the label or in ads," Tom Vanderbilt writes in his book *Traffic*. "By 2004, there were 504." He adds that what the food industry calls "on-the-go eating occasions" in the United States and Europe were slated to rise from 73.2 billion in 2003 to 84.4 billion in 2008. As ends have become harder to meet and more workers take on multiple jobs at less conventional hours, traditional meals and mealtimes have come to mean less and less. In addition to a nation of snackers, many Americans have become odd-hours diners. Between 2002 and 2007, for example, the number of McDonald's locations that operate twenty-four hours a day grew from 0.5 percent to 40 percent; meanwhile, a majority of franchises extended their core hours to accommodate very early mornings and very late nights.

According to industry estimates, the drive-thru window now generates 60 to 70 percent of all revenue at fast-food restaurants. These figures took hold in the late 1990s and have more or less remained steady ever since. These impersonal practices have created a gulf not just in the distance between Americans and their understanding of the food chain, but between citizens' understanding of each other.

In December 2014, a week before Christmas, a woman named Nadine was passing through a Whataburger drive-thru for breakfast in the Texas suburb of Liberty, when Cheryl Semien, the store's cashier, paid her a compliment on her coat. Nadine, otherwise unprompted, took off her $10,000 mink coat and passed it through the drive-thru window for Semien to keep. According to one fellow employee, Semien immediately commenced "yelling as if she won a million dollars." As she sashayed before a news camera in her sweet new coat, Semien told local media of Nadine, "She was a perfect stranger, I didn't know this lady from nowhere. I didn't see her come through my drive-thru window as long as I've been at Whataburger for nine years." As fate would have it, that December day was also Semien's birthday.

The stories of the impulsive charity of fast-food patrons are part of a genre of viral heartwarming tales that frequently carom around the internet. In 2015, six months after Semien received PETA's version of the Christmas massacre, 215 consecutive diners at a Chick-fil-A in Pooler, Georgia, picked up the tab for the customers after them in the drive-thru line in an epic pay-it-forward chain. That number was eclipsed a few months later when 250 straight drivers at a McDonald's in Lakeland, Florida, followed suit. Observing this trend back in 2013, the journalist Kate Murphy reported, "Serial pay-it-forward incidents involving between 4 and 24 cars have been reported at Wendy's, McDonald's, Starbucks, Del Taco, Taco Bell, KFC and Dunkin' Donuts locations in Maryland, Florida, California, Texas, Louisiana, Pennsylvania, Oklahoma, Georgia, Alabama, North Dakota, Michigan, North Carolina and Washington." Murphy suggests that it's an easy, affordable, and anonymous way to propel joy and goodwill out into an otherwise indifferent-seeming world.

These tales of lardy benevolence also sweep across a wide emotional gamut, from the lieutenant colonel on leave from Fort Benning buying dinners for two hungry kids he encountered at a Taco Bell in Greenville, Alabama, to Marshawn Lynch, the All-Pro NFL running back, who handed $500 to a McDonald's worker and aspiring fashion mogul in Dallas to buy a pair of the same Buscemi shoes that Lynch was wearing. Each act expresses a hopelessly American spirit of generosity in a country where fast food is the closest thing we have to a collective home, and where the closest thing we have to a collective safety net is each other.

All of these changes speak to the unwinding of a social order that began in kitchens and dining rooms and emanated out to the roadsides. When the twentieth century began, a plurality of Americans lived either on farms or in rural areas, and dining out constituted a rarefied luxury. By the century's end, a dynamic had emerged in which cooking and dining in had become the luxury. Explanations for these developments are political, cultural, economic, and sociological, and, as we'll later see, they would become divisive and controversial as the twenty-first century got underway.

While these transformations were setting in at home, the singular power of the United States was newly taking shape abroad in the final decade of the millennium. In many ways, American clout projected itself differently from that of all other behemoths before it; rather than just using brute force, America with its cultural and economic leverage spoke to adaptation and aspiration. The proliferation of American fast food into the world afar would draw all of these disparate strands together.

10 GLASNOST

The most beautiful thing in Tokyo is McDonald's. The most beautiful thing in Stockholm is McDonald's. The most beautiful thing in Florence is McDonald's. Peking and Moscow don't have anything beautiful yet.
—ANDY WARHOL

In early 1990, the Soviet Union was in the midst of a severe crisis. Its economy was in shambles and hyperinflation had rendered the ruble inconvertible to Western currencies. Amid intense internal political strife and disaffection, Soviet satellite states demanded and declared autonomy, and in a spiritual depression Communism flailed under the weight of its corruption and concentration of power.

But in January of 1990, in the Soviet empire's last days, a symbol of hope, freedom, and possibility first glistered in downtrodden Moscow: Russia's first McDonald's, of course. This would be no ordinary outpost. The product of fourteen characteristically unhurried years of negotiations with a Russian novel's worth of Soviet bureaucrats, the store would be a leviathan within a leviathan. Nine hundred seats. Twenty-seven cash registers. The largest Mickey D's in the world. The project had first been announced two years earlier with no less triumphalism. "The McDonald's Golden Arches will be appearing on the Moscow horizon," one McDonald's official declared. "A Big Mac will taste the same in Moscow as it does in New York, Tokyo, Toronto, or Rio."

In a now-famous image, over five thousand customers queued up that winter day for as many as six hours in a line that extended for blocks. Together they stood, waiting for nothing short of the promise of salvation in the form of American-style hamburgers, apple pies, and politesse. Together they huddled as comrades in Pushkin Square in the shadow of a bronze statue of the square's namesake, who, 170 years earlier, had been exiled to southern Russia by Czar Alexander for writing "Ode to Liberty," a tirade against despotism.

In the days leading up to its Moscow debut, America's most seductive emissary of soft power had been issuing this coded slogan on Russian television: "If you can't go to America, come to McDonald's in Moscow." And now the moment was here. When the doors finally swung open, an awakening began. "Connoisseurs of fast food and human behavior were doubly satiated today," one reporter wrote, "as anxious crowds of Soviet customers engaged in traditional pushing and shoving to place *Beeg Mek* orders at the nation's first McDonald's restaurant, only to be calmed by uniformed compatriots dictating that they have a nice day."

It was January 31, 1990—forty years to the day after President Truman publicly announced the escalatory intention to develop the hydrogen bomb—that tens of thousands of Muscovites, isolated by their regime, walked away as new members of an American-founded global fraternity, paper cups in hand as keepsakes. The final figure of customers served—thirty thousand on the first day—was not just a company record, but also a historic moment of Cold War thaw. After more than four decades, the United States had outlasted its foe and, as the lone world superpower, would never again be undermined by dastardly Russian schemes. America, sprinting toward the new millennium, would also become freer to satisfy its imperial urges in less oppressive forms than other global powers had. In lieu of colonies, there would continue to be American music and language, science, technology, and popular culture. To be sure, a few scattered military bases here and there and a little expression of economic and political clout. And there would be fast food.

The end of the Cold War arrived with exquisite timing for American fast-food companies, whose momentum had started to buckle as the sheer number of stores hit a saturation point in the United States. So, the chains turned their expansionist gaze outward toward countries with rising middle classes or newfound prosperity, expanded trade ties with the United States, or aspirations to enter the global market. One of the central complaints about the international expansion of fast-food chains (and along with the reach of processed-food peddling conglomerates) is that the footprint of US companies abroad is a form of cultural hegemony, a dynamic that upends traditional diets and foodways, kills national culinary traditions, and foists American dietary norms and values upon unsuspecting communities.

Though some recent studies of rising obesity rates in developing countries offer some alarming evidence of this effect, fast food's interactions abroad have been less monolithic and more culturally significant than some might expect. In many ways, fast food channels a quaint, almost certainly outdated national image of the United States around the world—approachable and agreeable, charismatic and casual, evangelical and democratic, hectoring and optimistic.

Yuri Chekalin was part of the original team at the Pushkin Square McDonald's. From a pool of the 27,000 applicants that responded to a newspaper ad placed by the company, Chekalin secured one of the coveted 630 crew jobs. In addition to learning technical skills, his training also included surreal-seeming instruction for a hospitality gig in the Soviet Union, such as lessons on smiling, making and maintaining eye contact with customers, and committing to a foreign-seeming palette of polite phrases such as "How can I help you?" and "Come back soon."

It might be too easy to read this American imperative for cheeriness as an attempt to *civilize*. But part of what made McDonald's inroads into the USSR so revolutionary was that it inverted a system in which the average consumer held no power. *(In Soviet Russia, you wait on waiter!)* The eternal shortages and rations of the state-controlled economy, which had worsened in the late 1980s, created a dynamic that placed customers arbitrarily at the mercy of commodity purveyors, whether it was a grocer, clerk, cashier, or waiter. "In the Soviet Union, when you walked into a restaurant, the first thing they would look at is your clothes," Chekalin told NPR's Alix Spiegel in 2016. "And then they would, you know, judge if they want you in this restaurant or if they'd just rather take break."

The assertive McDonald's diktat about smiling and manners wasn't just an effective signal of something new, but a form of democratic samizdat that, in many ways, made the food itself secondary to the experience. "There is a lesson to be drawn from this for the country," said Tatyana Podlesnaya, a school-teacher and a first-day pilgrim to the Pushkin Square Mc-Donald's. "What is killing us is that the average worker does not know how to work and so does not want to. Our enthusiasm has disappeared. But here my meal turned out to be just a supplement to the sincere smiles of the workers."

More than twenty-five years later, Chekalin echoed this sentiment. "A lot of Russian people walking into that Mc-Donald's, they also acted differently," he went on. "They were friendlier. . . . Everywhere else you go, it was just gloomy and there were troubles, stress. And you come to McDonald's and it's, you know, everybody's always happy, and you see smiles. You can stay there for as long as you want. Nobody's going to kick you out. And so it was just a great place to hang out. People really felt they could just relax and be themselves."

This subversively jaunty, American-style service standard attracted fast-food apparatchiks. Since its opening in 1990, the Pushkin Square store has vied for (and frequently held) the mantle of busiest McDonald's in the world.* Following the dissolution of the Soviet Union in 1991, the Golden Arches would spread to hundreds of locations within the country. By 2007, the average Russian McDonald's was annually serving 850,000 customers, more than double the average traffic of other McDonald's markets. "In a country where there was nothing available, McDonald's was everything," Russian restaurant magnate Rostislav Ordovsky, who claims to keep a copy of Ray Kroc's autobiography on his nightstand, told *The Wall Street Journal.*†

---

* It somehow also became a popular venue for wedding receptions.
† Ordovsky proved to be a worthy disciple; he founded a Russian fast-food chicken outfit

By 2010, the company's twentieth anniversary in the country, the tally of customers to the Pushkin Square store had surpassed an eye-popping 130 million. As the remembrances and tributes poured in that milestone year, the arrival of McDonald's came to embody a shorthand for how the country had transitioned from socialism to capitalism. "McDonald's was not so much a fast-food chain, but rather a symbol of freedom, a symbol of Western values coming to Russia," one journalist told Russia Today. "No wonder the Communist Party objected so fiercely, but at the end it didn't have a choice."

Now, despite sentiments like these, American fast food wasn't exactly the belated fulfillment of Patton's dream to march on to Moscow, and McDonald's did not exactly impose its will on the Russian landscape. After so many years of negotiations just to open up shop, the company also had to undertake major steps to adapt itself to its new environs. For instance, in nearly every market, fast-food companies rely on a network of private suppliers to provide food and materials for their operations. But since no private companies were allowed in the USSR, McDonald's was required to build the McComplex, a megafactory on the outskirts of Moscow, to produce the supplies for its own Russian stores, such as meat, dairy, and bread.* And whatever couldn't be produced there—some 80 percent of the three hundred or so ingredients required—had to be imported from abroad.

As the Russian economy shifted toward capitalism, Mc-

---

called Rostik's in 1993. After it opened over a hundred franchises, the chain was bought out by Yum! Brands and rebranded as KFC.

* The McComplex, which has been estimated to have cost anywhere from $35 million to $50 million to build, was reportedly known to locals as the McGulag because of the barbed wire surrounding the facility.

Donald's slowly cultivated an arsenal of private local suppliers. By 2014, around the time that Russia invaded Ukraine, 85 percent of the products served at the four hundred–plus McDonald's outlets in the country came from Russian suppliers. (The last items to be produced at the McComplex were the hamburger buns, which were outsourced just ahead of the twentieth anniversary in 2010.) Ultimately, rising diplomatic tensions with the United States over the Russian 2014 invasion of Ukraine prompted the Russian government to close a handful of local McDonald's outlets over "numerous violations of the sanitary code." As with most Putin-styled nationalistic gambits, the closures were criticized for being both politically motivated and self-destructive, given the successful network of local suppliers and that the company employed over thirty-seven thousand Russian workers.*

Among the shuttered stores was the Pushkin Square McDonald's, the closure of which inspired some laments about Russia's flirtation with renascent Soviet-era totalitarianism: "Everything about this particular branch of the American fast-food giant was iconic for a person born in Soviet Russia," wrote Mitya Kushelevich in the Calvert Journal. "Just as St. Petersburg was once considered our 'window to Europe,' this restaurant was our 'window to the world.'" He added, "The message is clear and it's not aimed at Americans, it's aimed at us: the window to the world is closing."

Although there's little doubt that McDonald's enjoyed paying a symbolic yearly rent of one ruble to open its doors in Moscow, not every chain has had to find a way to work within a

---

* In 2011, McDonald's had been honored by the government as Russia's best employer.

system as rigid as Soviet-style socialism. However, contrary to popular critique, any American fast-food entity that has found success in a new foreign market has done so by adapting drastically to appeal to the tastes, customs, and mores of the host countries. The results are a fascinating pageant of the world reflected and refracted through an American lens.

Any nineties film buff knows that a Quarter Pounder with cheese is called Le Royal Cheese in France* because of the metric system, but if you're on the hunt for its kosher counterpart, the McRoyal is available (sans cheese) at certain McDonald's outlets in Israel any day but the Sabbath. Meanwhile, metric system be damned, there are actually Quarter Pounders on McDonald's menus in countries like Jordan, Saudi Arabia, Lebanon, and the United Arab Emirates. The only little difference is that those burgers are certified halal.

One large part of why fast food has sustained its success across the decades is its adaptability. And so, more than just conforming to the native orthodoxies of a given country, fast-food chains also project their evolutions. In December 2015, Burger King began its takeover of Quick, the first-ever European hamburger chain, in an effort to expand its operations in France. What made this generally mundane news item into an international story was the detail that, in a nod to France's booming Muslim population, about 10 percent of the four hundred or so acquired stores would keep their Quick branding and serve strictly halal fare.† One year earlier, as BK first

---

* In *Pulp Fiction*, Vincent Vega (John Travolta) refers to it as a "Royal with cheese," but what are you gonna do?

† Unfortunately, a clearinghouse of far-right, conspiracy-minded news sites and Twitter accounts caused a stir by accusing Burger King of bowing to sharia law and calling for boycotts of the chain.

opened its doors in India to court the country's burgeoning middle class, the company unveiled a specialty menu that included six meat-free sandwiches with India's massive beef-eschewing, vegetarian-heavy population in mind. And just as Taco Bell in India exclusively serves its tacos and burritos with potatoes, chicken, and beans instead of beef, Burger King India offers paneer and bean burgers and swaps out the beef in its trademark Whoppers and replaces it with patties made of veggies, chicken, and even mutton.

Of course, the world is complicated and not everything translates perfectly. A visitor craving a Whopper in Australia might be surprised to find that Burger King is called Hungry Jack's because of a preexisting trademark there. A devotee of Church's Chicken honey-butter biscuit would instead have to seek it out at a Texas Chicken, which is what the company calls its stores outside of the Americas to preempt a potential holy war. (Both Hungry Jack's and Texas Chicken have nearly identical logos and signage to their parent companies.) Elsewhere, in Malaysia, religious authorities have compelled chains like A&W and Auntie Anne's to reintroduce their hot dogs and pretzel dogs as coneys and franks and sausages to avoid confusion with actual dogs, which are decidedly not halal.* Similarly, root beer, which has been A&W's calling card since 1919, is referred to as RB on menus in places like Malaysia and Indonesia to avoid any alcoholic connotation.

There's poutine on plastic trays across Canada. Gazpacho at the McDonald's outlets in Spain, and light, airy macarons across Western Europe. Your breakfast at an Ecuadorean Wen-

---

* In some ways, this seems like historical retribution for the rise of the "hot dog," which was bolstered by anti-German sentiment during World War I.

dy's could include sweet honey hotcakes or savory fried plan-
tains and salchichas. Meanwhile, at Domino's outposts in
Nigeria, you can get a pizza topped with jollof rice, the West
African staple. If you head south by southeast far enough, you
might find yourself hungry for a Burger King hoagie made of
boerewors, the classic South African sausage. From there, if
you change course due east down Oceania way, try a locally beloved Georgie Pie at a McDonald's in New Zealand or head to
Australia for an English muffin with Vegemite. If a traditional
porridge is what your heart truly seeks, A&W, KFC, and Mc-
Donald's outposts across Malaysia, Indonesia, and Singapore
have variations of bubur ayam. For a more portable snack, Popeyes outfits in Turkey boast sesame onion rings, which might
pair nicely with a roast-veal foot-long from a Subway in neigh-
boring Bulgaria.

From there, the possibilities for adventure are borderless.
Some mind-blowing limited-time offerings have included the
McZuri, a ground-veal burger with hash browns and mush-
room sauce at Swiss McDonald's locations, the fabled Birizza,
a pizza and biryani mash-up that once starred at Pizza Huts
in Sri Lanka and India, and Burger King New Zealand's Full
Meaty, a double hamburger with double cheese, a chicken patty,
and six stripes of bacon for good measure. More enduring international fast-food items include Steak Loaders, cheeseburgers that are topped with Philly cheesesteaks, wrapped in
tortillas, and live in Hardee's outlets in Saudi Arabia, Bahrain,
Oman, and Qatar. For a curious yin and yang of health and destruction, Wendy's stores in the Republic of Georgia have
salmon burgers and various iterations of the Double Down—
that infamous sandwich made of two fried-chicken buns and
bacon filling—at KFCs in South Korea. For a more understated

selection, the pepperoni hot dogs at Dairy Queens in Cambodia or Laos might seem a way to go, while nothing may befit the spirit of Middle Eastern ostentatiousness better than Pizza Hut's Crown Crust series, which are pizzas with crusts studded with various gauntlets such as mini-cheeseburgers, chicken fingers, alternating meatballs and cream-cheese balls, or hot dogs.

If these princely arrays of sodium-chaffed glory drive you to drink, you should do so at the hundreds of fast-food franchises across Europe and East Asia that serve beer. And for dessert, the sucrose is the limit. Taco Bells around the world have a lineup that would wet a stoner's dry eyes with tears of joy, including chocolate and Baby Ruth–filled dessert quesadillas across Central America and Spain and a Nutella-banana hybrid in Cyprus. Or just top it all off with a flavored Frosty from your local Wendy's—dulce de leche if you're in Argentina, coffee jelly if you're in the Philippines. And if you're still not sated, there are always Toblerone McFlurries in Switzerland, Speculoos milkshakes at Steak 'n Shakes in Portugal, and pork-and-seaweed doughnuts at Dunkin' Donuts in China. One *could* argue that the truest splendor of American fast food abroad is actually its tapestry of menu offerings around the globe. Simply put, it's a beautiful world out there.

In recent years, a term among marketeers and academics alike has come into favor in describing the deliberate modifications that global operations must make to function and prosper within a new community. For fast food, *glocalization*, which we can all agree is a terrible term, is more than adapting a menu to suit local preferences and norms. It's also adjusting store amenities, décor, advertising, service standards, and more.

Alongside the Pushkin Square location, another steady contender for the title of world's busiest McDonald's is a Parisian store on the majestic Champs-Élysées. It sits in the shadow of the Arc de Triomphe and on the former site of a nineteenth-century Rothschild mansion. Before we spit out our pastis in disgust, it's worth noting that it is not a run-of-le-mill Mickey D's. By some accounts, it's a tourist destination. A recent redesign of the store was conceived by acclaimed industrial designer Patrick Norguet, and in addition to its own custom furniture and light boxes, the outpost offers table service as well as specialty burgers with such cheeses as chèvre and Camembert, croques made with melted Emmentaler, a high-tech ordering system, and an eighty-two-foot window displaying 180-degree views of the vaunted Parisian strip. *C'est magnifique.*

But of all the places in the world that have tried to turn their fast-food culture up to 11, none come remotely close to competing with Japan. It's well understood that Japan is a place of high innovation and pop-cultural obsession—a combination that makes for a fast-food scene that is completely bonkers. In 2012, Burger King Japan ran a promotion that allowed customers to add fifteen slices of bacon to a burger for a little over a dollar. For breakfast, Spam-and-egg sandwiches are standard fare. When Wendy's Japan relaunched in 2011 after a two-year hiatus, it did so with a $16 burger topped with foie gras and truffles. A more steady item is the Roppongi, which is a cheeseburger topped with bacon, ketchup, a chunky mayo sauce, and a fried egg. At MOS Burger, the Japanese burger chain inspired by the incredible Los Angeles chili-burger chain Original Tommy's, the standard cheeseburger comes covered in meat sauce on a rice bun. At Taco Bell, huge plates of nacho fries are on order with Asahi beers on draft, and the stores have open kitchens, colored wood-panel walls, and specialty lounges. Dinner at McDonald's could be a MegaMac, Japan's four-patty Big Mac interpretation. Breakfast could include its morning counterpart, the MegaMuffin, which is an Egg McMuffin stacked with two pieces of bacon and two pieces of sausage, plus egg, cheese, and a slather of ketchup. Meanwhile, at Pizza Hut Japan, one of the most popular selections in recent years has been a seafood-themed pizza topped with shrimp, squid, tuna, mayonnaise, broccoli, onions, and tomato sauce.

The true dark-meat pièce de résistance of Japanese fast food is Kentucky Christmas—a bona fide, decades-long annual ritual in which millions of Japanese families eat KFC around Christmastime. The origins of Kentucky Christmas are intensely debated, but the best version of the legend is that after a successful spring trial at the 1970 World Expo in Osaka, Kentucky Fried Chicken Japan was established on July Fourth. Soon after, Takeshi Okawara, the manager of the country's first KFC franchise, overheard a few expats in his store who couldn't find turkey in Japan for their Christmas celebrations and had settled for fried chicken instead. Later, in a dream, Okawara was apparently struck by a vision of his countrymen sharing Christmas-themed barrels of fried chicken with their families. He woke up, wrote down the idea, then made it so. In 1974, KFC turned Okawara's successful concept into a national marketing campaign called *Kurisumasu ni wa Kentakkii!* (Kentucky for Christmas!), which promptly sent the country into a chicken-fueled bonanza.* The initiative quickly evolved into a

---

* Okawara would go on to serve as the head of KFC Japan for eighteen years.

full-blown Japanese institution with ubiquitous ads and highly choreographed television commercials featuring a signature jingle, dancing celebrities, and intergenerational tableaus of Christmas-entranced families sharing party barrels of fried chicken.

It's difficult to overstate the success and impact of KFC's Kentucky Christmas miracle. According to the company, an estimated 3.6 million families seek out their yuletide leg (or wing) at KFC each December, sometimes doubling the average sales of other months. The sales, which are mainly generated through company-branded Christmas dinner packages,* have come to account for a full third of KFC Japan's annual revenue. But these mind-boggling figures are only part of the story.

I met Yuko Nakajima, my KFC Christmas-spirit guide, early on the morning of December 24, hours before the madness would kick into its highest gear. Along the way to the company headquarters in Tokyo, I passed countless signs outside convenience stores, grocers, small restaurants, even a Wendy's, promoting Christmas-themed fried-chicken packages. Nakajima's tour started in the deserted warrens of the headquarters office, where she clarified that December 24 isn't a national holiday in Japan; the desks were empty because the vast majority of corporate employees had been dispatched to help out on a day when KFC foot traffic can surge to about ten times the size of an average day. "Everybody's at the stores today," she explained. "A large amount of people come [to corporate] from stores and so they're all used to it. So some people really go and

---

* The standard set is a $40 spread that includes a bucket of chicken, salad, a Christmas cake, wine, and a commemorative plate.

cook, some people are handling lines and making sure that customers are happy."

The irony is that December 25 isn't a national holiday in Japan either; the country's Christian population is thought to be around 1 percent. The brilliance of the *Kurisumasu ni wa Kentakkii!* gambit is that it created an itch for Western-style Christmas revelry that Japan never knew it needed to scratch. As a result, Christmas has become a cultural phenomenon in Japan, a surreal rite that centers around a meal of American fast food. Every year, the planning and menu development begin in July, and the ads start running in November. And each of the 1,150-plus KFC stores in Japan participates. Or, as Nakajima put it, "From Hokkaido to Okinawa, everyone is doing the same thing."

Part of what makes the messaging so effective is the simplicity of the imperative: On Christmas, families eat KFC chicken together. And since 1985, KFC has produced specialty collector holiday chicken barrels for each Christmas campaign. Overwhelmingly, these buckets feature renderings of Colonel Sanders in a Santa hat—mushing reindeer atop a flying sleigh, posing with V-fingers beside a Christmas tree, or framed by a wreath or bow. All told, Colonel Sanders does not look terribly unlike Santa Claus.*

The barrels are a crucial element of the ritual; about half of the 3.6 million Christmas customers order in advance, while others wait in line for takeout, sometimes for hours. Eating at the actual store isn't central to the experience, whether it's Christmas or not. "In Japan, about fifty or sixty percent of our business is takeaway," said Nakajima. "So people bring it back

---

* Japan's particular deference toward its elders only heightens Sanders's appeal.

and it's not a full meal anyway. Moms will prepare something else and things like that so it would never be a full, full meal that you'll just have KFC on your table and that's it."

At a KFC store in Ebisu district, the line for the Kentucky Christmas was already out the door and down the block. Inside, makeshift shelves were being filled with stacks of advance orders. At a table near a smoking section cordoned off by clear doors, crowds came and went and ate Original Recipe chicken, iced coffee, fries, and biscuits, which in Japan come with holes in the center and are served with honey. Outside, another line was made up of passersby that wanted to pose for pictures with the Colonel Sanders statue that sits outside every single KFC location in Japan. Each December, Sanders's iconic white Kentucky colonel outfit and string tie are covered by a Santa suit and hat. It's hard to imagine that Sanders would have minded this modification. After all, in Japan, the common perception is that Harland Sanders's real first name is Colonel.

If somebody told me that I'll live a year longer by
eating nothing but broccoli and asparagus from now on,
I would just say every day will seem like as long.
I'll stick with the Cheetos and the Coke.
—WARREN BUFFETT

In the early days of fast food, long before it would dominate the roadsides and suburbs and meander across cityscapes into schools and hospitals, White Castle cofounder and impresario Billy Ingram commissioned a medical study. In it, a healthy young medical student ate nothing but White Castle sliders and water for over three months. "The student maintained good health throughout the three-month period," Ingram announced at the end, "and was eating twenty to twenty-four hamburgers a day during the last few weeks." Gloating further, Ingram trumpeted that a food scientist had even signed a report suggesting "that a normal healthy child could eat nothing but our hamburgers and water, and fully develop all its physical and mental faculties."

This conceit may sound familiar. In 2004, filmmaker (and

non–medical student) Morgan Spurlock set out to prove the opposite of Ingram by not exercising and gorging himself on five thousand calories' worth of McDonald's every day for a month for his film *Super Size Me*. Unsurprisingly, the results of his nominally scientific stunt appalled and horrified viewers and briefly turned Spurlock into a household name.

Held together, these two stunts offer an alluring, perfectly tidy narrative arc for fast food in America: It begins in 1930 at the scrappy dawn of the industry with the dubious marketing of burgers as simple, affordable, family-friendly sustenance. The story then crescendoes seventy-five years later with the indictment of fast food's most recognizable conglomerate as corrupted by success, artificial ingredients, oversize portions, shareholder greed, and promotional fervor.

A few months after *Super Size Me* debuted, another fast-food flick hit theaters: *Harold & Kumar Go to White Castle*. It's the classic story of two twentysomething friends who, fed up with the stresses of life, embark on an elaborate, weed-fueled hero's journey to their favorite fast-food chain. Along the way, the two pilgrims undertake a medical-marijuana heist at a hospital, smoke weed with an escaped cheetah, and hang glide from a clifftop to a White Castle after the actor Neil Patrick Harris (appearing as himself, high on ecstasy) steals their car.

Harold & Kumar did not win an Academy Award.* But just because it lacks the subtle visual poetry of Fellini doesn't mean it was without its poignant flourishes. Zoomed out, it's basically a buddy flick about two sons of Asian immigrants, who find relief and release in the very American experience of a

---

* Despite its cultural currency, *Super Size Me* was also shut out at the Oscars and mightily outgrossed by *Harold & Kumar Go to White Castle*. Both spawned ill-fated sequels.

completely frivolous road trip. The joke is that White Castle is their white whale; it works because it is a totally relatable quest. "It was the first time we almost ran out of hamburgers since 1921," White Castle VP Jamie Richardson said of the aftermath of the release. "We knew about it and we worked with New Line Cinema, but when the film came out, we had been tracking up about two percent for the year, and instantly sales popped up for many weeks after that in the twenty-percent-plus range. It really had a dramatic impact on sales." *Super Size Me*, on the other hand, almost certainly caused fast food sales to drop, particularly for McDonald's, which just happened to abandon its *super size* menu options just weeks before Spurlock's documentary debuted.

Though admittedly it's silly to read too much into the particulars of two weird fast-food flicks, their coincidental timing is meaningful. By the early aughts, a new front in America's culture wars was in full bloom. The once-encompassing sway of national institutions and media had fractured. Minus a fleeting nanosecond of national unity after September 11, the strain of all-afflicting partisan timbre that had taken hold in the 1990s came on stronger. Values became further affixed to their red-blue, right-left designations and extended to all facets of life, including American diets. *Fast Food Nation* and its fellow discontents helped the dissatisfaction with the consumerism of the 1990s snowball into an open questioning of social tenets—with the corruption of the food system as a central pillar. During the lead-up to the Iraq War, a righteous citizen either supported french fries or freedom fries. This would be followed by the dividing lines between heritage corn or corn syrup. Kale chips or brownies at PTA bake sales. Calorie counts and food regulations or free will and free markets.

As *foodie-ism* entered the lexicon, fast food and processed foods became the official bill of fare at the sectarian barricades. With the future of public health and the environment at stake, food that was *wholesome* became not just chic in certain circles of righteous-minded diners, but necessary; sustainable, local offerings from small farms and organic producers weren't just an enlightened choice, but a moral one. Starting in the aughts, it became the duty of public intellectuals and civic leaders to nudge, steer, and shame consumers away from their big sodas and Happy Meals toward better food choices. Anything less, as Alice Waters, the sainted cofounder of Chez Panisse and the grand doyenne of the Slow Food movement, once put it, was to cede the ground to "fast-food values." In 2008, with food prices rising and the Great Recession underway, Waters implored economically disadvantaged consumers to "make a sacrifice on the cell phone or the third pair of Nike shoes" to find room in their budgets for more sustainable food.

The backlash against a behemoth so engirding as fast food created a huge market for an alternative way of eating. The revolution for *good food* arrived like a triumphant Lenin at Finland Station. Elevated cafés and high-minded gastropubs, *good* places, debuted with media-kindled fanfare and menus that read like album liner notes. Between 2006 and 2016, the number of listed farmers' markets in the US Department of Agriculture's national directory nearly doubled. Like the transition from minivans to SUVs before, consumer choices became part of an exclusive lifestyle that (wittingly or not) signified class, status, luxury, and virtue for an increasingly cloistered group of Americans.

* * *

The Northstar Café in Columbus, Ohio, is one of many *good* places. It features light wood accents that soften its gray industrial vibe, an open kitchen, big hanging light fixtures and tall windows, and a mishmash of seating arrangements. It also came recommended by the entire staff of a nearby yoga studio. On the day I visited, the sunny patio was filled with diners, drinking bright juices and tending to well-coiffed and very good dogs.

It's easy to see why Northstar wins the hearts and minds of the locals. In addition to looking like a set from a Nancy Meyers movie, it has all the rhetorical hallmarks of gastronomical-political awareness. "The clean lines and fresh colors of Northstar reflect our sincere commitment to pure and natural dining, rooted in our Ohio soil," noted its website, which contained a "philosophy" section and promises organic-focused, locally sourced, sustainable food, and compost-ready takeaway containers. Even its name is meant to convey reassurance and responsible stewardship. Inadvertently driving the point home, the café is located directly across a small street from a well-weathered White Castle store that looks a bit like a charred marshmallow.

As I stood in the ordering line, I watched plate after glorious plate make its way out—huge cheeseburgers made from Niman Ranch brisket and chuck, enormous ricotta-topped pancakes, smoothies flecked with bits of fruit, all of which were beautiful. When I asked what the most popular items were, I was recommended one of the three salads. At $14, the Village Salad was also the cheapest salad on the menu. With tax and a tip for the counter staff, the total came out to over $16. I headed out to the patio and snagged a small table next to an

Ohio State college student and her mother, who had come to town to see her off. At other tables, there were business lunches and student reunions afoot and idlers sunning in full Lululemon.

I waited for a runner to find me by my order number, which had been printed on a small laminated placard decorated with a passage from Michael Pollan's book *In Defense of Food*, a celebrated selection from the modern foodie canon. On it, Pollan is quoting Gyorgy Scrinis's explanation of his term *nutritionism*: "The most important fact about any food is not its nutrient content but its degree of processing. 'Whole foods and industrial foods are the only two food groups I'd consider including in any useful "food pyramid."'"

The $16-plus salad soon arrived, a profile in visual and gustatory glory. A heaping mass of greens with an array of different lettuces, thick strips of tomato, glistening almonds, dates, bits of corn, chunks of avocado, well-roasted chicken, an oversize peppered bed of goat cheese, and croutons, all with a coat of champagne vinaigrette and served with a huge wedge of bread. It tasted very *good* and almost certainly contained eight hundred calories.* Digging into it, I knew that I had invaded the terrain of the enlightened eater, where the accommodations felt delightful, high quality, Instagrammable, and somewhere between aspirational and inaccessible. The salad was way too big to finish.

A few months later, in what almost certainly must have been a publicist's mistake, I ended up having breakfast with Michael

---

* No nutritional information about the food at Northstar was available either in the store or online. Later when I called back to ask if they could give a ballpark estimate for their dishes for someone on a calorie-restricted diet, they politely declined.

Pollan in New York at one of the eateries in the progressive gourmet empire of restaurateur Danny Meyer. As we sat down, I mentioned encountering a quote of his in Columbus, Ohio. "Which one?" he asked, before guessing his most famous dictum: "Eat food. Not too much. Mostly plants."

It's easy to envision this quote plastered on the walls and menus (or crocheted on homemade samplers) at vegetarian or vegan restaurants across the United States. But this advice would have been out of place at Northstar, where the interpretation of *good* meant a menu touting loads of high-quality meat and dairy at Cadillac-sized portions. I asked Pollan how he felt about this trickle-down effect of his name, his words, and his work throughout the food and restaurant industries. "Good!" he said. "You could have seen McDonald's trying to do the same thing. I'm glad it was a good place."

One difficulty with *good* places—the trendy, moral, gourmet outfits—is that they have created a confusing glut of virtue. It's hard to distinguish a place like Northstar with its commitment to "pure and natural" dining from the countless shoppes, bougie larders, and corporate brands that purvey "fresh," "farm-raised," or "responsible" goods. Despite sounding wholesome and ethical, often these words are meaningless or a nice turn of marketing copy. Pollan joked about encountering "GMO-free" and "gluten-free" water for sale on shelves in his travels.

Take the *organic* designation, for example, which basically means an item produced with relatively little use of synthetic pesticides and fertilizers or an animal raised under certain guidelines. Despite being sacred to many consumers, *organic* often falls somewhere between useful and corrupt, depending on the item. After all, an *organic* label doesn't necessarily make food more nutritious, more environmentally sound, completely free of herbicides or pesticides, or even thoroughly vetted by inspectors. Neither the shortcomings nor the price of organic food has kept it from insane popularity. Eating organic has become a source of comfort, a shortcut to culinary absolution that went mainstream. In 2015, Whole Foods, a pioneer in the organic game, was supplanted by the mega-wholesaler Costco as the top purveyor of organic food.*

As a diner, it's nearly impossible to function in an era in which much of the reporting on the science of what's *good* is built on a foundation of sand (or quinoa). Every few months, a deceptive new study gets published about coffee, wine, chocolate, eggs, butter, fat, salt, sugar, sweeteners, genetically modified organisms (GMOs), vitamins, dairy, tree nuts, breakfast, and oils. As if by design, they shatter news cycles and clutter social media feeds, and in a blink, a fruit, a grain, a root, a spice, a legume, gets indexed as secretly good, actually bad, possibly carcinogenic, ecologically problematic, a new cure-all superfood, lacking all conviction, or full of passionate intensity.

All of this din and contradiction have created a disorienting uncertainty for consumers looking for alternatives to the evils of fast and processed foods. It's no surprise that food fads, purity-themed trends, and bizarro diets have become so enticing in a steadily changing climate of vaguely defined wellness. "Clean eating—whether it is called that or not—is perhaps best seen as a dysfunctional response to a still more dysfunctional food supply: a dream of purity in a toxic world," writes Bee Wilson in a dissection of wellness culture in *The Guardian*. "To

---

* Soon after, Whole Foods responded by creating "Responsibility Grown," its own proprietary produce-rating system, which includes nonorganic items.

walk into a modern western supermarket is to be assailed by aisle upon aisle of salty, oily snacks and sugary cereals, of 'bread' that has been neither proved nor fermented, of cheap, sweetened drinks and meat from animals kept in inhumane conditions."

What helps kindle the forces of extremism (both inside the food system and outside) is the comprehensive plunge in the credibility of government, which has never been a particularly effective arbiter or moral advocate of good-food policies anyway. It's fair to say that a food pyramid with a base that suggests six to eleven daily servings of carbohydrates might not have been terrific advice. Meanwhile, were a consumer to follow the FDA's guidelines for "healthy" foods, which have been in place since the early 1990s and have only come under review in the past few years, Pop-Tarts and Frosted Flakes would qualify as healthy items while almonds, salmon, and olive oil, all of which are high in fat, would be discouraged.

Even if public officials and institutions were savvier and more principled, the national credo of rugged individualism still rears its stubborn head. Americans hate being told what to do, especially by the government. New York, where Pollan and I met, is an ostensibly liberal city that had recently thrown a hissy fit when its previous mayor, Michael Bloomberg, had tried to limit the size of sugary drinks in the name of public health. "Look, food culture is emotionally very fraught," Pollan said, sighing. "People have very strong feelings and they don't want to be told by anybody how to eat. You have to be very careful how you have this conversation." He referenced an episode in the public health wars of 2006 when parents passed fatty snacks through the fence of a British school to students in protest of a healthy-eating initiative led by chef Jamie Oliver.

"Although it's worth pointing out that we tolerate social engineering from corporations about our eating in a way we won't tolerate it from our elected representatives. So you take something like Bloomberg's efforts to deal with soda—"

As if on cue, we were interrupted by a manager, who had clearly recognized Pollan and approached with the diffident shyness and tender nerves of a kid at a junior high dance to present our plates of $9 toast. Pollan, who must endure encounters like this regularly, made this man's young life by asking him where their bread comes from.

"We make it in-house," the manager said.

"Cool," Pollan replied.

"You'd be happy," the man stammered. "Flour, water, our own starter."

"Your own starter?"

"Yeah! About five years old."

"Wow! Cool."

"The bread is what makes everything," the man added, now in a full-on blush. "From the pizza to the bread."

The manager then skated away on air, trying to suppress a smile. Pollan picked up exactly where he'd left off. "So for Bloomberg, this was outrage. Essentially, he was asking people to pause and reflect before you go from [drinking] sixteen to thirty-two ounces of soda," Pollan said with some exasperation. "It's what in social sciences is referred to as a nudge, it's the mildest form of social reform. And beloved by the right, by the way. And they went all over it. Yet every time you step into the supermarket, you are being manipulated ten ways till Sunday, and this doesn't bother us. And I find that's a very curious thing."

* * *

In recent years, as consumer moods have grown more polarized and defensive, many of the larger national fast-food chains have tried to maintain their mass appeal while also making overtures to more politically conscious diners. To create distance between themselves and the negative perception of fast food, companies have employed the semi-clever tactic of disavowing the term *fast food* entirely.

The industry has long chafed at its given name (*fast food*), preferring the more credible, dignified *quick-service restaurant* (QSR). But in the years since the industry became a target of a larger examination by the mainstream, it's taken to some true rhetorical gymnastics. Here's a small sampling of some current and recent slogans: Dairy Queen (Fan food, not fast food), Wendy's (It's waaaay better than fast food. It's Wendy's), and Arby's (Fast crafted). An incredible 2002 commercial for KFC popcorn chicken features *Seinfeld*'s Jason Alexander and major league slugger Barry Bonds, who would later be accused of taking a regimen of cattle steroids, ripping on the blight of "mystery meat nuggets." It defiantly concludes with the tagline "There's fast food . . . Then there's KFC."

By 2015, McDonald's had rebranded itself as a "modern, progressive burger company" with "good food, served fast." Just like Northstar, even McDonald's now has a "philosophy" section on its company website to highlight its food-supply changes, which reads a bit like a hostage script that went through about fourteen rounds of focus-group testing: "At McDonald's, we're making changes based on what we're hearing from all of you. That's why we work hard to make tasty food with a 'less is more' philosophy. But what does that mean for our ingredients?" In lady-doth-protest-too-much fashion, the statement goes on to list menu items featuring "100% real beef," "real buttermilk," "sustainably-sourced Alaskan Pollack," and "a freshly-cracked egg" before concluding, "To put it frankly, it means—The Simpler The Better™."

In recent years, McDonald's has also verbally pledged to some more-than-cosmetic changes. Its announced plan to shift to cage-free eggs in the United States and Canada seems meaningful even before considering that the company uses about 2 billion eggs, or about 5 percent of all the eggs produced in the United States. It also moved from using margarine to butter in its Egg McMuffins, and like Taco Bell, KFC, Pizza Hut, and Dunkin' Donuts before it, it unveiled plans to eschew palm oil from sources linked to deforestation. In 2015, the company announced that it would stop serving chicken raised on medical antibiotics, a fiat that some health observers predicted would set a model for the entire poultry industry.

Understandably, Pollan was skeptical about the sincerity of these corporate appeals to a reform-minded generation of eaters. But he also took these new assurances as concessions extracted by the food movement. I asked if he thought fast-food chains, which command the loyalty of many millions and which may someday serve millions of Americans items like their first cage-free eggs, could be the most effective agents of change. "I think they're part of the solution, I don't look down on those ideas," he explained. "I think that this is how change comes in America. Basically you shift the center a little bit by staking out a position, a more radical or pure position here, and you see everybody move a little."

What's particularly challenging for fast-food companies is that it's not entirely clear its principal consumer base actually wants these changes. If you ask industry representatives about the various campaigns against fast food, they almost always tend to stress, with slight agitation, how limited the pressure for change seems to be, particularly beyond certain enclaves on the coasts.

Historically, American diners haven't been terribly kind to healthful gestures from their breaded overlords. In 1985, Wendy's spent $10 million on an ad campaign for a lower-calorie menu, which survived all of one year before Dave Thomas was starring in commercials for bacon cheeseburgers once again. Later, when true panic over American obesity first arose in the 1990s, it brought about a number of industry reactions. Dairy Queen introduced the Breeze, a lower-calorie version of the Blizzard that featured yogurt instead of ice cream. It bombed and was ultimately discontinued. In 1990, McDonald's, Burger King, and Wendy's broke (and saved) the hearts of millions by opting to cook their fries in 100 percent vegetable oil instead of a mix made almost entirely of beef tallow. Around the same time, Burger King introduced the B.K. Broiler, the first grilled-chicken sandwich to go national. It took off, at one point selling a million sandwiches a day (or half the number of Whoppers sold each day), before slowly fizzling out. In a solid 1990s flourish, Pizza Hut also introduced and scrapped an ill-conceived "light" pizza, with lower-calorie meat toppings. Unpopular adjustments with consumer health in mind have carried on into present day. In 2017, General Mills had to resume its use of Red 40, Blue 1, and Yellow 6 dyes in Trix cereal after customers revolted at a new, dystopian-looking blend that featured more muted colors extracted from radishes, purple carrots, and turmeric.

It was everyone's good fortune that Colonel Harland Sanders had long kicked the biggest chicken bucket of them all before his company, facing heat from a grilled- and rotisserie-chicken health craze, briefly started selling a skinless chicken offering called Lite 'n Crispy. In 1991, the company even took the extreme step of permanently shortening the Kentucky Fried Chicken name to KFC in an effort to limits its use of what had become an F-word in the early 1990s. That same year, McDonald's released the fabled McLean Deluxe, which it promoted as a burger with only 9 percent fat by weight. (Most burger mixes range between 15 and 20 percent fat.)

The McLean Deluxe had many of the hallmarks of popular burgers today: it was made to order, touted as higher quality, and cost more than an average fast-food burger. By many accounts, the 91 percent fat-free burger performed extremely well in four test markets, and McDonald's sank millions into national ads in major newspapers. The company ran an line of enthusiastic television commercials featuring NFL star Kevin Greene, who wore the jersey number 91. The McLean Deluxe also became the official sandwich of the NBA. But still, hesitation was in the air. "Securities analysts doubted whether the new sandwich would give an immediate lift to McDonald's sales, because, they said, most fast-food customers are not overly concerned about nutrition issues," one industry observer noted.

Once word got out that McDonald's was using carrageenan, a popular, basic seaweed derivate, to lock in the moisture lost in the leaner mix, consumers balked at this apparent betrayal to the country's pure-beef moral code. The McLean Deluxe spectacularly flopped.* By 1993, McDonald's had started test-

---

* Along with Johnny Carson, Hardee's poked fun at the seaweed in its own ads for its Real Lean Deluxe burger, which had slightly less fat. (Their lower-fat burger also flopped.)

ing the Mega Mac, a half-pound burger, its largest and fattiest ever. "Consumers have had their fill of healthier fare," Barry Gibbons, then the chairman and chief executive officer of Burger King, decreed in a 1993 interview with *The Wall Street Journal*. "They're saying, 'Thanks for the choice, thanks for the [nutrition] info. Whopper and fries, please.'"

But as diners, particularly millennials, use their growing consumer power to flock toward healthier or more sustainable options, a cautious brand of fast-food experimentation will continue. In recent years, White Castle has introduced veggie and vegan sliders, and Taco Bell has touted meatless items that would land on an official American Vegetarian Association–approved menu. Even Carl's Jr.–Hardee's, the brand that ran a several-year campaign with sexed-up ads and featured a burger topped with hot dogs and potato chips, was also recently seen promoting new burgers made with ground turkey and grass-fed beef.

As these chains test the progressive waters, others are still holding wholly fast to their sybaritic missions, which bank on value, speed, familiarity, and the gluttonous creativity of their menus. Beloved regional outfits like Cook Out, In-N-Out, and Freddy's still don't have token salads on their menus. Meanwhile, Sonic, America's fourth-largest burger chain, saw its sales boom in the midteens by doubling down on cheap burgers, sweet drinks, and hot dogs, instead of embracing salads and wraps. (Though in 2018, it started a strategy of healthful incrementalism by briefly testing smaller, lower-calorie burgers with mixed patties made of 25 percent mushrooms.) Meanwhile, Arby's reversed a years-long sales slump after ditching its Slicing Up Freshness slogan in favor of a more swaggering We Have the Meats mantra, voiced in commercials by a booming Ving Rhames. Its quirky ad campaigns have included a public apology to vegetarians, along with a call-in helpline for herbivores tempted by their offerings.

With some bemusement, Pollan told me even his acolytes don't love the idea of fast food transmogrifying into some kind of bland and polite adulthood. "It's funny, I've often asked audiences, 'So how would you feel if McDonald's announced tomorrow that they were going all organic: grass-fed beef, organic french fries, no high-fructose corn syrup in the soda?' And everybody is like, 'Aww . . .' They don't like that idea. 'It's not what we want,'" he said. "I find that very curious because that would represent a tremendous victory. If you think about all the pesticides that would not be sprayed on, all the atrazine no longer sprayed on cornfields, if you think about all the animals having much better lives, meat being much healthier."

Something poignant hums beneath this sentiment, this begrudging acknowledgment of the place that fast food now occupies in the American imagination as part of an inviolably holy (or unholy) tradition. At least one explanation for why some don't want fast food to change is that, as Pollan suggested, it represents a time-honored means of reward, an infrequent indulgence, a treat. "That is what fast food was for me growing up," he said. "And I loved it. I loved going to McDonald's. It happened once or twice a month. And we would have soda and french fries and several hamburgers. The hamburgers then cost like fifteen cents. I think that's true with all sorts of junk food. It's fine as a special-occasion food. I think when it becomes the default is when we get into trouble. And that's what happened in the last couple decades. One-third of American kids are [literally] having fast food today."

Navigating the push and pull of these two very different interpretations of purity has inspired some strange corporate behavior. In late 2015, Kraft revamped the recipe for its iconic blue-box mac and cheese, swapping out its dyes and preservatives for a combination of paprika, annatto, and turmeric. To avoid upsetting the faithful, Kraft waited three months and sold 50 million boxes before announcing what they had done. "We'd invite you to try it, but you already have," read one of the ad taglines. Franchises such as Chick-fil-A and McDonald's have tweaked their offerings to make them healthier by reducing portions and subbing for certain ingredients, while often avoiding publicly announcing all of the changes because of the potential affront to their fan bases. "We call it stealth health," one Chick-fil-A nutritional consultant told *Nation's Restaurant News* in 2013. "We didn't necessarily want the customer to know we've tweaked their favorite product." She added, "If customers ask, we'll tell them, but it's almost like you're forcing them to notice a change if you tell them."

America is torn between a constituency that demands serious, progressive change for the long-term health of the country, and another that views change as a mix of sanctimonious, overreaching, price-hiking, doomed-to-fail socialist poppycock. This physical and political division and disconnection in the United States extends deeply into food. For some, the craft-coffee craze might seem ubiquitous, but over 90 percent of Americans still buy their coffee pre-ground. And while tiny craft breweries have grown in fashion, as recently as 2015, eleven brewers were still producing over 90 percent of America's beer.*

Professor Shashi Matta researches consumer behavior at Ohio State University in Columbus, where he is also the faculty director of the school's MBA programs. Matta's research includes studying how parents make choices for their children in fast-food restaurants. In other words, he wants to know what influences parents' thinking as chains begin to offer more options in their kids' meals, such as "milk and not pop" or "fruit slices and not fries." These decisions, he explained, are significant because they tend to have lasting impacts on the long-term habits of children. It's also meaningful because studies suggest that many parents can't afford to serve food to their children that they might reject.

"The important factor contributing to what parents choose is what they think others in their social networks choose," he explained. "We actually measure choice [in our research], but they fill out information about themselves in the survey, information that asks them what others in their social group—friends, family, neighbors—how do they view fast food?" For Matta, these responses helped inform a theory of how the priorities are driven: "I would argue it's social. People, human beings, tend to compare themselves to others, and it's a continuum. Some of us like to compare ourselves to others a lot, and some of us do it a lesser extent, but people do compare themselves to others."

---

* Some other, semirelated eye-opening facts: The average age of first-time homeowners in the United States is about thirty-two. Only about 40 percent of US citizens have a valid passport. The average American only lives eighteen miles from his or her mother. By one slightly dated account, the average age that Americans become grandparents is somewhere between fifty and fifty-four.

This helps explain the wild array of responses to the fickle and shifting tides of American diets. Every company is angling to stand out by changing dramatically or by standing pat. "Fast food has now become so many different things," Matta explained. "White Castle is different from McDonald's is very different from Wendy's is very different from Taco Bell."

In the spirit of this specialization, Matta suggested a visit to Acre, a farm-to-table fast-food concept started by a former student of his on the onetime site of a KFC. The light, airy space had shiny wood tables and hanging lamps and was festooned with plants, books, and growlers. It had craft beers on tap and not one menu item that cost $10 or more. I ordered a mixed-berry smoothie, which at $4.50 cost about a dollar more than a large-sized berry smoothie at McDonald's. It took about five minutes to make—an amount of time that might have irritated me on a normal day.

While I waited, I wandered around the space ogling the chalkboards marked up with seasonal dishes and a list of local purveyors. Mounted near the entrance was a framed crop-themed illustration, featuring a giant carrot, a plump radish, and a huge head of kale sprouting from the earth. Floating above the crops, all too perfectly, was a quote by Michael Pollan: "The wonderful thing about food is that you get three votes a day. Every one of them has the potential to change the world."

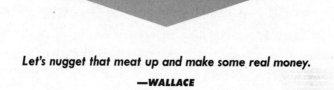

12 CRISP DIGITAL NUGGETS

Let's nugget that meat up and make some real money.

—WALLACE

Carter Wilkerson had no way of knowing how profoundly his life was going to change when the sixteen-year-old high school junior in Reno, Nevada, innocuously reached out to Wendy's over Twitter. "Yo @Wendys," he asked in 2017, "how many retweets for a year of chicken nuggets?" Within a minute, the Wendy's account, which has become one of the truer sages of the social media era, responded, "18 million." It was an impossible order; after all, only one tweet had even reached 3 million retweets before. But Wilkerson quickly took a screenshot of the exchange and tweeted it out to his 150 or so followers with a plea: "HELP ME PLEASE. A MAN NEEDS HIS NUGGS."

The cruel digital universe, which usually taketh, decided to giveth. By the next morning, Carter's call for nuggs had been retweeted fifty thousand times. His campaign gained a lovable hashtag slogan, #NuggsForCarter, and an unlikely coalition including social media influencers, young pop idols, Hollywood stars, Kathy Griffin, Senator Marco Rubio, and television anchor Jake Tapper amplified Wilkerson's tweet with their approvals. "It's good to have dreams," added actor Aaron Paul. Even the automatons joined in. Microsoft's Twitter account blasted out, "We're in. How about you, @Amazon and @ Google? #NuggsForCarter." Both conglomerates, along with the Apple Music and Twitter accounts, retweeted in kind. "Live your best life, Carter," Amazon wrote. "Follow your dreams." In a tweet, United offered to fly Wilkerson to a Wendy's anywhere in the world if he hit his target. After Wilkerson's tweet reached seven digits in just two days, Wendy's gave the plea new life with a retweet of its own: "1 Million?!?! Officially SHOOK."

Soon enough, Wilkerson's lonely request for nuggs approached striking distance of the most retweeted tweet of all time: Ellen DeGeneres's record-making tweet, a selfie taken live in the middle of the 2014 Oscars telecast, which had been viewed by 43 million people. As DeGeneres had explained in the moment to a bemused Meryl Streep, her hope had been that the selfie of herself with a hastily assembled crew of celebrities would become the most retweeted photo of all time. And backed by the wattage of nearly a dozen A-listers, including Bradley Cooper, Julia Roberts, and predivorce Angelina Jolie and Brad Pitt, DeGeneres's post was retweeted over 3 million times. It not only broke the standing Twitter record—a tweet featuring a picture of Barack Obama hugging his wife, Michelle, following his 2012 reelection—in roughly half an hour, it even briefly knocked down Twitter's server.

What Ellen's tweet showcased was the rare power of a monocultural moment, such as a presidential election, where a disparate population's shaky attention span is briefly fixed on one thing. But nothing, not the Super Bowl, the presidency, or the entire Hollywood apparatus stood a chance against the most fixed, basic, and all-encompassing station in the order— humanity's weakness for the perfectly calibrated siren song of fast food.

As Wilkerson's numbers drew closer, DeGeneres did not take the development lying down. Within the course of a week, she cycled through the entire Kübler-Ross spectrum of grief. Mentioning Wilkerson's tweet on her talk show, at first she downplayed its significance. Next, she brought out the actor and Oscar-selfie snapper Bradley Cooper to implore her viewers to retweet the Oscar photo to hold off this challenge to its supremacy. "Not today nugget boy," she declared on her Twitter account. But when she failed to stunt Wilkerson's momentum, DeGeneres brought him on her show as a guest to size him up. In a studio segment she asked him point-blank why he was trying to "sabotage my selfie." To the delight of the audience, he replied with a verbal shrug: "You know, honestly, I just want chicken nuggets." Next, a production assistant brought out a fifty-five-inch television and a year's worth of branded Ellen underwear as part of a proposed pact: Wilkerson could continue promoting his own tweet but only if everyone also retweeted her Oscar selfie. "If somehow you pass me," she warned, "I will come to your house. I will take that TV back, I will take the underwear back, and do more."

But in the following days, nugget fate won out and Wilkerson's tweet surpassed Ellen's with over 3.4 million retweets. Wendy's, no doubt pleased by this insane surfeit of free publicity, announced that Carter would get his free year of nuggs

and honored his record-breaking tweet with a $100,000 dona-
tion to the company's preferred charity, the Dave Thomas
Foundation for Adoption.

Carter Wilkerson's journey to digital sainthood offers just a
nugget, if you will, of how technology and social media have
entwined themselves with fast-food branding and identity.
About forty miles southwest from where Ellen DeGeneres was
selfieing at the Oscars in 2014, Taco Bell was preparing for the
audacious launch of its national breakfast service. To gin up
excitement, the company had created a menu item with the capacity for attention-grabbing internet virality. The Waffle
Taco, a hybrid concoction of a waffle shell studded with eggs,
cheese, sausage or bacon, and topped with syrup, was designed
to deliver the exact kind of frenzy that Taco Bell needed to pro-
voke intrigue and disgust.

As part of the company's largest marketing campaign in history, Taco Bell coordinated a massive publicity stunt in which
the company mailed out a thousand chunky small old-school
burner phones to Taco Bell loyalists, professional social media
stars, and various high-profile creatives across the country.
The phones were sent out via UPS with Taco Bell–branded
packaging marked URGENT and accompanied by a set of
serious-seeming directives. Recipients had to keep their
Breakfast Phones on their person at all times. They should expect that it might ring or buzz at any minute with a righteous,
clandestine mission to be executed for God and Crunchwrap.

The unveiling of the phones alone not only captured intense
media coverage, but brand devotees who had been left out also
oozed online with insane jealousy. In spite of all the intrigue,
most of the Breakfast Phone assignments were tasks in which

Twitter or Instagram were used to promote Taco Bell breakfast. In texts and automated calls, users were implored to blast out videos, selfies, and other content to compete for limited-edition company swag with prizes for the winners ranging from a Taco Bell skateboard deck, bedsheets, and Waffle Taco Nikes to a few paid-for trips and free breakfast for a year. Despite a few operational quirks, the Breakfast Phone campaign with its fan collusion and inherent exclusivity seemed to be a success; images of long lines on the day of the debut were seen far and wide across digital platforms in pictures, tweets, check-ins, and videos.

But this tale of Taco Bell's social media savvy doesn't end with the debut of its breakfast. As the unwashed masses gathered for their Waffle Tacos on the East Coast, the company's social insights team had gathered at 3:00 A.M. at the headquarters in Irvine, California, to monitor from afar how the first day of breakfast was going. Their command center is called the Fish Bowl, a high-tech chamber outfitted with a map that tracks the social media conversations about the chain (as well as its competitors). During the debut of breakfast, the Fish Bowl doubled as a situation room where the team worked for forty-eight hours straight to keep tabs on the newest campaign. "We launched at six A.M. East Coast time, and at about seven-thirty we started seeing emerging topics like 'running out of eggs, long lines,'" Ben Miller, who headed up the social insights team at Taco Bell, told me on a visit to the Fish Bowl in 2016. "So we started digging in and realized we underprojected on how many people were going to come to the restaurants for breakfast so we were literally running out of eggs." Next, the team called in Taco Bell's chief of operations to show him the conversations, and soon enough operators and managers around the country were notified to get more eggs and call in more staff to prepare for the crowds. "Basically that conversation [about the shortages and long lines] stopped just past the Mississippi River," Miller explained. "We were able to reforecast the projections for who was going to come into the stores for the morning."

On less intense days, the social insights team looks for trending topics on social media and drives the company's presence across platforms like Facebook, Twitter, YouTube, and Snapchat. These efforts are led by a squad of young workers and interns who know, with pinpoint accuracy, how long it will be before "raising the roof" or describing something good as "fierce" or "lit" or "dope" are no longer socially acceptable. This work involves much more than just being the gatekeepers of modern vernacular or dealing with irate customers; the social insights team creates custom content that places Taco Bell in the midst of ongoing conversations online, whether it's about a popular new meme, something in the news, or the glory of a new product. The team also curates fan-generated stories on the Taco Bell website itself. "They're very ingrained in the native platforms," said Miller, "so anything that happens within those they're pretty on point with."

Whether it's hamburgers, high-yield savings accounts, or mattresses, the social media accounts for most brands tend to be embarrassing. More than in traditional advertising, a company's digital presence can often seem forced and unsure of itself. But because the identities of fast-food companies are so tied up in their menus, they have a built-in capacity to express themselves a little differently. Sometimes, it's predictable and banal. Other times, it's completely insane. McDonald's, all-pleasing behemoth that it is, plays it safe on social media by deploying the voice of a cheerful corporation: "Mondays, am I right?" Unsurprisingly, Subway's social presence is kind of bland. Both Burger King's and Jack in the Box's Twitter accounts tell a lot of terrible dad jokes, while Chick-fil-A's feeds tend to be both family focused and extremely earnest. As regional chains, Whataburger and Bojangles' tend to tweet disproportionately about local sports. Owing to its cultish, low-profile nature, In-N-Out rarely posts on social media and doesn't even use Twitter. Perhaps knowing its target demo a little too well, Arby's official accounts post a lot about video games, the glory of meat, and anime.* In a nod to the sanctity of Harland Sanders's eleven-ingredient original recipe, KFC's Twitter follows exactly eleven accounts: six random guys named Herb and all five of the Spice Girls. (Six herbs, five spices.) Wendy's, which has positioned itself as the better-knowing older sibling of fast food, can be both thoughtful and not above hurling stinging barbs at other brands.

Amid all this, Taco Bell is perfectly poised for the social media ecosystem. After all, it's hard to be indifferent about a business with standard-issue sour-cream bazookas and meat and nacho-cheese rethermalizers in its kitchens. Whether these things inspire baseline revulsion or a deep and abiding emotional kinship, Taco Bell inflames strong passions. Or, as Miller put it, "You hear that it's either your favorite fast-food place or it's a diarrhea joke." But this dynamic liberates the company from the lame and onerous chore of pandering and instead endows it with the power to make its followers feel at home in the ethos of Live Más. It also frees Taco Bell to be as

---

* Nearly as popular is the parody account Nihilist Arby's, which limns on the bleakness and futility of life and then suggests that people eat at Arby's. (In 2017, Arby's marketing team brought the creator of Nihilist Arby's a peace offering of sandwiches and a puppy.)

ridiculous as it wants. "One of our brand-engagement strate-gies is to fuel the cult of the brand," Matt Prince, a senior public relations manager, added. "When you look at our brand versus others, it truly has a cult phenomenon where you have a lot of passion, but it works both ways—you either love or you hate. But I think that's a good thing."

In 2016, a few weeks before I visited the shiny Taco Bell headquarters, a historic billion-dollar lottery drawing had more or less dominated public conversation. It made for exactly the kind of topic that brands would capitalize on. "We had a plan, we had a setup, we had a storyboard of what we were going to do," Prince explained, "and then we kind of took a step back and thought, 'No, it's not authentic to our brand, it feels like we're just trying to be a part of something that's not authentic to Taco Bell,' and so we let it slide. And then the next day, we saw Burger King, KFC, a handful of brands, do the same thing. Our mind-set is, 'If you can take out our logo and put in another logo and it makes sense, the chances are we probably shouldn't do it.' We have a lot of flexibility in our brand, and not a lot of others do in this space, so we have to make sure we don't take that for granted."

When Taco Bell does choose to weigh in on a cultural moment (or tries to manufacture its own), it turns to Jozlynn Pfingst, who holds the futuristic title "social and digital experience specialist." Pfingst has been credited with fashioning *the voice of Taco Bell* from the boring heap of wet clay that defined the early days of social media, back when each and every company transmission had to be run by the legal department. What she emphasizes about a brand voice is a basic relatability that resonates with the customers who live their lives on these digital platforms: "It's done by a group of twentysomethings who really get the space. They're millennials themselves, so they understand what's funny, what people want to say, they really understand the customer, and they live and breathe the customer because they are the customer themselves."

This principle may seem simple and obvious until you observe how many companies either fail spectacularly at seeming casual ("How do you do, fellow kids?") or try to inhabit a voice of staid, aspirational distance. "When you look at companies like Lexus, and you look at their Instagram, their Instagram's so polished. It's so obvious it's a professional photographer in a set, closed studio," Pfingst went on. "Everything that we want to do, we want to make sure it felt like you could either have taken that Instagram photo or you could have responded back with that same response. We want everything to feel really authentic and real, and so we make sure that the lens we put on everything is just, 'How would a friend respond? How would a friend take this photo?'" If the Taco Bell feeds are any indication, your friend dresses hip, laughs a lot, and is not afraid to post pictures of their nachos with some spilled cheese or a stray bit of tomato or two on the table.

It seems significant that, in a way that's sometimes completely unrelated to food, Taco Bell generates loyalty by offering open seats in a cold and cliquish digital lunchroom. If you catch a Taco Bell fan in their virginal engagement with the company on social media, you might think Taco Bell were a celebrity inviting them to join it on vacation in St. Barts. "It's really incredible," said Pfingst. "People when they get a response from Taco Bell on Twitter or even if you like one of their Instagram photos, it's fascinating to see what they'll do. They'll take screenshots of it and put it as their cover photo on Twitter or Facebook, and then they'll update their bio and they will say, 'Oh my God, Taco Bell commented back to me on 6/6/16. . . .' So that's a lot of how we tailor our social strategy—who we talk to and really being focused on millennials because they're the ones who notice the most."

The cult of the Taco Bell brand is a powerful force. Take it from Jake Booth, an army veteran and onetime sheriff's deputy in Florida, whose first words to his family after miraculously waking from a forty-eight-day coma in 2016 were "I want Taco Bell." After he got his strength back, his devouring of eight tacos was seen as a symbol of his unlikely recovery. "We'd all been waiting an entire month for him to eat those tacos," his older brother told *USA Today*. "It was symbolic of the entire thing—more of a metaphor of him having woken up and being given a second chance at life." Later, on a sad night in 2018, an electrical fire at a Taco Bell in Montgomery, Alabama, burned the store to the ground. In what was originally intended to be a joke to mock a distraught roommate, one local woman created a Facebook event for a candlelight vigil to honor their lost institution. Then over one hundred shell-shocked mourners actually showed up in the bitter winter cold for the memorial service.

"I have seen a lot of things on social for other brands, but I've never seen the level of the craziness that I think Taco Bell fans have, of the love they have for the brand," Pfingst explained. "It's insane. They have tattoos, they create swag, there are people on Etsy who created lines of Taco Bell clothing, Taco Bell crocheted tacos. They're creating all this stuff out there and it's just because they love the brand, and it's just fascinating to see that level of love and craziness for a taco company. But it's out there and I think it's so unique, comparatively I mean, to anyone in our category. People out there don't do things like that for McDonald's."

Of course, long before the emergence of viral social media stunts, fast-food brands still lived with a mischievous thirst for publicity. In a 1996 April Fools' Day prank, Taco Bell set off a firestorm by announcing in a full-page ad in *The New York Times* that "in an effort to help the national debt" the company had purchased the Liberty Bell and renamed it the Taco Liberty Bell. Over a thousand media outlets picked up the story, and thousands of angry citizens called the Taco Bell headquarters as well as the National Park Service, which had been caught completely off guard by the ruse.* When asked about the story by reporters, White House spokesperson Mike McCurry quipped, "We will be doing a series of these. Ford Motor Company is joining today in an effort to refurbish the Lincoln Memorial. . . . It will be the Lincoln Mercury Memorial." Two years later, Burger King used April Fools' Day to introduce the Left-Handed Whopper in a full-page ad in *USA Today*. It featured a sketch of the redesigned burger, highlighting the "meticulous" placement of sesame seeds "to ensure the least amount of loss during consumption," as well as a "rearranged orientation of condiments" to favor lefties. The joke is that the Whopper is a circle. But that didn't stop thousands of people from showing up at their local BK to ask for the new version.

The arrival of social media and its permeation into every nook of waking life has turned the maintenance of brand rel-

---

* According to company estimates, Taco Bell's revenue jumped by $500,000 and $600,000 on the day of the prank and the following day, respectively.

evance into an existential imperative. It's also given the manufacture of internet virality a mystical importance. As a result, a brand's cries for attention now tend to ring a little on the dystopian side. In the years since the introduction of the Double Down, the infamous KFC sandwich made of two fried chicken breasts, bacon, and cheese, the company's bizarro promotions have included the invention of an edible chicken-flavored nail polish (it is "Finger Lickin' Good" after all), a chicken-scented firelog, and "Extra Crispy" sunscreen (all of which sold out in hours), and the mostly unexplained, high-profile blasting of a KFC sandwich to the edge of space in a high-altitude balloon. The company also produced low-smell packaging for self-conscious commuters in Japan and, in 2018, promised to give $11,000 to the first baby born on the Colonel's birthday. All the parents had to do was name their newborn baby Harland. (Not surprisingly, this gambit worked.) Many believed Burger King when, just before April Fools' Day 2017, the company announced it would release Whopper-flavored toothpaste.

After the popular dimension-bending Adult Swim cartoon series *Rick and Morty* repeatedly referenced Szechuan sauce, the nineties-era McNugget dip that lived briefly as a (geographically dubious) promo for the Disney movie *Mulan*, McDonald's was bombarded with online petitions and social media demands by the show's fans to bring the sauce back. In what was meant to be a shrewd publicity stunt, the company acquiesced with a special-edition run, but unfortunately, when stores hadn't carried nearly enough packets to meet the hours-long lines and unexpected hordes, customer riots led by chants of "We want sauce!" ensued. "We did not anticipate the overnight crowds, the cross-state travel and the amazing curiosity, passion and energy fans showed," McDonald's wrote in a ridiculous apology. "Our super-limited batch, though well-intentioned, clearly wasn't near enough to meet that demand. We disappointed fans and we are sorry." To make amends, the company produced and shipped 20 million packets of Szechuan sauce out to its stores a few months later. (In the interim, fans sold packets online for several hundred dollars.)

Carter's quest for nuggs and the great Szechuan Sauce Riots of 2017, along with these other bits of bottled social lighting, reveal how online modern wildfire spreads and digital mobs form, even in the commercial space. When everyone is vying for a connection and suffering from a perpetual and deathly case of FOMO, there will always be inventive and sinister ways for businesses to cash in. This dynamic isn't limited to fast food. The giddy fervor that greets the gimmicky arrival of high-end Cronuts, rainbow-colored bagels, heart-shaped pizzas, Starbucks Unicorn Frappucchinos, and pumpkin-spiced everythings are the instant-gratification versions of the trend toward picturesque food and restaurant set pieces—with twee cartoon menus and packaging, selfie-friendly low lighting, and decadent-looking dishes. Menus increasingly tilt toward items designed to be shared on the internet. Every meal gets consumed in a thousand ways by a thousand people, whether it's a $60 heritage-breed roast chicken for two or a six-piece box of nuggs for one lonely teen.

13 BELONGING

*You don't need to go to church to be a Christian.
If you go to Taco Bell, that doesn't make you a taco.*
—JUSTIN BIEBER

In the emotional realm beyond the fickle and fleeting joys of social media, there lies a deeper, more gratifying range of feeling. As any cult or professional association can attest, a sense of belonging is a powerful sensation. And fast-food chains are some of the most skillful cultivators of this kind of collective loyalty out there. In 2012, for example, the Chicago Bulls had all but pulled away from the Orlando Magic in the fourth quarter of an early-season game. As the clock wound down to the final minute, the crowd at the United Center grew loud, but also urgent. They weren't just cheering for the Bulls' imminent win, they wanted, nay, they needed, their team to score again. With less than twenty seconds left, the Bulls had 99 points, and if they broke 100, everyone in attendance would win a free Big Mac as a part of an ongoing McDonald's promotion.

As chants of "We want Big Macs, we want Big Macs!" rained down from the rafters, the Bulls' star power forward Joakim

Noah grabbed a stray rebound with seven seconds left and, instead of running out the clock, he pulled up from deep and took a long three-point shot, a shot that was well beyond his range. Not only did Noah miss (badly), but he was also summarily chewed out by his coach for taking a careless shot. "I just got caught up in the moment," Noah said sheepishly after the game, "and I was trying to get the people a Big Mac. They really wanted a Big Mac and I felt like, not only did I take the shot and miss the shot, we didn't even get the Big Mac." One month later, an entire arena of Philadelphia Sixers fans booed their own team when they ran out the clock during a 99–80 win over the Atlanta Hawks instead of trying for the free Big Mac. Perhaps to head off a potential riot, Sixers coach Doug Collins had the public address announcer tell the crowd that Big Macs were on him.

On the other side of the country, a similar chant is well-known. At Los Angeles Lakers games whenever the team wins a game while keeping an opponent beneath 100 points, everyone wins two free Jack in the Box tacos. "The 'We want tacos!' chant is as much a part of Lakers home-game traditions as Jack Nicholson sitting courtside," said Ben Smith, a professional sports gambler and team obsessive. In recent years, Lakers fans have had pretty good luck, scoring two free Jack in the Box tacos nearly two hundred times between 2006 and 2016. Assuming all fans cashed in their tacos, this promo had the potential to ding the company for over 7 million tacos.*

---

* This pales in comparison to the 1984 Olympics in Los Angeles, which featured perhaps the most disastrous fast-food giveaway. Ahead of the games, McDonald's handed out scratch cards that would guarantee a free item for every US medal won in a certain event. A gold meant a free Big Mac, silver meant fries, and bronze meant a free soft drink.

What the company hadn't anticipated is that over a dozen countries, led by the Soviet Union and its allies, would boycott the American-hosted Olympics after the United States

It's probably reasonable to see conspiracy in these performance-based promotions, which are popular at all levels of sports. "It's a trick," said onetime Lakers guard Sasha Vujačić after the team fell short of securing the taco promotion in 2009. "They give everyone spicy tacos and no drink. Maybe it would be better if they included a drink." But what's telling and brilliant about these promotions is that they elevate the significance of everyday, dopamine-releasing food—Big Macs, Jack in the Box tacos, Bojangles' biscuits, A&W burgers, Arby's curly fries, and Culver's custards—by attaching them to an even bigger sense of excitement and reward. Everybody wins, twice.

The Lakers giveaway is especially mind-blowing because the Jack in the Box taco might just be the single most divisive foodstuff in the fast-food totality. Indeed, the entire life of a Jack in the Box taco is sacrilege. The corn shells are produced at plants in Kansas and Texas and shipped to stores frozen, prefilled with a cooked "taco meat" mélange of indeterminate makeup.* At Jack in the Box stores, they are unfrozen, topped with lettuce, a haphazard spritz of hot sauce, and then, brace yourself, a slice of American cheese. Next, they are submerged completely in oil and deep-fried whole before being served in a taco-sized bag. The result is a slick-with-grease entity, somehow both wet and crisp, savory and spicy, horrifying, pasty, and

---

boycotted the previous Soviet-hosted Olympic Games in 1980. After winning 94 medals at the 1976 Olympics, the Americans cruised to 174 medals in 1984, including 83 golds. Over sixty-six hundred McDonald's outlets reported Big Mac shortages in the aftermath of the promotion.

* According to the company, it's a mix of beef, chicken, water, vegetable protein, and defatted soy grits, the texture of which allows some vegetarians and carnivores alike to persist in a delusion of their own choosing.

irresistible, all with the structural integrity of a bridge in rural New Hampshire.

In an interview with *The Wall Street Journal*, one addict likened the Jack in the Box taco to a "wet envelope of cat food." (That Jack in the Box was once owned by pet-food maker Purina for eighteen years has only added to the wicked mythology of its tacos.) When the tacos aren't free, they come as a pair for ninety-nine cents and are available twenty-four hours a day in some locations, making them both a harbinger of hangovers and a salve for them as well. But, for all of this, the Jack in the Box tacos are by far the most popular item at America's sixth-largest burger chain, whose menu already includes about a dozen decadent burgers, all-day breakfast sandwiches, and other profane objects like pork-and-cabbage egg rolls and fried jalapeños stuffed with molten cheese.

Menu popularity may actually be too weak of a metric for these tacos. They are yearned for. Coveted. Mimicked in copycat recipes on dozens of sites across the Web for home cooks. Jack in the Box sells over 550 million tacos every year, which evens out to more than a thousand every minute. This figure is roughly the same as the annual domestic sales of Big Macs; one key difference is that Jack in the Box operates in less than half of the states in the union and has less than one-sixth of the total locations that McDonald's does in America.

These stories of obsession emanate down from seemingly unlikely places. Even those who oppose chain restaurants on ideological grounds find themselves making grudging endorsements. Hang around enough vegetarians and you're almost certain to find one that harbors a fierce bias against fast food and yet remains a sucker for at least one of its offerings, usually McDonald's Filet-O-Fish. During his tenure as editor in chief of the revered food mag *Saveur*, James Oseland offered his terms of surrender to the humblest of seafood sandwiches. In spite of referring to McDonald's as the "Evil Death Star," he called the Filet-o-Fish "perfection on a bun" and a "miracle of food science," and recalled that "the first thing I wanted to eat upon returning to the States after spending ten months in a South Indian village sleeping on a mat and eating a strict vegetarian diet was a Filet-O-Fish sammy. They are that important to me."

This brand of I-can't-quit-you ambivalence sums up the primal, complicated temptation of fast food in all its shame and glory. The Filet-O-Fish sits alongside the Jack in the Box taco in the sanctuary of inventions that summon the deepest allegiances and most violent disgust. But the story of the weird piscine concoction also demonstrates fast food's complex relationship with evolving American identities—or vice versa—as well as the efforts taken by the industry to remain meaningful to its customers.

Despite its profane reputation, the Filet-O-Fish was actually designed for a spiritual purpose. In the early 1960s, a McDonald's franchisee named Lou Groen faced a dire crisis. Sales at his Cincinnati store would routinely tank every Friday, when his Monfort Heights customer base, nearly 90 percent Catholic, would abstain from eating meat. "On Fridays, we only took in about seventy-five dollars a day," he told the *Cincinnati Enquirer* in 2007.

Observing the popularity of a fish sandwich at a nearby Frisch's Big Boy, Groen crafted a sandwich of his own, made with battered fish and tartar sauce. He presented the concept to McDonald's chief Ray Kroc, a man not exactly known for his open, ecumenical spirit. "Hell no! I don't care if the pope himself comes to Cincinnati," Kroc told him. "He can eat hamburgers like everybody else. We are not going to stink up our restaurants with any of your damned old fish!"

But with his livelihood on the line, Groen persisted. He convinced two of Kroc's lieutenants to advocate for the sandwich. Kroc eventually agreed to consider the fish—with a catch. Groen's invention would have to square off against the Hula Burger, a meatless, grilled pineapple-and-cheese sandwich that Kroc had been working on. A challenge was set: On Good Friday in 1962, both sandwiches would be tested and the customers would decide. (The ever-confident Kroc made a side bet with his chief of operations that the Hula Burger would prevail; the winner would get a new suit.) "Friday came and the word came out," Groen recalled. "I won hands down. I sold three hundred and fifty fish sandwiches that day. Ray never did tell me how his sandwich did."*

Pumped as the "fish that catches people," the Filet-O-Fish quickly grew from a Friday offering to an everyday item and from regional to national to international, even as the company struggled to market it on its merits.† The sandwich saved Groen's business and aided in the be-all and end-all of rags-to-

---

* The total Hula Burger tally was six. Kroc, never one to be left out of a parade, later claimed that the odd half slice of American cheese that adorns the Filet-O-Fish was his idea.

† Worried that cod "brought back too many childhood memories of cod-liver oil," Kroc thought it best to label the fish as "North Atlantic whitefish." Also, one 1976 ad featured a confusingly Irish, net-wielding, anthropomorphic fish mascot named Phil A. O'Fish in a double-breasted sailor outfit and the tagline "For a surprisingly good taste ... try our Filet-O-Fish."

fishes stories: Groen, who had battled through homelessness as a teenager in the 1930s and had found out about McDonald's franchises through a magazine ad, would go on to open over forty new stores in the area, hire thousands of employees, and churn out millions in sales.

A recent company estimate put the annual sales of Filet-O-Fish at 300 million, a quarter of which are sold during Lent, when the company devotes a healthy advertising push to the sacred sandwich. Several fast-food chains now have specialty items and menus during Lent. To name a few: Wendy's, Arby's, KFC, Jack in the Box, Checkers/Rally's, White Castle, Del Taco, Carl's Jr., Culver's, Krystal, Church's, Whataburger, and Taco Bell.

But the symbolic life of the Filet-O-Fish extends far beyond its Good Friday embrace and subsequent triumph. What started as a local Catholic operator's solution to a local Catholic business problem helped galvanize the chain's expansion of menu items and a fuller consideration of the diversity of American markets. The Filet-O-Fish wasn't just the first non-burger addition to the original McDonald's menu, it was the first of a few pantheonic products—the Big Mac (Pennsylvania), Egg McMuffin (California), and apple pie (Tennessee)—to be dreamed up by individual franchisees, tested, and then brought to market nationally.

The Filet-O-Fish is more than a compelling piece of business trivia; it's a relic of living history and a social through line that carries us across the decades from 1960s America to the present day. Nestled among such artifacts as the original Star-Spangled Banner and the John Bull steam train, a blue polystyrene clamshell package that once held a Filet-O-Fish sandwich can be found at the National Museum of American

History in Washington, D.C.* That's right. Preservationists of American heritage deemed the story of the Filet-O-Fish worthy of enshrinement, partially because the sandwich represents a bygone chapter of the national story.

"You fellows just watch," Ray Kroc carped to a pair of Catholic executives after the Filet-O-Fish became a permanent item. "Now that we've invested in all this equipment to handle fish, the pope will change the rules." And, as it turned out, Pope Paul VI and the Second Vatican Council did slacken the fasting regulations in 1966 to modernize and adapt Catholic practice to accommodate postwar cultural shifts. While one result of Vatican II was a decline in the fish-on-Friday tradition, a broader decline in observance appears to have already been underway. The brief revival of faith that took hold in the United States in the 1950s ultimately diminished as the chaos of the 1960s unsettled the old order. Americans now sought out new ethics and different assurances.

Like the Filet-O-Fish origin story, the foam container on display at the museum is also something of a relic. In a nod to more earthly concerns that had taken root in the American mainstream, McDonald's declared that it would phase out the foam packing for its sandwiches in 1990. Later, in 2002, the Filet-O-Fish would appear in a thrown-out lawsuit by two Bronx teens claiming that McDonald's had made them obese. Not long after, the sandwich became a popular tool used by military interrogators to curry favor with detainees at Guantánamo Bay. Then, in 2013, McDonald's announced that its Filet-O-Fish would only feature wild Alaskan pollack that had been cer-

---

* A visitor can get a real Filet-O-Fish just across the National Mall at the McDonald's in the National Air and Space Museum.

tified as "sustainable" by the Marine Stewardship Council. (Like many purity-themed labels, the significance of the new designation was quickly challenged by critics.)

These tiny footnotes each reflect the evolution of American values and priorities. Like the sways of US politics or the Alaskan tides carrying wild pollack, they ebb and flow and contain multitudes. Plenty of devout, tradition-minded Americans still observe meatless Fridays, while other environmentally and health-conscious consumers have latched onto initiatives like the snappier, more hashtag-friendly Meatless Mondays to demonstrate their commitments. Fast food is one of the major connective threads between the two, offering a sense of affiliation.

The Filet-O-Fish and the Jack in the Box taco, items that are both over fifty years old, embody a bond that exists between fast-food chains and their fans that is special, aspirational, and bordering on abusive. Every year, companies experiment endlessly, laboring to create the next outrageous offering that might become equally sacred in the culinary canon. To stave off menu fatigue, they run new items through test markets and hope they catch on or reprise limited-time classics such as the McDonald's McRib to inflame old passions.

A successful fast-food item is not just a Herculean culinary feat. To invent just one of these fleeting marvels of taste and science, one not only has to nail the evolving sweet spot of a trend-obsessed population, but do so without allowing an item to become too expensive, too difficult to make, or too far beyond a set of core ingredients. To captivate consumers that are already texting while driving, fast-food companies rely on intricate, genius gimmickry and wacky marketing, jingles and slogans, baseline appeals to id and comfort, a hucksterism both grand and unflinchingly American. "We're in the temptation business with the LTOs [limited-time offerings], not the education business," said Jim Taylor, the senior vice president of product development and innovation for Arby's. "If people don't really know what it is, they are not going to be attracted to it. But by the same token, if what you're giving them is something they can get anywhere else, they're not going to pay attention and come into the store specifically for us on an extra visit."

This challenge can be quantified. According to industry research, nearly 60 percent of all trips to fast-food restaurants are on impulse. "You're not just coming up with the flavor of the day, you're telling stories with your food because that's how you connect with the consumer," Amy Alarcón, Popeyes' vice president for culinary innovation, explained. "So we're as much about the food and the inspiration and the story behind it that makes it relevant, that makes someone get off the couch or drive over three lanes of traffic to come to one of our restaurants."

However, given that fast-food fandom is symbiotic, once in a while the customers themselves bring the mountain to Muhammad. Or in the case of Arby's, they bring the Meat Mountain to Muhammad. In 2014, word began to spread about a secret, unofficial sandwich so ridiculous that no corporate innovation team could realistically have conjured it into being on its own.

At the time, the Ohio-born chain had been working to shake its trademark image as a roast-beef company. And so the company began posting tantalizing promotional photos of the chain's array of meaty offerings around its stores. It was summer, and around the country Arby's customers were standing in line, perhaps transfixed by sunstroke, but also transfixed by one image: a poster that featured corned beef layered atop chicken tenders atop ham atop bacon atop turkey atop roast beef atop steak . . . you get the picture. So did the customers. By the time they arrived at the counter to order, enticed diners would ask for a sandwich version of the picture they had seen. The resulting creation came to be known as Meat Mountain, whose wretched topography has since become a viral legend:

Two chicken tenders
1.5 oz. of roast turkey
1.5 oz. of ham
1 slice of Swiss cheese
1.5 oz. of corned beef
1.5 oz. brisket
1.5 oz. of Angus steak
1 slice of cheddar cheese
1.5 oz. roast beef
3 half strips of bacon

Today, the Meat Mountain still lives on, as many fabled creations do, as a $10 secret menu item. Like taco giveaways, secret menu items, which are often schemed up by customers themselves, are yet another manifestation of the cult of belonging that fast food inspires. Depending on the chain, these publicly classified artifacts range from relatively generic to extremely strange. For example, Burger King's unofficial Suicide Burger (four patties, four slices of cheese, and sauce) is not terribly different from the Quad Cheese at Krystal or the Meat Cube at Wendy's. In-N-Out Burger assumes the mantle of having not only one of the best fast-food burgers, but also one of the most extensive and worst-kept secret menus in fast food.

Like the others, In-N-Out has a 4x4 burger, but also the unofficial options of mustard-grilled burgers, well-done fries, whole grilled onions, and, famously, burgers and fries served "animal-style" (covered with cheese, special sauce, pickles, and grilled onions).

Elsewhere, a down-low favorite among Hardee's—and Lipitor—devotees is the Harold, a mix of biscuits, gravy, eggs, hash browns, and shredded cheese, while at Chick-fil-A, they will happily blend a slice of its blueberry cheesecake into a vanilla milkshake if asked nicely. Perhaps the best sub-rosa offering of them all is Fatburger's Hypocrite, which is a veggie burger topped with bacon. Then there's Long John Silver's, whose secret item is free upon request: fried crumbs, also known as crunchies, krums, or crispies, which are simply collected bread chaff from its fried fish and shrimp.

But in the now-century-long history of fast food, one fan-driven creation story supersedes all others. It combines the zeal felt for Jack in the Box tacos with the spiritual character of the Filet-O-Fish and the disparate, communal longing for Arby's Meat Mountain, then stipples it with the artificial alchemy of Doritos flavoring and the greatness of a rare human spirit. It is the story of Todd Mills and the Doritos Locos Taco.

Todd Mills's stint in the air force had not been uneventful. He had trained bomb-sniffing dogs and served as a security escort for Bill Clinton when he took trips home to Arkansas during his presidency. After a bomb went off at the 1996 Olympics in Atlanta, Mills and his dog Henry were the first on the scene to investigate and make sure no other bombs had been planted. But in 2002, he was thirty, living in Arkansas, and still hadn't used his G.I. Bill benefits yet. His wife, Ginger, convinced him to finally go to school, where he studied business writing and information technology and set himself on a new career path. A relentlessly good-natured guy, Mills made friends with his professors. "It really bugged me sometimes how friendly he was," Ginger said. "We'd go to a gas station, he'd run in for a Dr Pepper and stay in there for an hour. And I'll have to go in after him and say, 'Hey, are you coming?' He's like, 'Oh, I just made this friend.'"

"No airs about him at all," his best friend and air force buddy Jimmy added. "The most easygoing, gregarious person. Always had a laugh for everybody. I'll never forget that, he was like that with any stranger. If he was here right now, you'd be on the floor." Ginger tells the story about Todd going to a Photoshop conference and befriending a fellow conventioneer, who eventually wrote a book about Photoshop. The book's dedication went to Todd. "The guy knew him for a week."

It was Todd's Photoshop prowess that would eventually place him in the pathway of Taco Bell history. "He loved taco salad," Ginger remembers. "He always made them with Doritos." According to the legend, Todd's eureka moment arrived one day as he was eating a Taco Bell taco in front of his television. A commercial for Doritos came on, and immediately a lightning quiver of genius trembled through the universe. Doritos and Taco Bell. Taco Bell and Doritos. Two American titans of chemical gastronomy. Todd's subconscious had been depositing clues for years, and finally, as a true visionary does, he saw an entire galaxy where others had only seen a star.

"Imagine this . . . taco shells made from Doritos," he scribbled in a letter he sent to Frito-Lay, the parent company of

Doritos. "I know. . . . It's an amazing thing to ponder." And it was. But the suits at Frito-Lay were not receptive. "They were all 'Thanks, but no thanks,'" Ginger recalled. "'We don't take suggestions.'"

So Todd took matters into own hands. In 2009, he founded the Taco Shells Made from Doritos Movement. He would photoshop Nacho Cheese Doritos–colored taco shells onto famous tableaux and share them on Facebook. In one doctored photo, a taco shell sat inside a frame before adoring crowds at the Louvre right beside the *Mona Lisa*. In another entry, a shell was superimposed onto the hands of Chuck Norris in the midst of a flying ninja kick. There was an alloy-orange taco at Norman Rockwell's iconic Thanksgiving table, and another being demanded by the protesting crowds at Occupy Wall Street. Another piece showed the hallowed shell levitating within an Albert Einstein thought bubble. The masses were smitten and the food sites swooned. Todd's movement went viral in those few years when that designation was still meaningful. And somewhere in the distance, a Bell was beginning to sound.

According to David Peterman, who served as the vice president of new concept operations for Taco Bell in the 1990s, the product that ultimately became the Doritos Locos Taco might have been developed twenty years earlier—back when Taco Bell and Frito-Lay were satellite siblings under the aegis of PepsiCo— were it not for some intercompany chest-puffing and corporate politics.* As he later wrote:

---

* Disputes over the authorship of the Doritos Locos Taco have roiled pretty much since the product was introduced. Taco Bell maintains that the idea was revived and developed independently in preparation for the company's fiftieth birthday, which took place in 2012.

You should know that in approximately 1992, the idea of
taco, tostada and taco salad shells coated with a variety of
Doritos flavorings from our sister company, Frito-Lay, was
evaluated and pursued. At that time, Frito-Lay had recently
completed a factory in Mexico that was capable of manufacturing the shells.

Unfortunately, according to Peterman, Frito-Lay opted not
to produce the hybrid shells. However, in 2012, with Taco Bell
now working in earnest to develop the once-shelved Doritos
concept, the company took notice of Todd and the thousands
of fans he was collecting. "He called me freaking out," Jimmy
recalls. "I'm like, 'Calm down, what's up?' He's like, 'I'm going
to Irvine!' I couldn't believe it, man. I could not believe it."

Taco Bell flew Mills out to their shiny Southern California
headquarters, a modern massive complex once occupied by a
Ford factory. They introduced him to the CEO, took him out
for a steak dinner, and showed him the test kitchen where his
dream vessel, the Nacho Cheese–flavored Doritos Locos Taco,
was being finalized for voyage. Mills became one of the first
people in the world to try it, texting Jimmy all the way through.
"So he's sending me pictures: 'Yeah, I'm going into the moth-
ership!' And there's a mariachi band when he gets in! This guy
just won a golden ticket. And then he gets up there and goes
into the kitchen and gets to eat the first one. He's kinda live-
tweeting this stuff the whole time. He met the CEO. They gave
him a T-shirt, and you know what? He gave that away, too. . . .
That's just the way he was."

After his trip, Todd posted a picture of the Doritos Locos Taco
shell superimposed on the deck of the USS *Abraham Lincoln*
beneath a MISSION ACCOMPLISHED banner. To the distress of

some of his friends, like Jimmy, Todd never sought compensation or credit. "My thinking, just because I had little girls, was 'Lawyer up, man! You don't even have to ask for a million, you could probably just put your kids through college.' He was like, 'Nah, I'm not gonna do that,' and that was just the way he was. That was one of the great things about him. I probably would have showed up with a lawyer and gotten booted out. [I told him,] 'This is such a great idea, this is gonna be freakin' huge!'"

And it was. In the first ten weeks following its much-ballyhooed launch, Taco Bell sold a staggering 100 million Doritos Locos Tacos. Two more varieties—the transcendent Cool Ranch and the serviceable Flamas—were later introduced. The company boasted that the new national obsession led to the creation of some fifteen thousand jobs. Even those who might not have been expected to take these russet-colored shells seriously did so with aplomb. "The shell is paper-thin, with a delicate crunch," William Grimes wrote in *The New York Times*. "The shell does not overpower the taco filling. So far, so good . . . The meat filling just lay there like ballast, but the lettuce was fresh and crisp and the grated Cheddar had an assertive tang. In other words, for what it is, the Doritos Locos taco is pretty good."

Back in Arkansas, the realization of Todd's dream stirred serious excitement. Jimmy tells a story of how his daughter's thrill over the Doritos Locos commercials offered the chance to teach her not to feel limited about her ambitions. "You can do it!" he told her. "It's not just those special people that get to become famous or go to the moon. Anybody can do it."

Less than two years later, in late 2013, Doritos Locos Taco sales had surpassed the $1 billion mark, making it the most successful product rollout in Taco Bell history. Meanwhile, in Arkansas, Todd, just forty-one years old, lay ailing of cancer. The father of two young daughters, he had attained some small degree of celebrity as the champion (and, by some belief, the creator) of a wildly successful product.

As his friends and relatives worked to form a network and begin crowdfunding efforts to help pay for Todd's treatment and for the family's future, the story got more complicated; all the attention that had been so instrumental in promoting the idea before now took on a different tenor. After Taco Bell donated $1,000 to the fundraising efforts, it attracted media attention and ignited a firestorm of criticism about whether the company could or should do more.

Ultimately, Todd's struggle was brief. He went to the doctor with a headache in July and passed away on Thanksgiving. Following his funeral, those close to Todd sought a less somber way to salute him, a celebration more befitting his youth and punch. "We went to Taco Bell. What better place to go?" Jimmy told me. "I don't remember who came up with it, everybody knew that was what we needed to do. It was a big send-off, a lot of us hadn't seen each other in years. Seemed like the natural thing to do. I've got a picture of it somewhere, my daughter's got a face full of Locos Tacos. It just seemed like the proper send-off. It's one of those clichés, it's what he would have wanted."

Word of the honorary excursion to Taco Bell emanated out from Little Rock and into a world desperate to feel a connection. For months after Todd's passing, Ginger received condolences from near and far. "I got a ton of strange messages from random people all over the country. A lot of them were widows who said, 'I know what you're going through'; people who had lost children who would say, 'I know the grief.' It was weird to me that they were contacting me, but for the most part they were kindhearted, they meant well. A lot of them were also photos of strangers eating Doritos Locos Tacos. It was still kind of neat, the attention that he got. He would have gotten a kick out of it, I know. He would have cracked up."

From funeral cakes and shiva spreads to Irish poteen and Mormon potatoes, food has often comforted during times of mourning. Regardless of whether tributes are affixed to an ancient tradition or customized to modern taste, they enact a feeling of membership and solace. That the Doritos Locos Taco could be a national sensation and still hold a deeply intimate meaning reflects the degree to which our inherent American identity is intertwined with these products. They span far beyond our likes and dislikes to symbolize memories of life's significant moments. A universal and accessible collective memory to which we can all belong.

14 THE FAST-CASUAL FRONTIER

My favorite restaurant is the one that loves me the most.
—DANNY MEYER

Not far from Northstar Café in Columbus, there's a Wendy's that served as a test prototype for the company's new futuristic-looking stores. For a newcomer who once drew comfort from the bland, retirement-home motif of a classic Wendy's store, seeing its new model is like discovering that your childhood house has been turned into a vape lounge. Gone are the earthy tones, that iconic brown mansard roof, the brick columns, the clumsy, curved black sunroom front, and the parapets. Nowhere is there a mention of "old-fashioned hamburgers." In their place are tall, black glass windows and red signage. Simple text declares, "Quality is our recipe."

As you approach, the store entrance is a black automatic sliding door. (A black automatic sliding door at a Wendy's!) And inside, instead of Kenny Loggins, Top 40 hits play from speakers above. There's also a tall red plank adorned with a shiny large flat-screen television, a long rectangular gas fireplace, and a mishmash of seating configurations that include low tables and lounge chairs, Starbucks-style high-top tables with outlets for plugs, some cushy padded dining booths, and a set of small tables with movable chairs. At the counter, the menu boards are bright digital white, and cylindrical lamps hang from a wood-paneled ceiling above like Courbets at the Musée d'Orsay. Simply put, Wendy's no longer looked like an elderly relative's sitting room; it was now the lair of someone who'd become either a late-in-life swinger or a villain in a Liam Neeson movie.

The development of this new Wendy's model—four new, equally mod configurations are in wide adoption around the United States—can be seen as a direct result of the rise in popularity of fast casual, a newer, trendier segment of the restaurant industry. Fast casual has forcefully emerged to capitalize on the negative associations of fast food as impersonal, unhealthy, and mass-produced. Part of its appeal, particularly among millennials, is that fast-casual chains such as Chipotle and Panera tend to strike a holier-than-fast-food posture. A customer pays slightly more and waits slightly longer for food with ingredients that are said to be better and that gets served by workers who tend to make ever-so-slightly higher wages.* The spaces look less like square and traditional dining rooms and more like coffee shops. And like in the original White Castles and Steak 'n Shakes, the food is often prepared in an open or visible kitchen to reassure diners about its quality.

Wendy's isn't the only fast-food chain plugging deep into this new aesthetic. In Louisville, one of KFC's new model stores had the similarly sleek look of the lobby of a hotel for business

---

* A 2013 survey by the market-research firm Mintel said that 92 percent of respondents cited "treating employees well" as one of the reasons they choose fast-casual restaurants. (Although statements and lawsuits by former employees have alleged that this perception may be unearned.)

travelers, albeit one with an enormous chicken-bucket lighting feature. Over on one wall, in the center of a neatly arranged
small display of historical company paraphernalia and a stately
looking photo of the Colonel, was some lettering billing Harland Sanders as THE ORIGINAL CELEBRITY CHEF. Meanwhile, by
the counter, a mounted chalkboard listed the name of the
store's cook that day as well as the provenance of that day's
chicken.

Elsewhere, in recent years, chains like Chick-fil-A and Arby's have debuted large modern stores set in the dead middle
of city centers. For the many younger Americans who have
moved back into cities and eschewed owning cars, these new
urban concepts have been built without drive-thrus. The first,
full-scale Chick-fil-A store in New York City, for example,
opened in 2015. At three stories and five thousand square feet,
it was the largest store in the franchise's system when it opened.
(On an early visit, one executive bragged that the store runs
through thirty thousand pickles a day.) Quickly, it became one
of the few anointed Manhattan institutions with a nearly permanent out-the-door line. In 2018, it was eclipsed by an even-
larger five-story unit with a rooftop in Lower Manhattan, just
a few blocks east of the World Trade Center.

A few months after Manhattan's first Chick-fil-A arrived,
Arby's opened a branch in the grimy shadow of Port Author-
ity; the store had been modeled after an experimental design
in Pittsburgh. In a surreal turn for a brand that Jon Stewart
once called "a dare for your colon," this sparkling-new Arby's
features Edison bulbs, wood accents, an open kitchen, and coffee sourced from a local roaster. "Overall, we had a strategy to
bring Arby's into more urban environments," Arby's CEO, Paul
Brown, told me at the opening. "We started a few years ago,

making sure we could get the design right and making sure we could do it without a drive-thru."

Like a number of fast-food chains, Chick-fil-A and Arby's scheme to capture younger and more discerning customers by relying in part on innovations once unthinkable for purveyors of $4 sandwiches: apps that let you use your phone to order and pay ahead, employees that take your order and money while you're still in a line, automated cashiers, fast-food home delivery via Uber and other services, and even office catering. "The fact that we do sixtyish percent of our business through drive-thru is because people are in their cars," Brown explained of traditional markets. "Here in New York, we'll be getting all this foot traffic. I'm not worried at all."

Another heavily stressed component of the fast-casual experience is the ability to obsessively customize what you order. This consumer-empowering possibility has always existed in fast food, but what many fast-casual restaurants have done is make every customer the manager of the restaurant assembly line. You walk in, you complain about the line, you wait in the line anyway, you hurriedly gesture at the toppings you want inside or on top of your salad, burrito, burger, or bowl, and you try not to seem like too much of a demanding jerk about it.

Although fast-food restaurants have built this kind of customization into their apps, few chains have taken a wholesale leap toward the fast-casual model. Back in Columbus, Wendy's was in the midst of test-marketing that very concept at its new store. As I approached the counter, I came upon a "Build Your Sandwich" menu, an emulator of fast-casual burger joints like Five Guys. For a set cost, a fussier diner could ignore the traditional Wendy's menu and design his or her own burger or chicken sandwich from a long list of bread, cheese, sauce, and toppings options. Forget Dave's Hot 'n Juicy! Suddenly, the dream of ordering a weird three-patty burger with Asiago cheese and barbecue sauce on a pretzel bun was not only possible, but encouraged.*

Beneath the beef and chicken options on the "Build Your Sandwich" board, however, an even bolder, more progressive consumer experiment was underway: Wendy's was test-marketing a black-bean veggie burger. For some vegetarians and public-health warriors alike, the veggie burger has stood in as the impossible dream, a vessel of corrective (and gas-inducing) hope and normalcy, the one item that, if adopted by the mainstream, could perhaps shift the dark balance of the fast-food world toward the light.

In 2014, White Castle raised some eyebrows when it introduced sliders made with Dr. Praeger's brand premade veggie patties. Burger King has also offered a Morningstar Farms–produced veggie burger since 2002, and for a brief moment, it had been rumored that the company might start selling some of its more successful vegetarian sandwiches from its Indian menus to other vegetarian-heavy markets around the world. Despite some pressure, McDonald's has only had short-lived flirtations with veggie burgers over the years, although some vegetarians rejoiced when the company introduced its all-day breakfast in late 2015, which immediately made sought-after protein more widely available. But if successful, Wendy's black-bean burger—a "custom blend with black beans, corn, and

---

* While chains have long claimed their customers could customize or "have it your way," the outright listing of toppings and combinations is pretty rare in the fast-food world, most likely because it would slow everything down.

bell peppers"—might just be the first internally developed national fast-food veggie burger offered in the United States.

The cashier at Wendy's explained that the veggie burger was being tested at only one other store, not far from where we were. Next, she patiently shepherded me through the building process, suggesting that I try spring mix as a topping, along with the toasted multigrain bun, a big heavily sesamed affair with rolled oats and quinoa. I paid my $5 tab and took a paper cup to the store's specialty Coca-Cola Freestyle machine, which looked like a NASA-built Wurlitzer jukebox. It had 127 mesmerizing, head-scratching flavors of soda, including Coke Raspberry, Diet Barq's Vanilla, and Sprite Zero with Orange.

From the lounge-like décor to its tyranny-enabling customizable burgers, this tiny Wendy's seemed like the epicenter of an evolution, signaling the future of quick-service dining. Then there was the black-bean burger. Americans weren't just consuming more lean proteins like chicken, they were also eating less meat overall. A few months later, in early 2016, Wendy's expanded the test market for its black-bean burger from two stores to three cities—the rest of Columbus, along with Salt Lake City, Utah, and Columbia, South Carolina—placing PETA and vegetarian blogs in the unlikely position of advocating that its followers run out to a fast-food chain and make a product there successful. By the end of the summer, however, the test had run its course. The Wendy's black-bean burger was unceremoniously discontinued, survived by its vegetarian kin of baked potatoes, fries, and salads.

So long as the hamburger remains the national meal, there will always be a market for places like Freddy's, the Wichita-born steakburger-and-custard chain. Before surrendering at a Colo-

rado federal prison in 2012, disgraced former Illinois governor Rod Blagojevich stopped at one to indulge in one last bite
of freedom before starting his fourteen-year sentence. If
Blagojevich's goal was to corrupt himself one last time before
serving time for corruption, he could certainly have done worse
than a Freddy's double-patty melt.*

In recent years, Freddy's has quickly grown into a regional
juggernaut, garnering some messianic praise and appearing
on a growing number of lists of America's best burgers and
best chains. The company's namesake is Freddy Simon, a smiling ninety-four-year-old Kansan and World War II vet, who
makes a habit of touring the Wichita-area stores at least once
a week, handing out "Freddy Bucks" to children. The franchise
was founded by his two sons and a business partner to honor
their love of custard, the frozen dairy-land staple they'd eaten
growing up, and a recipe for steakburgers that Freddy had
made for the family. And if all this didn't sound wholesome
enough already, add in a 1950s retro-diner motif with black-
and-white-checkered floors, red chairs and tables, and old pictures of Freddy. At a store in Wichita, the booths were squeezed
full with pockets of kids still out for summer, older couples,
and a few high school football players likely in the middle of
preseason two-a-days. At one table, there was literally a mail-
man in high socks drinking a milkshake.

Part of what's intriguing about Freddy's is not just that it's
a burger place from Wichita—the place of origin for White
Castle and, by some interpretations, the hamburger itself—it's

---

* Blagojevich's last request wasn't so unusual. According to a 2012 study, 24 percent of
death-row inmates have burgers as their final meals; takeout from fast-food chains makes
up another 4 percent, although that number is almost certainly limited by the requirement
of many states that the food for final meals be prepared on-site.

also a newer small chain in rapid ascent. In the weeks before my visit, the 150-unit company had launched 21 new franchises in twenty-one weeks, and one trade publication had declared it the fourth-fastest growing chain in the country. "We opened our first Freddy's when I was fifty-two, so the same as Ray Kroc," Randy Simon, one of the cofounders explained. "My wife said, 'Why did you wait until fifty-two to get into the burger business?' I said, 'That's what Ray did.' She thought we were retired at that point."

The invention of the steakburger is widely credited to Steak 'n Shake, a classic Midwestern fast-food institution and a by-product of the Wichita-inspired burger boom. The first Steak 'n Shake was inaugurated in Normal, Illinois, in 1934 by Gus and Edith Belt, the perfect names for the creators of the steak-burger. Gus would wait until the restaurant was full, then roll in barrels of meat, including finer cuts of round, sirloin, and T-bone, and grind them in view of onlooking guests. The lav-ish assemblage of beef would be formed into burger patties (hence the *steakburger* name), then prepared in a kitchen with an open view. Belt's enduring burgerly maxim: "In sight it must be right."*

Ever since, true burger obsessives have had their own imag-inings of what makes an ideal steakburger. "Well, it's a leaner beef and it's a higher-quality cut of the beef," Simon explained. "Generally, steakburgers are considered somewhere between eighty-five/fifteen to ninety/ten [in the ratio of meat to fat]. To me, traditionally, a steakburger is a smash burger, so it sizzles

---

* In interviews, Shake Shack founder and restaurant mogul Danny Meyer has cited Steak 'n Shake as his inspiration.

and grills quickly. That's why the double is so popular, people want to taste the meat, they don't just want a little chip in theirs."

What's incredible about a smashed steakburger is the texture; because it's flattened thin, the heavily seasoned meat crisps on the edges and browns in what gastronomes and scientists characterize as the Maillard reaction. The result is a marriage of savory, salty, and the best kind of flaky, almost like bread crust. A Freddy's steakburger is then topped with American cheese by default, which devilishly compensates for the fat lost in the leaner meat. Follow that with layers of chilled and crunchy lettuce, pickles, onions, and a squeeze of sharp yellow mustard, then throw it all on a butter-toasted bun. It's difficult to imagine that people who live in a world with this kind of possibility would ever do things like go to war or eat black beans.

In addition to its burgers, Freddy's is also useful for clarifying the somewhat blurry boundaries between the fast-food and fast-casual segments. Before Simon and I had sat down, I had ordered a Freddy's No. 1 Combo, which is a double steakburger with cheese, fries, and a soda. Based on the speed of service (five minutes) and the price point of the food ($7.59) as well as the very existence of combo meals, Freddy's seemed to be firmly in step with the Whataburgers, Chick-fil-As, and In-N-Outs, the brightest and glossiest lucidas of the fast-food constellations. These chains are typically regional, either privately held or family owned, beloved, and often slightly more expensive than their big national brethren such as McDonald's, Burger King, and Wendy's.

Meanwhile, fast-casual burger joints like Shake Shack or Five Guys generally have no combo meals. There, what I had ordered at Freddy's would easily have cost $11 to $13 and would likely have taken at least twice as long, depending on how lucky I'd gotten with the line. "My preference would be for people to think of us as fast casual, but I think that it's probably more perceived as fast food," Simon explained. "Face it, you generally don't go through a drive-thru on fast casual and expect to have any kind of speed of service. The same with inside the house. We feel like for the quality of the product that we deliver, part of it is because we smash it, we cook it fast."

For Simon, to be fast casual was to enviable; when we met, that segment was in the midst of a flush period of surging sales. But in the following weeks and months, Chipotle, the singular poster child for the meteoric rise of fast casual and whose mantra was locally sourced Food with Integrity, suffered through one of the more astonishing stretches of food-borne illness outbreaks. Within a short time, at least seven different episodes from California and the Pacific Northwest to the Midwest to the East Coast involved norovirus, salmonella, and *E. coli*. Roughly five hundred people were poisoned or sickened, one incident drew a grand jury subpoena, Chipotle's stock plummeted, and their co-CEOs had their 2015 salaries cut in half.* Finally, in 2018, with its recovery still flailing, it poached Brian Niccol, the head of the ostensibly villainous Taco Bell, to become its new CEO.

To this point and beyond, Chipotle and its snowballing fast-casual kin have been benefiting from the perception that

---

* Most ignominiously, one outbreak happened in the midst of the company's annual Halloween promotion where patrons who arrive in costume are granted $3 Boo-ritos. In 2015, Chipotle added a twist to their promotion, instructing customers to add an unnecessary object on their costume to highlight the company's recent pledge to serve food without additives or genetically modified organisms (GMOs).

because their food by all appearances is more "wholesome," it's also healthier than fast food. But this idea may have some wishful eating baked into it. In 2016, researchers at the University of South Carolina studied over three thousand entrées from fifty-two chains and found that main items at fast-casual restaurants averaged two hundred calories more than their fast-food counterparts. It's a complicating revelation for an industry that has been marketed as a healthier response to fast food. "While being aware of calories and sodium can be helpful, there is a dark side to an overemphasis on numbers," one dietitian told Reuters in response to the study. "It can distract customers from what makes foods healthy—nutrient density, fiber content, antioxidants, quality of the fat, et cetera. It's important to look at health more holistically." Nevertheless, another study, by *The New York Times*, in 2015 estimated that the typical order at Chipotle is 1,070 calories, which is nearly double that of a Big Mac, which, at 560 calories, is roughly the average for a fast-food entrée. "Most orders at Chipotle give you close to a full day's worth of salt (2,400 milligrams) and 75 percent of a full day's worth of saturated fat," the study noted. Simon, who spent much of his early career opening locations of the fast-casual chain Panera, confirmed this dynamic: "I can say Panera does a great job on salads, and Panera is perceived to be very healthy. But I could take you over to Panera and fix you a sandwich it would take two Big Macs to catch up to. And probably fries, too."

With neither better nutrition nor better food safety nor better wages guaranteed at fast-casual restaurants, one effective way to differentiate between fast food and fast casual might be to reduce it to a $5-plus lunch and a $10-plus lunch, respectively. And often, that price point can mean the difference between a social experience that transcends financial and generational divides, and one where the clientele generally resides within the same age and financial brackets. According to data released by the food-industry research firm Technomic, consumers aged forty-five or older constituted either 43 to 44 percent of the customer base of McDonald's, Burger King, and Wendy's in 2015. At Smashburger, the fast-casual comparison brand, that age range only represented 35 percent of customers in 2015. To eat fast food is to be in the midst of everything and everyone.

"It's funny," said Simon. "We get construction workers and billionaires. And you go from families to people that come in by themselves. People ask, 'What's your target market?' And [I say], 'Well, probably kid driven, family driven.' If there's any target, that would be it. But demographically, everybody seems to come here. The old people like the ice cream and the younger people like the ice cream and everybody in between likes the burgers and fries."

*I get an ice cream cone for a dollar. Then I will usually buy a
medium french fries. I love the salt and the sweet. And that's
what you get here, too—the salt and sweet of humanity.*
—SISTER ELAINE GOODELL

Although she was technically on her shift, it was slow and so
Sara Dappen said she didn't mind spending a few minutes
chatting. She explained that she'd grown up on an Iowa farm,
not far from the McDonald's where we were sitting. Dappen
had been born in October 1920, a month before Warren Hard-
ing won the presidency in the first national election in which
women could vote. She had lived through the Depression and
the droughts, heat waves, and black blizzards of the Dust Bowl
years. During the war years, her husband, Bob, had served as
a navigator in the Pacific on the Bethlehem Steel–built USS
Leedstown and been awarded seven Bronze Stars. After thinking back, she conceded that she couldn't quite recall where they
had gone on their first date. "It wasn't the first date, but one of
them was to see Clark Gable in *Gone with the Wind.* We saw it
when it came out first."

Seven years earlier, back when Dappen was eighty-seven, she had started working at this McDonald's in Story City, an hour north of Des Moines. "I wipe off all the tables and sweep up the crumbs, and if there's a spill of water or food, I'll clean that up. I'll greet the customers and visit with different ones and have to check the bathroom every twice in a while." She pointed over to the counter with a slow hand. "Sometimes you have to go to the counter for some of the customers, and some of 'em can't find the lids to their pop. It's right up above it, but they don't [always] see it, so I help them with that."

Dappen now works three shifts a week, usually in the afternoons. "It's the time of day when it's kind of melancholy. My husband died in '12, and now more than ever I guess I appreciate it because it's the time of day when I'm just kind of lonesome. I come in here about three and I work until seven or eight, it fills that void." Though she hadn't had a meal outside of home until she was fourteen and hadn't eaten much McDonald's prior to working there, Dappen had since grown fond of finishing her shift with a Bacon McDouble. "I watch my diet. I don't take the fries neither, I just take a sandwich."

At nearly ninety-four years old in 2015, Dappen was unique because she was thought to be the oldest McDonald's worker in the world, but she was also part of a trend that encompasses many of her cohorts. By dint of demography, sociology, and financial necessity, the American workforce matured as the twentieth century drew to a close. Between 1977 and 2007, the employment rate of workers sixty-five years and over shot up 101 percent in the United States, according to the Bureau of Labor Statistics. (Over that same span of time, total employment increased only 59 percent.) Baby boomers and their generational forebears were aging, and if they weren't controlling the government, they were doing other jobs. By the second quarter of 2017, nearly one-fifth of retirement-age Americans were working, the highest rate since the early 1960s.

Part of this drift has to do with a disappearing segment of the workforce. In the 1980s, as more and more American teenagers started to delay their entrance into the job market to go to college or collect pogs or whatever, a number of lower-wage businesses and retailers, including fast-food companies, focused on recruiting, hiring, and training workers in their postretirement years. It was an easy, calculated, and inexpensive fix for a growing labor problem. For employers, filling open positions and eliminating high turnover rates made them more efficient. (Not to mention that older workers are often thought to be more reliable and productive than younger ones.)

For a population with a lengthening life span and fewer careers with fixed pensions, part-time jobs offer different incentives from those of previous generations. Through low-wage gigs older workers in the United States can theoretically earn some income and still receive their Social Security benefits. In an only-expanding catastrophe of more and more Americans squeezed by debt and decades of stagnant wage growth, employment increasingly offers a small measure of protection against falling into poverty. Perhaps most affectingly though, in a time of increasing social isolation, jobs enable retirement-age citizens to plug themselves into their communities and interact. "It's really interesting," Dappen said of her work. "You see people that will say devotions before they eat, and then you'll meet friends that you haven't seen in a long time, and every once in a while some of your relatives that you haven't seen in a long time will come through."

* * *

The trend away from teen employment that started in the 1980s has accelerated in the twenty-first century. Between 2000 and 2018, the number of American teens (ages sixteen to nineteen) with a job dropped from 45 percent to just 30. The vanishing of teens from behind fast-food counters, even just for summer gigs, has had a more pronounced effect on the industry in part because fast food has steadily outgrown the population of younger Americans since the 1990s. In addition to older Americans, this gap has been filled in part by foreign-born workers and immigrants, a new wave of Aslam Khans from all over the world, who have stepped into the breach. Increasingly though, as economic conditions in the United States have worsened and social mobility has been stunted by flat wages and a decline in full-time work, fast food has become a career for American adults. The median age of a fast-food worker, according to the National Employment Law Project and others, has risen in recent years to somewhere near twenty-nine years old.* With this change, the image of fast-food work itself (in many quarters) has devolved from that of an honest job for workforce aspirants to the "McJob" pejorative now formally recognized by some dictionaries—a dead-end career purgatory for laggards or the unlucky.

Of course, it wasn't always this way. Still cataloged on the "They're Just Like Us" corner of the internet are lists of anointed luminaries for whom the fast-food industry represented a small

---

* One result is that as many as half of fast-food workers now receive public assistance, rounding out a restaurant industry in which 40 percent of workers live in near-poverty.

According to an analysis of Department of Labor data, seven of the ten lowest-paying jobs in the United States in 2012 were in the food industry. This includes farm laborers, fast-food workers, and servers at full-service restaurants—most of whom are women working for tips—as well as the salaried and unsalaried dishwashers, barbacks, busboys, and chefs from greasy roadside diners to the glimmering Michelin-starred temples.

character-building way station toward careers of unfathomable success. Jennifer Hudson and Queen Latifah logged time at Burger Kings in Chicago and Newark, respectively, while Gwen Stefani and Martina McBride pulled shifts and soft serve at Dairy Queen. Eva Longoria threw her own quinceañera with money made from working the counter at Wendy's in Corpus Christi. Brad Pitt's first starring role in Hollywood was as a dancing chicken outside an El Pollo Loco. Throw Madonna (Dunkin' Donuts), Barack Obama (Baskin-Robbins), and Rahm Emanuel (Arby's)* into the mix and you're on your way to a pretty impressive minyan.

Given its huge size and reach, McDonald's has a particularly dizzying roster of distinguished graduates. In 1996, McDonald's estimated that one of out every eight American workers had worked for the company. Recipients of a theoretical Golden Arches alumni newsletter would include Jay Leno, Rachel McAdams, Lin-Manuel Miranda, Shania Twain, Seal, Keenen Ivory Wayans, Sharon Stone, Macy Gray, Tony Stewart, Pink, and James Franco. Amazon overlord and world's richest person Jeff Bezos once gloated that he can still crack eggs with one hand from working the Saturday-morning shift at McDonald's. "Time is very important . . . you couldn't let the fries get cold," said former grillman and top Olympian Carl Lewis, stressing the crucial precision required for the world's best fries. "If I was ten seconds off, I'd have no gold medal."†

"I remember thinking that McDonald's was unique as a

---

* The infamously profanity-prone Chicago mayor and former White House chief of staff was, quite literally, diminished in his capacities to both swear and serve as President Obama's right-hand man because he lost part of his middle finger to an Arby's meat slicer.
† Among those who might appreciate this quest for speed is eight-time gold medalist Usain Bolt, who infamously ate one thousand Chicken McNuggets in ten days during the 2008 Beijing Olympics and still broke the world record in the 100-meter dash.

great equalizer," said Andy Card, the former McDonald's worker and White House chief of staff under George W. Bush. "Wealthy and poor, black and white, all came to McDonald's and stood in the same lines and sat at the same booths." Even Joe Kernan, the former Democratic governor of Indiana and a onetime Mickey D's employee, might have nodded at this line. As a vice-presidential hopeful on the campaign trail in 2012, Paul Ryan punctuated his Randian case for fewer social programs by calling back to his time working beneath the Golden Arches: "I don't know about you, but when I was growing up, when I was flipping burgers at McDonald's, when I was standing in front of that big Hobart machine washing dishes or waiting tables, I never thought of myself as stuck in some station in life."

Quietly, slowly, subtly, in a country where work is religion, the national fetish over teenagers learning the value of hard work has given way to a fetish over older Americans still contributing economically to society in their golden years. According to a recent Pew study, most retirement-age Americans tend to hold jobs in management, sales, and legal fields. But among the more popular images of graying workers in the United States are that of Walmart greeters, park rangers, and, of course, fast-food workers. The motif of the fast-food semi-retiree is the type of too-irresistible story that ends up becoming a national sensation. In 2017, coverage of Loraine Maurer, a ninety-four-year-old widow and great-grandmother who was being honored for decades of work at a McDonald's in Evansville, Indiana, noted that she regularly wakes up at three in the morning to make it for her Friday and Saturday shifts that begin at five. Her story inspired such headlines as "A 94-Year-Old

Woman Who's Worked at McDonald's for 44 Years Is Making the Rest of Us Look Bad" and "Evansville Woman, 94, Still Going Strong 44 Years into McDonald's Job." One regular interviewed in a dispatch by a local ABC affiliate cheerily dubbed her "the sunshine of this place."

But, like Dappen, beneath all of this wondrous cooing is a story about someone feeling cloistered. In one interview, Maurer said that she often mulls retirement in the winter, but would never bring herself to quit because she would get depressed. In another, Maurer told the *Evansville Courier & Press* that she "would never be a manager because I want to deal with my customers." She added, "I want to be in contact with them, I don't want to be behind the lines."

This touching sentiment is reminiscent of the story of Joel Presson, a ninety-three-year-old worker at a Wendy's in Oxford, Ohio. Presson started with the chain in 1989, when he was nearly seventy, and as he told the *Dayton Daily News* in 2014, he resisted the opportunity to become a supervisor there because he felt it was isolating: "I'd been in the food business all my life. They wanted me to go into management, and I said no. I didn't want to do that because I'd had sixty years of it, and that was enough." In an echo of both Dappen and Maurer, Presson added, "I don't like to be lonesome. . . . I love people. When you lived on a farm during the Depression years, and you didn't have anybody visiting you except a mule, you swore then you were going to find a place where you could be around people."

Ultimately, the elderly low-wage worker represents just one tiny droplet in the social lives of American seniors. But in ways that don't necessarily seem obvious, fast-food chains are also essential to the lives of retirees for reasons far beyond employment. Sociologists frequently refer to gathering spots outside of work and home as "third places." For the elderly cohort, oftentimes sectioned off by age at places like senior centers, the dining room of a fast-food restaurant is a ready-made community center for intergenerational mingling. The cost of admission is already low—the prices beckon those on fixed incomes—and crucially, the distance for the less mobile is often shorter, particularly in urban centers that are resource strapped or rapidly gentrifying.

Every Friday, local retirees at a Burger King in Oahu are famous for breaking out their ukuleles and guitars for an early-morning *kanikapila*—a traditional Hawaiian jam session. At the same time, nearly half a world away, seniors at a McDonald's in Fort Kent, Maine, have become a cult fascination among cardplayers for their marathon sessions of Charlemagne, or Charlie, a weird French-Acadian fusion of bridge and cribbage. "We are sort of like a family," Judy Levasseur, a Fort Kent regular, told the *Bangor Daily News*. "If one of us does not show up, we notice and try to make sure they are okay."

Everywhere in between paradise and the pines, groups assemble in places with year-round climate control to talk about the weather or sports or politics or to gossip over discounted meals. In 2014, a large diplomatic flare-up erupted in Queens, when the management at a McDonald's in Flushing sought to eject the members of the elderly Korean community who had made the store their regular meeting point, routinely for all-day sessions and, apparently, at the expense of seating for other customers during peak hours. Police officers were summoned, threats were announced, global boycotts were issued. News of the spat went as far as San Francisco, then carried all the way to Seoul before a local state assemblyman was called in to broker a truce between the community and the franchise's owner.

The episode also triggered a host of skull sessions among urban sociologists about city resources, assimilation, demography, and the cultural nuances between the American and the Korean treatment of the elderly. But at its heart, it was a story about access, proximity, and independence. Nearly all of the McFlâneurs lived within two blocks of the store, while the local library was a mile away, and the closest senior center was even farther away and located in the basement of a church.* "It's how we keep track of each other now," one habitué told *The New York Times* of their hangout sessions. In a familiar trope, he added, "Everybody checks in at McDonald's at least once a day, so we know they're okay."

One wild irony here is that the entire fast-food enterprise is built around speed: the assembly-line processes, blaring fryer timers, and hotfooted kitchen staff. The crowds pooling impatiently near the pickup counters, the cars and trucks jamming up drive-thru lines with that one back-seat driver speculating aloud about whether it would be quicker to just go inside. For many franchises, the success of every transaction is gauged first and foremost on the swiftness of the service. It's by size *and* velocity that McDonald's averages seventy-five hamburgers sold every single second of the day. Sonic, whose first slogan was Service with the Speed of Sound, was named to convey stratospheric quickness. Among the many studies on the topic, a 2008 study published in the *Journal of the American*

---

* According to the Department of Health and Human Services, the United States has only about twenty-five hundred more public libraries than McDonald's.

Dietetic Association found that speed of service (92 percent) and convenience (80 percent) were the most popular reasons people gave for eating fast food. But two other explanations were surprising: A full third responded that fast-food restaurants offer a way to socialize with friends and family, and another 12 percent said that fast-food restaurants are "fun and entertaining."

Chris Arnade, a photographer and writer who studies addiction and poverty around the country, often makes local branches of fast-food restaurants his entry point for the communities he visits. There he'll often encounter morning clubs, particularly featuring an older membership, who are seeking some kind of physical social network. Writing in *The Guardian* in 2016, Arnade chronicled his visits to a McDonald's in Natchitoches, Louisiana, where an informal crew called the ROMEO club—short for Retired Old Men Eating Out—hold court. The ROMEO club wasn't the only social game at the Natchitoches Mickey D's. "On Tuesdays, there is a bingo game," he wrote. "On weekends, a Bible group sets up in the opposite corner, and offers prayers and Bibles to whoever wants to come."

This raises a reasonable question: Who would want to sit inside a Burger King or a Bojangles' for hours on end? The plastic seats, the harsh lighting, and, in many cities, the semi-enforced time limits for diners. Yet, in spite of all this, people sit and stay and stay and stay. "If you give people a world of sterile fast-food places, they'll form networks and communities within them," Arnade told me. "People adapt. I always say that you can put me in any McDonald's anyplace in the country and don't tell me where I am. I can open my eyes and tell you where I am by the people. I can't tell you by the restaurant, they all look the same, but I can immediately tell you what town I'm in because the people make the place."

In other words, despite being designed to have no character, the restaurants have character. Some of that character manifests itself in those wholesome tableaux—birthday parties, first dates, father-daughter breakfasts, and teen hangs. Other times, it's supervised visitations and the custody swapping of kids, the meet-ups of recovering addicts, widows, exhausted workers, and semi-homeless, and the ingathering of lonely souls.

The McDonald's on West Florissant in Ferguson, Missouri, is an average-looking store. On the Sunday afternoon that I arrived, a few days after meeting Sara Dappen, the store was serving as a respite from ninety-seven-degree Missouri heat and what must have been at least 95 percent Missouri humidity. About thirty people were inside, a mix of ages, mostly black, but also white, people in Cardinals hats, people talking on phones, people playing Vince Staples and Kendrick Lamar from small speakers at tables. In one corner by the counter sat a computer terminal, which had been set up so people could apply for jobs there. In the men's room, two twentysomethings were rolling blunts. If the crowd was bigger than normal for the time of day, it had a reason to be; that Sunday was the one-year anniversary of the shooting death of Michael Brown a few blocks away, and a flurry of events, memorials, and protests were happening on the avenue outside.

In the days following the 2014 shooting, the Ferguson McDonald's had served a different function, as a harborage of sorts for people seeking food or normalcy, for cops on coffee breaks, for reporters needing tables and internet to write and file their dispatches, and for demonstrators escaping the heat of the protests and the clashes with police.*

"When a protestor blasted with tear gas comes moaning through the door," Matt Pearce of the *Los Angeles Times* reported at the time, "there are bottles of soothing McDonald's milk to pour over his or her eyes." One worker had been a classmate of Michael Brown's and knew his regular order: a McChicken, medium fries, medium drink.

Some McDonald's employees had quit to join the demonstrations or had protested in their uniforms before or after their shifts. Despite the extensive damage and tumult around it, the store itself had been spared, becoming a drop-by destination for Jesse Jackson and a mishmash of community and national leaders, media personalities, and celebrities. On this Sunday, the same large-screen television on which observers, rioters, and demonstrators had watched President Obama address the unfolding unrest a year before, a local channel was now showing a documentary on wounded American soldiers returning from the war in Afghanistan. Outside in the parking lot, a group of people held court, smoking cigarettes and drinking booze in the heat, listening to music, watching the crowds and the afternoon pass.

It's not just that fast-food restaurants are culturally pluralistic social hubs or places for unremarkable meals, meaningful rituals, and uncommon encounters. Or that they act as community centers of first and last resort. They also function as hallowed, neutral territory, where people can set about build-

---

* The Burger King and the twenty-four-hour McDonald's near New York City's Zuccotti Park were similarly depicted as unexpected safe asylums for demonstrators during the months-long encampment of the Occupy Wall Street protests in 2011.

ing connections and performing the work of whatever their interpretation of repairing the world might be.

In the recent, particularly fraught years, law enforcement agencies have (formally and informally) used fast-food restaurants as bases to step up their community outreach efforts. The most highly orchestrated version of this effort is Coffee with a Cop, a national initiative started in California by working police officers to respond to the tension and anxiety between police and the communities they serve. Funded in part by the US Department of Justice, these social outings take place in scattered town halls, churches, and (naturally) coffee shops. Nevertheless, an overwhelming number of these meet-ups happen at fast-food franchises in far-flung places. A Whataburger in northwest Florida; a Burger King in Pasco, Washington; six McDonald's in New Orleans, three in Rockford, Illinois, and one in Hagåtña, Guam. Chick-fil-As in North Carolina, Tennessee, Indiana, and Maine.

The officers buy the coffee and sometimes work the drive-thru, taking orders, answering questions, dispensing friendly hellos, and startling the bejesus out of any addled customers. In announcing its participation in the initiative, the City of Dayton, Ohio, promised "no speeches or agendas, just a chance to get to know the men and women who patrol your neighborhood." Responding to a public Facebook comment from an irate citizen who asked why taxpayers are paying for cops to serve drinks instead of preventing crime, the police department of Albany, Oregon, explained, "When our officers engage people in different ways (like serving them coffee), it provides a unique opportunity for connection. It also gives people the chance to talk about issues on their minds which they may not have otherwise called us about." A mother of two from Kankakee, Illinois, expanded on this sentiment in an interview with the *Daily Journal*, offering, "My husband and I want to make sure our kids are not afraid to approach a police officer when they need help."

Ultimately, fast food succeeds and has succeeded in large part because its appeal transcends nearly all demographic bounds. More than its innovation, imagination, convenience, value, or capacity to decode the national appetite, fast food's greatest virtue—and what people fail to appreciate most about its significance—is its creation of America's most successful democratic gathering points: small matchbox chapels with practically no barrier to entry or belonging, regardless of race, age, class, gender, religion, or other. There is no velvet rope, no palm to grease, and no tracking shot of VIPs being ushered through the kitchen. There is no waitstaff injecting a sense of hierarchy, no dress code, no reservation book, and no culinary norms. You are welcome to bumble in wearing last night's clothes and order seven small cheeseburgers and an apple pie at ten thirty in the morning.

For these reasons eating fast food is an experience with which nearly everyone is familiar. It's both an intimate common reference point and, somehow at the same time, the least countercultural thing imaginable. Some countries have the unifying trials of compulsory national service; America has a paper tray mat turned translucent by stripes of french-fry grease and tiny stars from dabbed-up ketchup. It's a secular communion and an inimitably American haven, something beautiful, terrible, perfect, and imperfect that cannot be replicated with nearly the same spiritual fidelity anywhere else in the world.

*The destiny of nations depends on the manner
in which they nourish themselves.*
—JEAN BRILLAT-SAVARIN

My fast-food story begins in the late 1990s with a simple ritual. I'm the first of my friends with a driver's license. It's 11:00
P.M. on a weekend night and we're all crammed into a green
Volvo with time for one last insinuation of independence before we dutifully rush across the Houston sprawl to make our
midnight curfews. In the car sit members of the graduating
high school class of 2000, Eagle Scouts and AP-course survey-
ors, yearbook staffers and youth-group nerds, sheltered kids
in the last American generation to come of age without ubiquitous cell phones and portable internet. For us and for many
in the pre-millennium adolescent corners of Texas, eleven
o'clock meant one uncomplicated thing only: Whataburger.
And for our $2, nothing held a candle to the Whataburger
taquito—a perfect, made-to-order eggy breakfast taco loaded
with delicately crisp hash browns (or bacon or sausage), melted

American cheese, and a slather of company-branded picante sauce so good it's sold in local grocery stores.

If we had enough time to spare, my friends and I would go inside to eat the taquitos. The cashier would hand us small numbered Whataburger plastic table tents to hold while we waited for our orders, markers that, if you were sixteen, you might sneak into your pocket to decorate your room with later. Then we'd all jam into a booth and devour our taquitos and talk about the otherworldly basketball exploits of Hakeem Olajuwon or high school politics or the unremarkable dramas of our romantic lives.

And if we were running behind schedule, there was always the drive-thru. And if the drive-thru line was jammed because of a concert, a high school football game, the rodeo, or the frequent 11:00 P.M. crush, we'd just speed away into the Texas night with the windows down and the CD player skipping at every bump, toward the next Whataburger, which was never more than an eight-minute drive away.

There are stories like this all across America. "Two potato taquitos with cheese, please" was mine. As a Texas kid, I felt about Whataburger the way a kid in Ohio might have felt about Steak 'n Shake, the way a kid in North Carolina might have felt about Cook Out, the way a kid in California might have felt about In-N-Out, the way a kid in Wisconsin might have felt about Culver's, and so on. I was young and mostly polite, my metabolism was boundless, my ritual was sacred and my curfew corruptible. I hadn't the slightest clue about what all had gone into making my ritual possible. I had the luxury of not knowing how lucky I was.

*　*　*

The current discourse about fast food mirrors all political discourse—highly polarized, fragmented, and partisan. Broadly speaking, arguments against fast food are defined by principled positions on issues like wages, health, the environment. For some, fast food stands for an enfeebling, artificially inexpensive product irresponsibly peddled by an industry that has become a byword for corporate greed and economic injustice. "If you want an example of how the one percent have gotten wealthier on the backs of working people, here you have it: the fast-food industry," New York City mayor Bill de Blasio, who has used a slate of anti-fast-food bills to burnish his progressive bona fides, said in 2016. Meanwhile, for their supporters and devotees, places like Jack in the Box and Milo's and Burgerville largely speak to convenience, ceremony, comfort, and perhaps a defiant rejection of elitist-seeming cultural signifiers.

If this rift didn't seem apparent before, its apotheosis was reached with the 2016 election of Donald Trump, whose very public love for quick-service fare led him to be dubbed "the nation's fast-food president" by *The New York Times* that same year. Throughout his campaign, the thrice-married Manhattan billionaire real-estate mogul blasted images of himself on social media eating KFC and McDonald's on his private jet to project an everyman persona and forge a genuine connection with voters. (Taking a cue from his running mate, in 2016 Mike Pence also posted a picture of himself on a plane, eating KFC with his mother.) Trump's calculated fast-food high jinks stoked extensive media coverage, of course, but they also struck a nerve with people across America. Those who felt alienated and overlooked by establishment figures were endeared; others who wanted their presidents' meals to have larger cultural and environmental significance were horrified.

The fast-food kingdom doesn't just contain all of these contemporary energies; it's also the product of a century of competing social forces. Almost a hundred years ago, White Castle embarked on a tech-forward quest to serve accessible, mass-produced burgers and completely uniform experiences. As cars entered the mainstream, fast food became a partner and companion of American mobility and, later, a savior of suburbia during the baby boom. As the roads prospered into the giant interstates of the postwar era, roadside chains became an economic equalizer for midcentury endeavorers, arriving immigrants, and urban entrepreneurs left behind in the cities. With the labor force democratizing, fast food answered the question "What's for dinner?" in young households with working parents. Within the past half century, the arches and curbside marquees have evolved into avatars of American corporatism and global dominance to be seen as admirable, menacing, or both. Domestically, fast food is now a symptom of a national lifestyle that seems as frenzied as it is unhealthy. Yet, at the same time, it's an unexpected antidote, offering lonely, isolated, and otherwise forgotten people venues to pursue connections and community in a cold, stratifying world.

Where other countries can be defined and distilled down to their theologies, norms, state parties, and militarism, the drive-thru lane is the American panopticon—a half-circle channel where most everything seems visible. Over the past few decades, fast food has become a prism through which American economic anxiety and cultural despair can be interpreted. In public perception and popular culture, fast-food work has gone from an exemplar of possibility to a consequence of the

American worker's decline in power. At the consumer level, the topic of fast food plays an outsize role in the arguments about how Americans are supposed to eat, live, and conduct themselves, whether by way of individual destiny and free will or guided by social responsibility and sustainability.

And then, there is the food—addictive, unnatural, majestic, gratifying. Most any honest person, no matter how refined the palate or how anointed the social status, can own up to harboring at least one fast-food pleasure, guilty or otherwise. One will-weakening item that their resistance is useless against and their fealty is set to. In spite of all the politics, controversies, and stigmas, some of the best yarns about fast-food kryptonite have been spun by figures in the upper echelons of the culinary world, gastronomes who, despite their stature, could never fully disavow the merits of lowbrow, everyman grub.

The burgers at In-N-Out have enchanted the fabled likes of Julia Child, Alice Waters, and Alton Brown as well as Thomas Keller, who salutes the California icon as "the perfect example of classic American fast food." Laurent Tourondel, the celebrated French chef and restaurateur, is partial to the Burger King Whopper, while British baker and anti-clean-eating evangelist Ruby Tandoh calls their fries "the jewel in the King crown." Celebrity fusionist Dale Talde carries the McRib, the Golden Arches' limited-time white whale, in his heart. Doffing his toque to Popeyes, *Top Chef Masters'* Michael Schlow asks, "Who doesn't like spicy, delicious, perfectly greasy, crunchy fried chicken?" Meanwhile, Craig Hopson, the one-time executive chef of Manhattan's exclusive Le Cirque, favors Jack in the Box: "Crunchy, rich, creamy, totally not good for you, delicious."

In its temptation and horror, fast food is a reflective pillar of a country that changes with the times and somehow manages to stay the same. An engine of change and a sacramental anchor to the comforts of the past. Whether you're hungry or not, it's possible to both shudder at the sodium levels in a Burger King Croissan'wich and marvel at how the first cage-free egg consumed by millions of Americans will likely come by way of it. Most of all, fast food is an institution designed to be in tune with the scrambled frequencies and priorities of everyday life.

Between these poles are places like the small McDonald's adjacent to the Phillips 66 on West Cemetery Avenue. It's the first stop off Interstate 55 in Chenoa, a central Illinois town surrounded by corn and soy fields. The gas station is about half the short distance between I-55 and the old Route 66. It's where I stood pumping gas in the August heat and was startled for a second when out of the corner of my eye I suddenly saw a woman rushing across the parking lot toward the store entrance. She was harried, as if she were chasing a bus she absolutely had to catch and that was already halfway down the block and speeding away. She did this wholly unselfconsciously and in sandals, while in her arms she balanced a white paper box as if it held everything fragile and dear in the world. She couldn't have been more than a few years older than me, but looked as though she had lived life in ways I hadn't even begun to imagine.

Inside the McDonald's in Chenoa, three elderly women in shirts of varying floral patterns were eating ice cream at a table on the hot Saturday afternoon while employees idled behind the counter waiting for a rush that didn't seem likely to come. Through another door in back was a small, high-ceilinged indoor playground that had been decorated with a few stray streamers and some *Frozen*-themed Mylar balloons. There were three Elsas and one Anna. Above a well-worn painting of a cartoon Hamburglar, simple paper lettering that spelled out HAPPY BIRTHDAY hung limply, blowing in the AC. Nearby, a chubby toddler with a side part and a button-front shirt tucked into shorts was being stuffed in a booster seat. The woman I'd seen moments earlier was now setting out paper plates and plastic forks around a sheet cake she had pulled from the paper box and topped with candles.

What she didn't know as she had careered across the parking lot was that when she arrived, two boys would be wigging out joyfully twelve feet up in the plastic-bottomed turret of the indoor playground. That a young girl who had clambered up a ladder and across a minibridge would be hanging from netting and cawing like a crazed rooster. That over by a poster on the playroom wall, two boys would be devising a way to help Olaf the snowman find his carrot nose. That parents clustered together in booths would be eating McNuggets and cheering on two girls locked in a vicious race to scoot down the double slide first. That this gas station McDonald's by the highway, the only game in town, would be the happiest place in Illinois and a berth through which a new generation of memories would pass.

As the social fibers fray, as fights are waged in impersonal isolation, thicketed by social, digital, geographic, and economic divisions, there will be fast food. As diners fluent in the pieties about ethical food systems watch someone with no paid sick leave and no health insurance meticulously stir their $22 polenta, as the fast-casual quinoa dispensaries go cashless and leave more people behind, there will be fast food. Against our better interests and angels, there will be fast food.

Like our arteries, the American landscape will always be clogged with beacons to indulge, to sin, to repeat. Like going to the Grand Canyon or falling asleep at a baseball game, fast food will always be part of the national rite of passage. It will always be where a weekly family meal still represents a familiar ritual and a consistent means to an end. It's where high school fund-raisers, jobs, and dates will happen along with senior breakfasts, Bible studies, and retirement parties. So long as there's still democracy, it's where some citizens will continue to cast their ballots. On the great roads between home and away, there will always be affordable, ready-made pit stops with playgrounds for kids, who, like wound-up tops, spin out their pent-up energy before the parks, gator farms, and grandparents that await them. We will remain torn about it because that is who we are. A fast-food nation stuffed with fries, full of kindness and drive-thru dreams.

ACKNOWLEDGMENTS

I owe a tremendous debt to Bryn Clark, who mercilessly cut a ton of terrible dad jokes from this book (and kindly let more than a few stay) and who edited this manuscript with both vision and patience. Thanks also goes to the rest of the Flatiron team, including Marlena Bittner, Noah Eaker, Kimberly Escobar, Jasmine Faustino, Keith Hayes, Bob Miller, Jeremy Pink, and Tal Goretsky, who designed this book's rad cover. Anyone in this world is lucky to have advocates as savvy and irrepressible as Keith Urbahn and Matt Latimer at Javelin Literary, who went to the mattresses for this project.

Exceptional, very special praise is due to Emily Saladino, who read about and graciously shared more Taco Bell with me in the past few years than any human should reasonably be asked to. At this time, I would also like to honor my various credentialed and uncredentialed mental health teams including Hadass Gerson, Michael Maze, and Jacob Silverman. For their friendship, support, and help, I'm grateful to Scott Beauchamp, Lisa Bonos, Alex Bregman, Carlos Correa, Hassan Damluji,

ACKNOWLEDGMENTS

Nicholas Dawidoff, Jason Diamond, Naomi Firestone-Teeter, Michael Furman, Rebecca Goldfarb, Jorge Hernandez, Liel Leibovitz, Nicole Loving, Paul Lucas, Lilit Marcus, Sara Mirsky, Gabrielle Moss, Lizzie O'Leary, Spencer Peeples, Jonathan Polland, Brooks Rich, Albert Rubinsky, Dan Sacks, Joe Saka, Sadia Shepard, Maya Sigel, Ben Smith, Charlie Smith, Nicole Soussan, Evan Susser, Adam Teeter, Andy Weil, Bari Weiss, the crew at the Atlantic Avenue McDonald's, the regulars at Fresh Salt, and anyone not listed here who may feel slighted. Speaking of which, thank you for everything, Nada Chandler and Amelia Cohen-Levy, Robert Lewy and Noma Blechman, Jason and Molly Methner, Ellen and Paul Orseck, and the rest of the fam.

Additional love to assorted colleagues and teachers: James Bennet, Jo Ann Beard, Russell Berman, Nicky Besuden, Jeremy Elias, Caitlin Frazier, Samuel Freedman, Kathy Gilsinan, Brad Girson, Jeffrey Goldberg, David Graham, Jennie Rothenberg Gritz, Jim Hamblin, Alana Newhouse, Joe Pinsker, David Samuels, Vijay Seshadri, David Sims, and Sarah Yager. I'd also like to shout out the vital work of the many who tirelessly report on the goings on in the food industry and the fast-food world. Lastly, I'd like to thank everyone who gave me their time, especially Sara Dappen, John Helling, Aslam Khan, Jimmy Looney, Ginger Mills, Shashi Matta, Mark Ocegueda, Michael Pollan, Bill Samuels, Jr., and Randy Simon.

INTRODUCTION

1 *apparently embroiled in a seven-layer feud with a diabolical hoaxer:*
    Mark Thiessen, "Hoax Prompts Free Tacos in Alaska Town,"
    Associated Press, June 30, 2012, http://archive.boston.com/news
    /nation/articles/2012/06/30/hoax_prompts_free_tacos_in
    _alaska_town/.

1 *"That's right. Officially, Bethel is not getting a Taco Bell":* KYUK,
    June 12, 2012, https://archive.kyuk.org/bethel-taco-bell-rumor-a
    -hoax/.

2 *the local Chamber of Commerce told the* Los Angeles Times: Kim
    Murphy, "Taco Bell Hoax: Alaska Town (Pop. 6,000) Left
    Reeling," *Los Angeles Times,* June 14, 2012, http://articles.latimes
    .com/2012/jun/14/nation/la-na-nn-taco-bell-alaska-20120614.

2 *the dramatic transport of 950 pounds of beef:* "Hoax Prompts Free
    Tacos in Alaska Town," Associated Press, June 29, 2012, https://
    www.cbsnews.com/news/hoax-prompts-free-tacos-in-alaska-town/.

2 *"If we can feed people in Afghanistan and Iraq":* Ibid.

2 *The marketing genius of Operation Alaska:* Jerry A. Hendrix,
    Darrell C. Hayes, and Pallavi Damani Kumar, *Public Relations
    Cases* (Boston: Wadsworth, 2013), 311.

3 *Operation Alaska would be adapted:* Elie Ayrouth, "Taco Bell's
    #OperationAlaska Is Now a Commercial, Here Are the Official

Videos," *Food Beast*, July 9, 2012, https://www.foodbeast.com
/news/taco-bells-operationalaska-is-now-a-commercial-here-are
-the-official-videos/.

3 *a sign more recognizable worldwide than the Christian cross:*
"McDonald's Bigger Than Jesus Christ," *Marketing Week*, July 21,
1995, https://www.marketingweek.com/1995/07/21/mcdonalds
-bigger-than-jesus-christ/.

3 *about 1 percent of the entire world's population breaks bread:* Mamta
Badkar and Gus Lubin, "18 Facts About McDonald's That Will
Blow Your Mind," *Business Insider*, April 20, 2012, https://www
.businessinsider.com/19-facts-about-mcdonalds-that-will-blow
-your-mind-2012-4.

4 *80 percent of Americans frequent at least monthly:* Andrew Dugan,
"Fast Food Still Major Part of U.S. Diet," Gallup, August 6, 2013,
https://news.gallup.com/poll/163868/fast-food-major-part-diet
.aspx.

4 *96 percent of Americans annually embrace:* Ibid.

4 *Not even the internet comes close:* Monica Anderson, Andrew Perrin,
and Jingjing Jiang, "11% of Americans Don't Use the Internet.
Who Are They?," Pew Research Center, March 5, 2018, http://
www.pewresearch.org/fact-tank/2018/03/05/some-americans
-dont-use-the-internet-who-are-they/.

5 *some of the straightest highways ever built:* John Metcalfe, "The
Straightest Roads in the World Are in Midwest America,"
CityLab, March 11, 2015, https://www.citylab.com/transportation
/2015/06/the-straightest-roads-in-the-world-are-in-midwest
-america/395582/.

5 *"Potatoes deep-fried while raw, in small cuttings":* Michael Specter,
"Freedom from Fries," *New Yorker*, November 2, 2015, https://
www.newyorker.com/magazine/2015/11/02/freedom-from-fries.

CHAPTER 1: THE NATIONAL MEAL

7 *Pete Saari picked up his phone:* Author interview with White Castle
VP Jamie Richardson, April 12, 2017.

8 *"Literally, you hear some of these things":* Ibid.

8 *the two would steal away to the nearby White Castle:* White Castle,
"New Jersey Woman Honors Sister's Memory with White Castle

Urn," Cision, May 2, 2016, https://www.prnewswire.com/news
-releases/new-jersey-woman-honors-sisters-memory-with-white
-castle-urn-300261325.html.

8 *"It might seem a bit silly to some people":* Ibid.

9 *set his comic strip about anodyne mischief in Wichita:* "Dennis, the
Menace of Wichita," *Washington Post,* November 7, 1990,
https://www.washingtonpost.com/archive/lifestyle/1990/11/07
/dennis-the-menace-of-wichita/5756c5ce-f746-42fe-a320
-b7fff2eb4a1e/.

9 *one of the few US cities where the water isn't fluoridated:* Dion Lefler
and Annie Calovich, "Wichita Voters Reject Fluoridated Water,"
Wichita Eagle, August 5, 2014, https://www.kansas.com/news
/article1102401.html.

9 *and where it's illegal to serve cherry pie:* Kris Kobach, *Kansas: Then
and Now* (Topeka: Kansas Secretary of State, 2011), https://www
.kssos.org/other/pubs/KTAN.pdf; Dawn Volkart, "Odd State
Laws" (Bel Air, Md.: Harford Community College, 2006),
https://ww2.harford.edu/faculty/DVolkart/Handouts/odd_state
_laws.htm.

9 *crucial catalyst for the reforms and regulations of the Progressive Era:*
Daniel E. Slotnik, "Upton Sinclair, Whose Muckraking Changed
the Meat Industry," *New York Times,* June 30, 2016, https://www
.nytimes.com/interactive/projects/cp/obituaries/archives/upton
-sinclair-meat-industry.

10 *"I aimed at the public's heart":* Ibid.

10 *with authorities on food and dining like Duncan Hines:* David
Gerard Hogan, *Selling 'Em by the Sack: White Castle and the
Creation of American Food* (New York: NYU Press, 1997), 32.

10 *buying his first day's provisions of beef and bread:* Ibid., 26.

10 *made a public display of grinding fresh meat:* John T. Edge, *Hamburger
& Fries: An American Story* (New York: G. P. Putnam's Sons,
2005), 42.

11 *often mercenaries driving cattle from Texas ranches to Kansas cow
towns:* Josh Ozersky, *The Hamburger: A History* (New Haven,
Conn.: Yale University Press, 2008), 11–13.

11 *Industrialization and urbanization reinforced each other:* David
Kyvig, *Daily Life in the United States, 1920–1940: How Americans*

Lived Through the Roaring Twenties and the Great Depression (Chicago: Ivan R. Dee, 2002), 46–47.

11 *Higher-paying manufacturing jobs brought masses into the cities:* Jane Ziegelman and Andrew Coe, *A Square Meal: A Culinary History of the Great Depression* (New York: Harper, 2016), 7–8.

12 *would be confirmed by the 1920 US Census:* US Census Bureau, *1920 Census,* https://www.census.gov/history/www/programs /geography/urban_and_rural_areas.html.

12 *had he not crossed paths:* Philip Langdon, *Orange Roofs, Golden Arches* (New York: Knopf, 1986), 29–30.

13 *"When you sit in a White Castle, remember":* Ibid., 30.

14 *who conformed to the standards of a rigorous:* Hogan, *Selling 'Em,* 33–34.

14 *A Model T cost a prohibitive $825 in 1909:* Kyvig, *Daily Life,* 29–31.

14 *would allow them to cook quicker and more evenly:* Langdon, *Orange Roofs,* 29.

14 *unlike bread, absorbed the juiciness of the beef:* Ronald L. McDonald, *The Complete Hamburger: The History of America's Favorite Sandwich* (Secaucus, N.J.: Carol, 1997), 14.

15 *the number of cars on American roads:* Kyvig, *Daily Life,* 30.

15 *shameless slew of regal- and sterile-sounding imitators:* Hogan, *Selling 'Em,* 48.

15 *burgers would shift from fresh beef to frozen pucks:* Ozersky, *Hamburger,* 35.

15 *Aunt Sammy . . . was dishing out questionable:* Ziegelman and Coe, *Square Meal,* 92–93.

15 *Ingram hired a dynamic saleswoman:* Hogan, *Selling 'Em,* 75–78.

16 *"it was not unusual to see businessmen and housewives":* Ibid., 79.

17 *They wanted to load their pantries with national brands:* Ibid., 48.

17 *Billy Ingram had a conservative approach to growth:* Author interview with Richardson.

18 *the company celebrates its most loyal fans:* Ibid.

18 *"We get to be a part of people's lives":* Ibid.

19 *Pete Saari was so moved by the two sisters' story:* Ibid.

19 *White Castle would make a $10,000 donation:* White Castle, "New Jersey Woman."

19 *"A ritual creates a freedom from anxiety that isn't rote":* Author interview with Richardson.

CHAPTER 2: THE COLONEL

21 *"I fed truck drivers and millionaires all at the same table":* Harland
    Sanders, "My First Restaurant," video, at 1:01, https://www
    .youtube.com/watch?v=7pOEW6bGK1I.

21 *Originally, Adams wanted the book to be titled* The American Dream:
    Timothy Noah, "The Mobility Myth," *New Republic,* February 8,
    2012, https://newrepublic.com/article/100516/inequality-mobility
    -economy-america-recession-divergence.

22 *"The American Dream is that dream of a land":* James Truslow
    Adams, *The Epic of America* (Boston: Little, Brown, 1931), 214–15.

22 *a forty-year-old man named Harland Sanders:* Harland Sanders,
    *Colonel Harland Sanders: The Autobiography of the Original
    Celebrity Chef* (Louisville, Ky.: KFC, 2012), 37.

23 *The four-room shack where Sanders spent his early years:* Jon Ed
    Pearce, "Colonel Sanders: The Man Who Would Be Colonel," in
    The Human Tradition in the New South, ed. James C. Klotter
    (Lanham, Md.: Rowman & Littlefield, 2005), 130.

23 *his father, Wilbert . . . came home from work sick with a fever:* Ibid.

23 *leaving five-year-old Harland to look after his two younger siblings:* Ibid.

23 *"So I set my yeast, made the sponge":* Sanders, *Colonel Harland
    Sanders,* 10.

24 *"Being that close to that many mules was bad enough":* Harland
    Sanders, *Life as I Have Known It Has Been Finger Lickin' Good*
    (Carol Stream, Ill.: Creation House, 1974), 21.

24 *trains accounted for 98 percent of intercity travel:* The Golden Age of
    American Railroading, exhibit (University of Iowa, 1989),
    https://www.lib.uiowa.edu/exhibits/previous/railroad/.

25 *Sanders decided to study law by correspondence:* William Whitworth,
    "How Colonel Sanders Built a Fried-Chicken Empire," *New
    Yorker,* February 14, 1970, https://www.newyorker.com/magazine
    /1970/02/14/kentucky-fried.

25 *"He was particularly proud of the time":* Alan Bellows, "Colonels of
    Truth," Damn Interesting, March 15, 2016, https://www
    .damninteresting.com/colonels-of-truth/.

25 *he went on to build and sell a successful ferryboat operation:* Victoria
    Dawson, "How Colonel Sanders Made Kentucky Fried Chicken
    an American Success Story," *Smithsonian,* July 6, 2015, https://

www.smithsonianmag.com/smithsonian-institution/how-colonel
-sanders-made-kentucky-fried-chicken-american-success-story
-180955806/.

25 *Sanders would make a promotional, sales-generating spectacle of
himself:* Josh Ozersky, *Colonel Sanders and the American Dream*
(Austin: University of Texas Press, 2012), 18.

25 *he had stitched his own scalp back on:* Pearce, "Colonel Sanders,"
134–35.

26 *"Lincoln was not great because he was born in a log cabin":* Adams, *Epic
of America*, 381.

26 *"What separates the successful from the unsuccessful":* J. D. Vance,
Hillbilly Elegy (New York: Harper, 2016), 193.

27 *Two of the more spectacular nicknames for Sanders's section of Corbin:*
Bellows, "Colonels of Truth."

27 *"Bootleggin's, fights, and shootin's was as regular":* Ibid.

27 *Sanders kept a pistol under the cash register for safety:* Pearce,
"Colonel Sanders," 137.

27 *"good old boys riding around like to shoot up signboards":* Ibid.

27 *Ironically, Sanders's penchant for strategic advertising:* Pearce,
"Colonel Sanders," 138.

28 *Sanders would make a grand production of wiping their windshields:*
Ibid., 135.

28 *"I got to thinking":* Dawson, "American Success Story."

28 *"tourists, businessmen, farmers, and everyday travelers alike":* Tammy
Ingram, *Dixie Highway: Road Building and the Making of the
Modern South, 1900–1930* (Chapel Hill: University of North
Carolina Press, 2014), 16.

29 *"He told stories about the local moonshiners":* Phil Patton, *Open Road*
(New York: Simon & Schuster, 1986), 180–81.

29 *Sanders rebuilt his café:* Author visit to the Harland Sanders Café and
Museum, Corbin, Ky., August 12, 2015.

29 *Sanders even installed a model motel room:* Ibid.

29 *It appeared listed on the menu as "$1.70":* Author visit, Corbin, Ky.

30 *Austrian-American economist Joseph Schumpeter popularized
"creative destruction":* Joseph Schumpeter, *Capitalism, Socialism
and Democracy* (New York: Harper & Brothers, 1942).

31 *Ruby Laffoon . . . commissioned Sanders with the ceremonial honor:*
Bellows, "Colonels of Truth."

31 *The pious, teetotaling Sanders often ventured:* Patton, *Open Road,* 179.

31 *he would engage in some "coloneling":* Ibid., 181.

31 *so he labored with Bertha:* Author visit to KFC headquarters, Louisville, Ky, August 11, 2015.

32 *Bertha cut the cook time from thirty minutes:* Ibid.

32 *Sanders would also end up with an official patent:* Sanders, *Colonel Harland Sanders,* 70.

32 *later recommended as "a very good place to stop":* Dawson, "American Success Story."

32 *"I figured I couldn't do worse":* Ibid.

CHAPTER 3: SOFT MARKET

33 *Warren Buffett . . . went to dinner at the Pool Room:* Stephanie Smith, "Warren Buffett Ordered Dairy Queen, a Coke at Four Seasons," *New York Post,* April 24, 2014, https://pagesix.com /2014/04/24/warren-buffet-ordered-dairy-queen-a-coke-at-four -seasons/.

33 *culinary historians credit the Four Seasons:* Paul Freedman, *Ten Restaurants That Changed America* (New York: W. W. Norton, 2016), 325.

33 *"the most expensive restaurant ever built":* Ibid.

34 *the term "power lunch" has actually been pinpointed:* William Grimes, "Four Seasons, Lunch Spot for Manhattan's Prime Movers, Moves On," *New York Times,* July 8, 2016, https://www .nytimes.com/2016/07/10/nyregion/four-seasons-lunch-spot-for -manhattans-prime-movers-moves-on.html.

34 *according to the tabloids, Buffett ordered a steak:* Smith, "Buffett Ordered Dairy Queen."

35 *He . . . eats like an eleven-year-old:* Kathleen Elkins, "Warren Buffett Is 88 Today—Here's What He Learned from Buying His First Stock at Age 11," CNBC, August 30, 2018, https://www.cnbc.com /2018/08/30/when-warren-buffett-bought-his-first-stock-and-what -he-learned.html.

35 *Page Six reported that Buffett's off-menu order "caused a scene":* Smith, "Buffett Ordered Dairy Queen."

35 *The Four Seasons even humblebragged about its failure:* Four Seasons, "For the first time in our 55 year history, we were unable to satisfy

a special request, but we tried," Facebook, April 25, 2014,
https://www.facebook.com/FourSeasonsRestaurantNYC/.

35 *the first Dairy Queen stand opened in 1940 in Joliet:* "Joliet Makes
Site of 1st Dairy Queen a Landmark," Associated Press, January 1,
2011, https://www.dailyherald.com/article/20101231/news
/101239886/.

35 *J. F. McCullough . . . was an old-time Dairy Man:* Sherb Noble,
"History of Dairy Queen," 1973, http://www.noblestores.com/Early
DQHistorywrittenbySDN1973.

36 *when it was about twenty-three degrees cold:* Nancy Ryan, "From Soft
Ice Cream Came Franchise Queen," *Chicago Tribune*, April 29,
1991, https://www.chicagotribune.com/news/ct-xpm-1991-04-29
-9102080038-story.html.

36 *"The reaction was very good":* Noble, "History of Dairy Queen."

36 *"the queen of the dairy business":* "History of Dairy Queen," Dairy
Queen, https://www.dqtoronto.com/history-of-dairy.php.

36 *"In June of 1942 I went into the service":* Noble, "History of Dairy
Queen."

37 *the so-called Roosevelt Recession of 1937–38:* Robert J. Samuelson,
"Lessons from the 1937–38 Recession," *Washington Post*, https://
www.washingtonpost.com/opinions/lessons-from-the-1937-38
-recession/2015/03/25/09b663ca-d303-11e4-ab77-9646eea6a4c7
_story.html.

37 *only about half of US homes had indoor plumbing:* "In Census Data,
a Room-by-Room Picture of the American Home," Associated
Press, February 1, 2003, https://www.nytimes.com/2003/02/01
/us/in-census-data-a-room-by-room-picture-of-the-american
-home.html.

37 *Less than a quarter of the population had a high school degree:* David
Morgan, "1940 U.S. Census Data Released Online," CBS News,
April 12, 2012, https://www.cbsnews.com/news/1940-us-census
-data-released-online/.

37 *the Fair Labor Standards Act went into law:* Jonathan Grossman,
"Fair Labor Standards Act of 1938: Maximum Struggle for a
Minimum Wage," *Monthly Labor Review*, June 1978, https://www
.dol.gov/oasam/programs/history/flsa1938.htm.

38 *"constitutes a step in the direction of communism, bolshevism, fascism,
and Nazism":* Peter Cole, "The Law That Changed the American

Workplace," *Time*, June 24, 2016, http://time.com/4376857/flsa
-history/.

38 *In 1940 . . . only 15 percent of the average American budget:* Tracie
McMillan, *The American Way of Eating: Undercover at Walmart,
Applebee's, Farm Fields, and the Dinner Table* (New York: Scribner,
2012), 196.

38 *that figure would nearly double to 28 percent:* McMillan, *American
Way*, 196.

39 *the big-name chains . . . cumulatively hosting fewer:* Robert L.
Emerson, *The New Economics of Fast Food* (New York: Van
Nostrand Reinhold, 1990), 7.

39 *"Soft serve requires a machine":* Michael A. Parks, "Dairy Queen:
Small-Town Texas Institution," *Atlantic*, April 5, 2010, https://
www.theatlantic.com/health/archive/2010/04/dairy-queen-small
-town-texas-institution/38350/.

39 *"What I remember clearly is that":* Larry McMurtry, *Walter Benjamin
at the Dairy Queen: Reflections on Sixty and Beyond* (New York:
Simon & Schuster, 1999), 13–14.

40 *"All day the little groups in the Dairy Queen":* Ibid., 15.

40 *how the chain has been paired in country songs:* "Dairy Queen," Lyric
Finder, https://www.lyricfinder.org/search/lyrics/Dairy+Queen.

41 *Martina McBride . . . actually left the family farm at sixteen:* "Celebrities'
First Jobs," *Oprah*, November 3, 2009, https://www.oprah.com
/entertainment/oprahs-live-newscast-and-celebrities-first-jobs/all.

41 *"Clichés lend structure and ritual and glue":* Leslie Jamison, "Why
Do We Hate Cliché?," *New York Times*, January 6, 2015, https://
www.nytimes.com/2015/01/11/books/review/why-do-we-hate
-clich.html.

42 *"I've been running a quality check for decades":* Bianca Golodryga and
Michael Milberger, "Secrets of America's Favorite Restaurants:
DQ's Top Secret Sweet Tooth Testing," *Good Morning America*,
September 14, 2010, https://abcnews.go.com/GMA/Consumer
/dairy-queen-sweet-secrets-lock-key-secrets-americas/story?id
=11624947.

42 *Dairy Queen . . . would spring from a handful of stores:* Joe Muñoz
and Edward Southerland, "Dairy Queen," *Texoma Living*,
September 1, 2008, https://www.texomaliving.com/dairy-queen.

43 *Kroc became intimately familiar:* Ray Kroc with Robert Anderson,

Grinding It Out: The Making of McDonald's (New York: St. Martin's, 1977), 87–88.

CHAPTER 4: FREEDOM FROM WANT

45 *In 1950 . . . Harmon Dobson opened:* Mark Mazzetti, "Whatabusiness!," *Texas Monthly*, July 2000, https://www.texasmonthly.com /articles/whatabusiness/.

45 *Dobson served up his heavyweight rebuke:* Greg Wooldridge, *The Whataburger Story* (San Antonio: Whataburger, 2011), 42.

46 *he had to start a side business with a local baker:* Mazzetti, "Whatabusiness!"

46 *A quarter-pounder for a quarter:* Ibid.

46 *ground beef was on its way to becoming as cheap:* Consumer Price Index, "Price Inflation for Uncooked Ground Beef Since 1947," US Bureau of Labor Statistics, https://www.officialdata.org /Uncooked-ground-beef/price-inflation/.

46 *the last year that all the Academy Award nominees:* Academy for Motion Picture Arts and Sciences, "The 22nd Academy Awards," https://www.oscars.org/oscars/ceremonies/1950/.

47 *"American workers produced 57 percent of the world's steel":* Joshua Freeman, *American Empire: The Rise of a Global Power, the Democratic Revolution at Home* (New York: Penguin Books, 2012), 50–51.

47 *By 1956, nearly 8 million Americans:* Keith Olson, "The G.I. Bill and Higher Education: Success and Surprise," *American Quarterly*, December 1973, 596–610.

47 *And by 1966, 20 percent of single-family homes:* Freeman, *American Empire*, 34.

47 *newspapers around the country reported:* Associated Press, "Marines Ready All Hands Call," *Austin American*, August 8, 1950, 1.

48 *a tiny plane up in the ether:* Wooldridge, *Whataburger Story*, 57.

48 *"I would sit in the back seat":* Author interview with Whataburger chairman Tom Dobson, August 27, 2015.

49 *"Folks, we priced our burgers":* Cindy Jones, "Whataburger," Texas State Historical Association, June 15, 2010, https://tshaonline.org /handbook/online/articles/dgw02.

49 *Whataburger is (as of 2018) now the country's sixth-largest:* Sam Oches, "The QSR 50 Burger Segment," *QSR*, August 2018,

https://www.qsrmagazine.com/content/qsr50-2018-burger
-segment.

49 *Bob Wian . . . created a double-decker burger*: Ozersky, *Hamburger*,
45–46.

49 *"A meal in one on a double-deck bun"*: "'A Meal in One on a Double-
Deck Bun' at Manners Big Boy," *Cleveland Plain-Dealer*, November 1, 2011, https://www.cleveland.com/remembers/index.ssf
/2011/11/a_meal_in_one_on_a_double-deck.html.

49 *Yancey moved west in the Great Migration*: Dennis McLellan, "Fatburger Founder Expanded South L.A. Eatery into Chain,"
Los Angeles Times, February 2, 2008, http://articles.latimes.com
/2008/feb/02/local/me-yancey2.

49 *She opened Mr. Fatburger with her boyfriend in 1947*: Ibid.

50 *"The name of the store was my idea"*: Ibid.

50 *In 1954, they took over Insta-Burger King*: Robert D. Hershey, Jr.,
"David Edgerton, a Founder of Burger King, Is Dead at 90," *New
York Times*, April 16, 2018, https://www.nytimes.com/2018/04/16
/obituaries/david-edgerton-90-dies-helped-start-burger-king-in
-the-60s.html.

50 *Edgerton sank a hatchet into the fritzing conveyor belt*: Ibid.

51 *"I suggested that we call our product a Whopper"*: James McLamore,
The Burger King: Jim McLamore and the Building of an Empire
(New York: McGraw-Hill, 1998), 45.

51 *the first signature fast-food item to truly go national*: Tim Carman,
"The 55-Cent Whopper and the Evolution of Burgers," *Washington
Post*, December 3, 2012, https://www.washingtonpost.com/blogs
/all-we-can-eat/post/the-55-cent-whopper-and-the-evolution-of
-burgers/2012/12/03/8dffc456-3d68-11e2-bca3-aadc9b7e29c5
_blog.html.

51 *consumer willingness to pay a then eye-popping amount*: Andrew F.
Smith, *Fast Food and Junk Food: An Encyclopedia of What We Love
to Eat*, vol. 1 (Westport, Conn.: Greenwood Press, 2006), 66.

51 *"The pressures of prosperity were inexorable"*: Ozersky, *Hamburger*,
87.

51 *the Whopper inspired countless other signature creations*: Carman,
"55-Cent Whopper."

52 *the bestselling book in the United States*: Christopher Lane, "The
True Mission of Donald Trump's Pastor," *Daily Beast*, January 15,

2017, https://www.thedailybeast.com/the-true-mission-of-donald
-trumps-pastor.

52 *legal tender printed with the newly adopted national motto:* US Department of the Treasury, "History of 'In God We Trust,'" March 8,
2011, https://www.treasury.gov/about/education/Pages/in-god-we
-trust.aspx.

CHAPTER 5: ARE WE THERE YET?

53 *"I was fifty-two years old":* Kroc, *Grinding It Out,* 13.

53 *In 1956, the long-planned expansion:* Richard Weingroff, *Public Roads*
(Washington, D.C.: Federal Highway Administration, 1996),
https://www.fhwa.dot.gov/publications/publicroads/96summer
/p96su10.cfm.

53 *the system's nearly forty-seven thousand miles:* Earl Swift, *The Big
Roads: The Untold Story of the Engineers, Visionaries, and Trailblaz-
ers Who Created the American Superhighways* (Boston: Houghton
Mifflin Harcourt, 2011), 5.

54 *spending on the interstates was credited:* Ishaq Nadiri and Theofanis
Mamuneas, "The Effects of Public Infrastructure and R&D
Capital on the Cost Structure and Performance of U.S. Manufac-
turing Industries," *Review of Economics and Statistics* (Cambridge,
Mass.: MIT Press, February 1994), 26.

54 *a majority of Americans became homeowners:* US Census Bureau,
"Historical Census of Housing Tables," https://www.census.gov
/hhes/www/housing/census/historic/owner.html.

54 *from about seventy thousand to 6.7 million:* Joseph R. Conlin, *The
American Past: A Survey of American History* (Boston, Mass.:
Wadsworth, 2009), 760.

54 *by 1957, there would be 55 million cars:* Smith, *Fast Food and Junk Food,*
31.

54 *Los Angeles had nearly a million cars:* Eric Schlosser, *Fast Food Nation*
(New York: Houghton Mifflin, 2002), 16.

55 *Between 1920 and 1940, California's population tripled:* Frank Hobbs
and Nicole Stoops, "Demographic Trends in the 20th Century,"
US Census Bureau, 2002.

55 *in 1954, Ray Kroc famously first set:* Kroc, *Grinding It Out,* 6–7.

55 *"The mental picture of eight Multimixers":* Kroc, *Grinding It
Out,* 6.

56 *Dick and Mac McDonald . . . had struck out for California:* David
    Halberstam, *The Fifties* (New York: Random House, 1993), 155.

56 *In 1948 . . . the two brothers shut down:* Ibid., 157–58.

56 *assembly-line operation to befit the "age of jet propulsion":* Lisa Napoli,
    *Ray & Joan: The Man Who Made the McDonald's Fortune and the
    Woman Who Gave It All Away* (New York: Dutton, 2016), 20.

57 *"The kids loved coming to the counter":* John F. Love, *McDonald's:
    Behind the Arches* (New York: Bantam, 1986), 16–17.

57 *the first McDonald's neon marquee:* Halberstam, *Fifties*, 159.

57 *In 1958 . . . the service industry overtook manufacturing:* Patton, *Open
    Road*, 17.

58 *"Kroc saw immediately that that prime customers were families":*
    Halberstam, *Fifties*, 163.

58 *"When I saw it working that day in 1954":* Kroc, *Grinding It Out*, 71.

58 *one year later he opened his first McDonald's:* Smith, *Fast Food and
    Junk Food*, 280.

58 *Kroc bought them out for a cool:* Napoli, *Ray & Joan*, 93.

59 *McDonald's now feeds more people daily:* Specter, "Freedom from Fries."

59 *there are more than thirty-six thousand McDonald's stores:* McDonald's,
    "About Us," https://www.mcdonalds.com/us/en-us/about-us.html.

59 *Kroc simply opened a McDonald's across the street:* Napoli, *Ray & Joan*, 95.

60 *he lied about his age:* Kroc, *Grinding It Out*, 16–17.

60 *One of his Red Cross comrades:* Schlosser, *Fast Food Nation*, 35.

60 *Ray Kroc—whose father had "worried himself to death":* Kroc,
    Grinding It Out, 106.

60 *"We have found out":* Schlosser, *Fast Food Nation*, 5.

60 *Kroc was shrewd enough to capitalize on his franchisees' creativity:*
    Ozersky, *Hamburger*, 75.

61 *He broke up with his second wife:* Napoli, *Ray & Joan*, 118.

61 *"If they were drowning":* Schlosser, *Fast Food Nation*, 41.

61 *was nearly boycotted by his players:* Bob Wolf, "Kroc's Tirade Shook
    Up '74 Padres," *Los Angeles Times*, June 20, 1990, http://articles
    .latimes.com/1990-06-20/sports/sp-132_1_owner-ray-kroc.

61 *he would fly over communities in a light plane:* Robert Pearson,
    "McDonald's Chief Ray Kroc Dies," *Washington Post*, January 15,
    1984, https://www.washingtonpost.com/archive/local/1984/01/15
    /mcdonalds-chief-ray-kroc-dies/5c5007d4-9cad-4fad-8a7f
    -08b8a785a33b/.

61 *"If you see a man in a three-hundred-dollar suit"*: Ralph Novak, "The McDonald's Man: What Ray Kroc Hath Wrought Around the World," *People*, May 19, 1975, https://people.com/archive/the-mc-donalds-man-what-ray-kroc-hath-wrought-around-the-world-vol-3-no-19/.

61 *Kroc sought out hungry young operators*: Smith, *Fast Food and Junk Food*, 280.

62 *"Instead of a structured, ritualistic restaurant"*: Jacques Pepin, "Burger Meister Ray Kroc," *Time*, December 7, 1998, http://content.time.com/time/magazine/article/0,9171,989785,00.html.

62 *Esquire named him to a list*: Kroc, *Grinding It Out*, 208.

62 *Kroc was hardly the sole lurking admirer*: Smith, *Fast Food and Junk Food*, 172.

62 *"Our food was exactly the same as McDonald's"*: Schlosser, *Fast Food Nation*, 22.

63 *Dave Thomas . . . exorcised his ancient demons*: Nicole Duncan, "The Immeasurable Legacy of Dave Thomas," *QSR*, May 2017, https://www.qsrmagazine.com/growth/immeasurable-legacy-dave-thomas.

63 *Wilber Hardee resisted a call*: Dennis Hevesi, "Wilber Hardee Dies at 89; Founded Restaurants," *New York Times*, June 26, 2008, https://www.nytimes.com/2008/06/26/business/26hardee.html.

63 *Glen Bell . . . rode the rails looking for work*: Dennis Hevesi, "Glen W. Bell, Jr., Founder of Taco Bell, Dies at 86," *New York Times*, January 10, 2010, https://www.nytimes.com/2010/01/19/business/19bell.html.

63 *Ed Hackbarth (Del Taco) was the ninth of ten children*: Kathleen Luppi, "At 78, Del Taco Founder Can Still Bring It," *Orange County Register*, March 19, 2012, https://www.ocregister.com/2012/03/19/at-78-del-taco-founder-can-still-bring-it/; Mike Lamb, "'Mr. Del Taco' Dies," *Daily Press*, May 23, 2014, https://www.vvdailypress.com/article/20140522/NEWS/305229974/.

64 *Carl Karcher . . . parlayed a humble hot dog stand*: "Carl's Jr. Founder Dies of Parkinson's Complications," Reuters, January 11, 2008, https://www.reuters.com/article/us-cke-karcher-carls-jr-founder-dies-of-parkinsons-complications-idUSN1023817220080112; Schlosser, *Fast Food Nation*, 13.

64 *William Rosenberg . . . dropped out of middle school*: Myrna Oliver,

"William Rosenberg, 86; Dunkin' Donuts Founder Pioneered Franchising Businesses," *Los Angeles Times*, September 23, 2002, http://articles.latimes.com/2002/sep/23/local/me-rosenberg23/.

64 *S. Truett Cathy . . . spent part of his teenage years:* Kim Severson, "S. Truett Cathy, Chick-fil-A Founder, Dies at 93," *New York Times*, September 8, 2014, https://www.nytimes.com/2014/09/09/business/s-truett-cathy-93-chick-fil-a-owner-dies.html.

64 *he later started his Atlanta chain:* Ibid.

64 *"I never forget being poor":* Douglas Martin, "Al Copeland, a Restaurateur Known for Spice and Speed, Dies at 64," *New York Times*, March 25, 2008, https://www.nytimes.com/2008/03/25/business/25copeland.html.

64 *Edith and Gus Belt sold beer:* Laurie Lucas, "Here's the Scoop on the New Steak 'n Shake," *Riverside (Calif.) Press-Enterprise*, August 16, 2016, https://www.pe.com/2016/08/16/heres-the-scoop-on-the-new-steak-n-shake/.

65 *Esther and Harry Snyder were practically newlyweds:* Myrna Oliver, "Esther Snyder, 86; Co-founded the In-N-Out Burger Chain," *Los Angeles Times*, August 6, 2006, http://articles.latimes.com/2006/aug/06/local/me-snyder6.

65 *Esther Snyder . . . kept the books:* Ibid.

CHAPTER 6: BIG BUSINESS

67 *he learned that the route:* Patton, *Open Road*, 182.

68 *Sanders had started signing franchise agreements:* Pearce, "Colonel Sanders," 144.

68 *Sanders . . . would now (literally) suit up:* Ibid.

69 *Samuels rode around with Sanders:* "Bill Samuels, Jr., Talks About Being Col. Harland Sanders' First Employee," *Bourbon Story*, video, March 29, 2014, https://youtu.be/cKLEMTPBf2Y.

69 *his second wife, Claudia, who had worked as a waitress:* Pearce, "Colonel Sanders," 144–46.

69 *"I'm not talking about craft":* Author interview with Bill Samuels, Jr., Loretto, Ky., August 12, 2015.

70 *the largest fast-food operation in the world:* Dawson, "American Success Story."

70 *McDonald's only breached the triple-digit mark in 1959:* McDonald's,

"A Brief History of McDonald's," http://www.mcspotlight.org/company/company_history.html.

70 *The first KFC franchisee was a café operator:* Ozersky, *Colonel Sanders*, 39–41.

70 *Harman rearranged his entire business:* Ibid.

70 *Harman also came up with the brand's eternal tagline:* Ozersky, *Colonel Sanders*, 41.

70 *Harman conceived the brand's iconic chicken bucket:* Ibid.

71 *"If there was anything that got Kentucky Fried Chicken":* Robert Darden, *Secret Recipe: Why KFC Is Still Cookin' After 50 Years* (Littleton, Mass.: Tapestry Press, 2002), 44.

71 *By 1962, 90 percent of American households had one:* Freeman, *American Empire*, 125.

71 *Ahead of his election in 1952, Dwight Eisenhower:* James Ciment, *Postwar America: An Encyclopedia of Social, Political, Cultural, and Economic History* (New York: Routledge, 2007), 448.

71 *Television created a gold rush in advertising billings:* "1950s TV Turns on America," *AdAge*, March 28, 2005, https://adage.com/article/75-years-of-ideas/1950s-tv-turns-america/102703/.

71 TV Guide *reigned as one of the bestselling periodicals:* Daniel Niemeyer, *1950s American Style: A Reference Guide* (Boulder, Colo.: Fifties Book Publishers, 2013), 250.

71 *a fellow fast-food traveler:* Douglas Martin, "Dave Thomas, 69, Wendy's Founder, Dies," *New York Times*, January 9, 2002, https://www.nytimes.com/2002/01/09/business/dave-thomas-69-wendy-s-founder-dies.html.

72 *Thomas attended Cook and Baker's School:* Wendy's, "Dave's Legacy," https://www.wendys.com/daves-legacy.

72 *"He introduced himself and asked if I knew him":* Ozersky, *Colonel Sanders*, 34.

72 *Thomas would later be enlisted:* Wendy's, "Dave's Legacy."

73 *Thomas eventually sold back his stake:* Martin, "Dave Thomas."

73 *he appeared in roughly eight hundred television spots:* Kate Macarthur, "Wendy's Dave Thomas Dies," *AdAge*, January 8, 2002, https://adage.com/article/news/wendy-s-dave-thomas-dies/33533/.

73 *"Popeye wasn't my hero":* Martin, "Dave Thomas."

73 *"He saved me":* Joel Engardio, "'Colonel Sanders Saved Me'—

Wendy's Founder Dave Thomas on KFC Icon," *POV Magazine*,
June 1997, https://youtu.be/f7u8HjdvUpk.

74 *Sanders next managed unfathomable fame in his seventies:* Pearce,
"Colonel Sanders," 149.

74 *"He was as much at home":* Ibid., 150.

75 *His archives at the KFC headquarters:* Author visit to KFC headquarters.

75 *an independent survey in 1976 found him:* Simon Meiners, "Ali,
Sanders Legacies Began on Same Day," *Courier-Journal*, March 2,
2017, https://www.courier-journal.com/story/opinion
/contributors/2017/03/02/ali-sanders-legacies-began-same-day
-meiners/98574926/.

75 *a coterie of businessmen:* Pearce, "Colonel Sanders," 149.

76 *he got himself booked on the* Tonight *show:* Patton, *Open Road*, 183.

76 *Sanders's body was ordered to lie in state:* J. Y. Smith, "Col. Sanders, the
Fried-Chicken Gentleman, Dies," *Washington Post*, December 17,
1980, https://www.washingtonpost.com/archive/local/1980/12/17
/col-sanders-the-fried-chicken-gentleman-dies/64925eb3-3a20
-4851-afbc-ba4fe16e9770/.

76 *"not only our founder and our creator":* Ozersky, *Colonel Sanders*, ix.

CHAPTER 7: INTO THE CITIES

77 *"I had heard for years from our girls":* Schlosser, *Fast Food Nation*, 32.

77 *The company first offered shares at $22.50:* Phil Han, "McDonald's
IPO: 51 Years Later," CNBC, April 21, 2016, https://www.cnbc
.com/video/2016/04/21/mcdonalds-ipo-51-years-later.html.

78 *Jack in the Box founder Robert Peterson sold:* Hogan, *Selling 'Em*,
156.

78 *Among the dearly departed are:* Samantha Leffler, "25 Fast Food
Restaurants You'll Never Eat in Again," *Eat This*, February 21,
2018, https://www.eatthis.com/closed-fast-food-restaurants/.

78 *The biggest to fall was the Midwestern chain Burger Chef:* Ozersky,
Hamburger, 99–100.

78 *grew to become the second-largest chain in the United States:* Ibid.

79 *KFC would be listed on the Stock Exchange in 1969:* Beverly Fortune,
"Fifty Years Later: The Tale of the KFC Business Deal," *Lexington
Herald Leader*, August 3, 2014, https://www.kentucky.com/news
/business/article44500860.html.

79 *"Let's face it, the Colonel's gravy was fantastic":* Whitworth, "How
     Colonel Sanders."
79 *Sanders likened KFC gravy to "sludge":* Dan Kauffman, "Is a Chicken
     Wing White Meat?," *Louisville (Ky.) Courier-Journal,* October 8,
     1975, 17.
80 *suburban strips . . . were already bloated:* Andrew Small, "How Fast
     Food Cornered the Urban Market," CityLab, March 31, 2017,
     https://www.citylab.com/life/2017/03/how-fast-food-chains
     -cornered-the-urban-market/521148/.
80 *Between 1950 and 1960 alone, the nation's dozen:* Walter LaFeber,
     Richard Polenberg, and Nancy Woloch, *The American Century: A
     History of the United States Since 1941,* vol. 2 (London: Routledge,
     2013), 261.
81 *over 80 percent of African Americans lived in cities:* Ibid., 59.
81 *a study of the businesses in fifteen black neighborhoods:* Ibid., 62.
81 *These initiatives were undertaken:* Chin Jou, *Supersizing Urban
     America: How Inner Cities Got Fast Food with Government Help*
     (Chicago: University of Chicago Press, 2017), 55–57.
81 *A 1969 initiative led by a minister:* Nishani Frazier, "A McDonald's
     That Reflects the Soul of a People: Hough Area Development
     Corporation and Community Development in Cleveland," in *The
     Business of Black Power: Community Development, Capitalism, and
     Corporate Responsibility in Postwar America,* ed. Laura Warren Hill
     and Julia Rabig (Rochester, N.Y.: University of Rochester Press,
     2012), 74–75.
82 *"Perhaps the most obvious explanation":* Jou, *Supersizing,* 19
82 *"Our nation is moving toward two societies":* National Advisory
     Commission on Civil Disorders, *1968 Kerner Report,* https://
     haasinstitute.berkeley.edu/1968-kerner-report.
83 *Johnson directed the Small Business Administration:* Jou, *Supersizing,*
     29.
83 *Nixon established the Office of Minority Business Enterprise:* "Histori-
     cal Highlights," Minority Development Business Agency, US
     Department of Commerce, https://www.mbda.gov/page
     /historical-highlights.
83 *Nixon couched the philosophy behind these initiatives:* Jou, *Supersizing,*
     75–76.
83 *Thousands upon thousands of government-backed loans:* Ibid., 1.

83 *The availability of these loans were:* Ibid., 15–16.

84 *the number of minority-run fast-food franchises sextupled:* Robert Yancy, *Federal Government Policy and Black Business Enterprise* (New York: HarperCollins, 1974), 82.

84 *More than a few minority franchisees would later:* Jou, *Supersizing,* 106–9.

84 *McDonald's debuted new store designs:* Langdon, *Orange Roofs,* 140–41.

85 *"The moment when the fast-food industry":* Alex Park, "How the Fast-Food Industry Courted African American Customers," *Washington Post,* June 11, 2018, https://www.washingtonpost.com /news/made-by-history/wp/2018/06/11/the-origins-of-fast-foods -enduring-popularity-with-african-americans/.

85 *"Within hours after the curfew was lifted":* Edwin Reingold, "America's Hamburger Helper," *Time,* June 24, 2001, http://content.time .com/time/magazine/article/0,9171,159962,00.html.

86 *"Our businesses there are owned":* Ibid.

86 *"They are one of us":* Chuck Ebeling, "Rodney King Death Today Reminds of a Positive Lesson from LA Riots," Apple Pressings, June 17, 2012, https://applewoody.wordpress.com/2012/06/17 /rodney-king-death-today-reminds-of-a-positive-lesson-from-la -riots/.

CHAPTER 8: "YES, IT CAN BE DONE"

87 *Congress passed the Immigration and Nationality Act of 1965:* Tom Gjelten, "The Immigration Act That Inadvertently Changed America," *Atlantic,* October 2, 2015, https://www .theatlantic.com/politics/archive/2015/10/immigration-act-1965 /408409/.

87 *In 1960, roughly seven out of every eight immigrants:* Ibid.

87 *the United States went from being 84 percent:* Pew Research Center, "Immigration's Impact on Past and Future U.S. Population Change," September 28, 2015, http://www.pewhispanic.org/2015 /09/28/chapter-2-immigrations-impact-on-past-and-future-u-s -population-change/.

88 *a fifteen-year period (1965–80) in which:* Marlene A. Lee and Mark Mather, "U.S. Labor Force Trends," *Population Bulletin,* June 2008, 3.

88 *the Cajun-themed Popeyes brand:* "Our Story," Popeyes, https://popeyes.com/our-story/.

88 *the North Carolina biscuit-and-chicken chain:* "A Heaping Helping of History," Bojangles', https://www.bojangles.com/about-us/history/.

88 *the Mexican roast-chicken chain El Pollo Loco:* "About Us," El Pollo Loco, https://www.elpolloloco.com/about-us/.

88 *the immigrant-founded Golden Krust:* Louise Kramer, "For Ex-nurses, Real Money's in Takeout," *New York Times*, April 4, 2004, https://www.nytimes.com/2004/04/04/jobs/home-front-for-ex-nurses-real-money-s-in-takeout.html/.

89 *Between 1976 and 1986 alone:* Jou, *Supersizing*, 89.

89 *"It took me eighteen years to figure out":* Author interview with Church's franchisee Aslam Khan, July 30, 2015. Unless otherwise noted, all quotes and data about Khan come from the July 30 interview.

93 *the world's oldest-operating McDonald's:* Author visit to Downey, Calif., August 7, 2014.

93 *no indoor seating and no drive-thru window:* Author interview with McDonald's franchisee Ron Piazza, August 7, 2014.

94 *the only McDonald's location where a customer can still:* Melanie Dunea, "The Oldest McDonald's in the Country Serves Up Fried Apple Pie and Fifties Charm," Yahoo, July 28, 2014, https://www.yahoo.com/lifestyle/the-oldest-operating-mcdonalds-in-the-country-93107756477.html.

94 *the National Trust for Historic Preservation even listed it:* "America's 11 Most Endangered Historic Places," National Trust for Historic Preservation, https://savingplaces.org/11most-past-listings#.XBa1Q3pKiL4.

94 *"Ray Kroc used to pride himself on saying":* Author interview with Piazza.

95 *"McDonald's has made more African American millionaires":* Sharon Bernstein, "Restaurant Group Plans to Fight Fast-Food Restrictions in Los Angeles," *Los Angeles Times*, November 11, 2010, http://articles.latimes.com/2010/nov/11/business/la-fi-fast-food-fight-20101112.

95 *June Martino . . . who started as Ray Kroc's bookkeeper:* "June Martino, McDonald's Pioneer, Passes Away," McDonald's, http://www.junemartino.org/site/epage/21891_504.htm.

95 *Her Majesty has technically owned:* Rose Fitzmaurice, "We Went to the McDonald's Owned by the Queen—and It's One of the Poshest We've Ever Seen," *Business Insider*, October 20, 2017, http://www.businessinsider.com/welcome-to-the-queens -mcdonalds-in-banbury-britain-2017-10.

96 *a much higher percentage of Americans hold:* Richard Wike, "5 Ways Americans and Europeans Are Different," Pew Research Center, April 19, 2016, http://www.pewresearch.org/fact-tank/2016/04 /19/5-ways-americans-and-europeans-are-different/.

98 *the middle class slipped out of the economic majority:* Pew Research Center, "The American Middle Class Is Losing Ground," December 9, 2015, http://www.pewsocialtrends.org/2015/12/09 /the-american-middle-class-is-losing-ground/.

98 *Khan would be named the CEO of TGI Fridays:* Ron Ruggless, "TGI Fridays Names Aslam Khan CEO," *Nation's Restaurant News*, April 27, 2017, https://www.nrn.com/people/tgi-fridays-names -aslam-khan-ceo.

CHAPTER 9: DRIVE-THRU AMERICA

99 *Its meager price of forty-nine cents:* Hilary Stout, "Not Just a Hot Cup Anymore," *New York Times*, October 21, 2013, https://www .nytimes.com/2013/10/21/booming/not-just-a-hot-cup-anymore .html.

100 *Burns covered 16 percent of her body:* Ibid.

100 *the total award was later cut $680,000:* Stout, "Hot Cup."

100 *"Now she claims she broke her nose":* Susan Saladoff, *Hot Coffee* (HBO, 2011).

100 *Her ordeal would be alluded to:* Ibid.

100 *at least one such campaign was spearheaded by Karl Rove:* Saladoff, *Hot Coffee*.

101 *the American workforce approached unprecedented gender parity:* Casey B. Mulligan, "A Milestone for Working Women?," *New York Times*, January 14, 2009, https://economix.blogs.nytimes.com /2009/01/14/a-milestone-for-women-workers/.

101 *about 25 percent of American women with children:* Tyler Cowen, *An Economist Gets Lunch: New Rules for Everyday Foodies* (New York: Dutton, 2002), 34.

101 *"The working person doesn't have time to come in":* Isabel Wilkerson,

"New Funeral Option for Those in a Rush," *New York Times*,
February 23, 1989, https://www.nytimes.com/1989/02/23/us
/chicago-journal-new-funeral-option-for-those-in-a-rush.html.

102 *Red's Giant Hamburg . . . is credited:* Geoff Pickle, "No. 19 Red's
Giant Hamburg Farewell," *Springfield (Mo.) Business Journal*,
July 26, 2010, http://sbj.net/stories/no-19-reds-giant-hamburg
-farewell,23622.

102 *Others suggest the title belongs to Kirby's Pig Stand:* Blake Stillwell,
"You Can Thank the Military for the McDonald's Drive-Thru,"
Business Insider, October 28, 2015, https://www.businessinsider
.com/you-can-thank-the-military-for-the-mcdonalds-drive-thru
-2015-10.

102 *In-N-Out Burger used what it claims:* Oliver, "Esther Snyder."

102 *Jack in the Box married the McDonald brothers':* Langdon, *Orange
Roofs*, 104.

102 *Der Wienerschnitzel, which solved concerns:* Ibid.

102 *"I thought, 'Where is all this business going'":* Robert L. Emerson, *Fast
Food: The Endless Shakeout* (New York: Lebhar-Friedman Books,
1979), 87.

103 *By the late 1980s, nearly 90 percent:* John A. Jakle and Keith A.
Sculle, *Fast Food: Roadside Restaurants in the Automobile Age*
(Baltimore: John Hopkins University Press, 1999), 329.

103 *34 percent of American food budgets:* Ibid.

104 *Wendy's introduced pita wraps, KFC invented:* Ibid., 62.

104 *quick-service restaurants like Checkers:* Ibid., 132.

104 *these express burger spots have parlayed:* Ibid., 61.

104 *By the late 1980s, the number of McDonald's:* Emerson, *New Economics*, 90.

105 *Its creator, a former adman:* Stephen Miller, "At McDonald's, He Was
the Egg McMuffin Pioneer," *Wall Street Journal*, April 5, 2008,
https://www.wsj.com/articles/SB120734439838190797.

105 *Ray Kroc had just finished lunch:* "The Birth of the Egg McMuffin,"
McDonald's, https://corporate.mcdonalds.com/mcd/our
_company-old/amazing_stories/food/the_birth_of_the_egg
_mcmuffin.html.

105 *Lemuel Benedict, the hungover Wall Street stockbroker:* Russell
Kronkhite, "Eggs Benedict and Beyond," *Washington Post*, April 2,
2002, https://www.washingtonpost.com/archive/lifestyle/food

/2002/04/24/eggs-benedict-and-beyond/d3240d9f-74ea-4c64
-a199-d240d17f441a/.

106 *roughly 25 percent of all breakfasts:* Lane Crothers, *Globalization and
American Popular Culture,* 3rd ed. (Lanham, Md.: Rowman &
Littlefield, 2013), 150.

106 *Chrysler, which released the first successful:* Bob Sorokanich,
"30 Years Ago Today, Chrysler Invented the Minivan, and
Changed History," Gizmodo, November 2, 2013, https://gizmodo
.com/30-years-ago-today-chrylser-invented-the-minivan-and
-1457451986.

106 *After selling an impressive two hundred thousand–plus minivans:* Nick
Kurczewski, "Driving Down Memory Lane in the Original
Minivan," *New York Times,* December 15, 2016, https://www
.nytimes.com/2016/12/15/business/driving-down-memory-lane
-in-the-original-minivan.html.

107 *The cupholders in early-model minivans:* Ibid.

107 *"When we began doing the new minivan":* Richard Truett, "The Art
of Cupholders," *Orlando Sentinel,* May 14, 1992, http://articles
.orlandosentinel.com/1992-05-14/topic/9205130156_1_cup
-holders-coffee-cup-cup-of-hot.

107 *"crannies for drinking cups":* Sam Dean, "The History of the Car
Cup Holder," *Bon Appétit,* February 18, 2013, https://www
.bonappetit.com/trends/article/the-history-of-the-car-cup
-holder.

107 *"In a car that has so many thoughtful design details":* Henry Petroski,
Small Things Considered (New York: Vintage Books, 2003), 64.

108 *the tide of cupholder adoption turned forever:* Dean, "Car Cup
Holder."

108 *In 1992 . . . the country had fewer than two hundred Starbucks:*
Florence Fabricant, "Americans Wake Up and Smell the Coffee,"
New York Times, September 2, 1992, https://www.nytimes.com
/1992/09/02/garden/americans-wake-up-and-smell-the-coffee
.html.

109 *"insecure, vain, self-centered and self-absorbed":* Ben Greeman, "Road
Killers," *New Yorker,* January 12, 2004, https://www.newyorker
.com/magazine/2004/01/12/road-killers.

109 *From 1992 until 1999, the US economy grew:* Kurt Andersen, "The
Best Decade Ever? The 1990s, Obviously," *New York Times,*

February 6, 2015, https://www.nytimes.com/2015/02/08/opinion
/sunday/the-best-decade-ever-the-1990s-obviously.html.

109 *an average of over 1.5 million jobs:* Ibid.

109 *Median household income grew by 10 percent:* Ibid.

110 *union membership dropped from a quarter:* Freeman, *American Empire*, 387.

110 *the minimum wage, relative to all wages:* US Department of Labor, "Minimum Wage and Maximum Wage Hour Standards Under the Fair Labor Standards Act," quoted in Emerson, *New Economics*, 104.

110 *from 1980 to 2005 saw more than 80 percent:* Scott Winship, "Making Sense of Inequality," Brookings Institution, August 3, 2012, https://www.brookings.edu/opinions/making-sense-of -inequality/.

110 *"The S.U.V. boom represents, then":* Malcolm Gladwell, "Big and Bad," *New Yorker*, December 12, 2004, https://www.newyorker .com/magazine/2004/01/12/big-and-bad.

111 *"There's this notion that you need to be up high":* Ibid.

111 *"The catchphrase in the auto-design community is* McDonaldability," Gerald Scott, "Cupholders Proliferate, Light Up and Chill Out": *Chicago Tribune*, February 8, 2004, https://www .chicagotribune.com/news/ct-xpm-2004-02-08-0402070177 -story.html.

112 *PricewaterhouseCoopers surveys had found:* Mary A. Nichols, "Cup-holders Are Everywhere," *Atlantic*, April 22, 2018, https://www .theatlantic.com/technology/archive/2018/04/cupholders-are -everywhere/558545/.

112 *"the biggest Subaru yet":* Ibid.

112 *"In 2001, there were 134 food products":* Tom Vanderbilt, *Traffic: Why We Drive the Way We Do (and What It Says About Us)* (New York: Vintage Books, 2008), 16.

112 *the number of McDonald's locations that operate:* Michael Arndt, "McDonald's 24/7," Bloomberg, February 5, 2007, https://www .bloomberg.com/news/articles/2007-02-04/mcdonalds-24-7.

113 *60 to 70 percent of all revenue:* Sam Oches, "The 2016 QSR Drive-Thru Study," *QSR*, 2016, https://www.qsrmagazine.com/reports /2016-qsr-drive-thru-study.

113 *"yelling as if she won a million dollars":* Steve Campion, "Woman

Gives Mink Coat to Fast-Food Employee," ABC 13, December 18, 2014, https://abc13.com/society/woman-gives-mink-coat-to-fast -food-employee/442587/.

113 *215 consecutive diners at a Chick-fil-A:* Tedi Rountree, "Hundreds Pay-It-Foward at Pooler Chick-fil-A," WTOC 11, July 23, 2015, http://www.wtoc.com/story/29620874/hundreds-pay-it-foward-at -pooler-chick-fil-a/.

114 *250 straight drivers at a McDonald's:* Ken Suarez, "Hundreds 'Pay It Forward' at Lakeland McDonald's," Fox 13, December 14, 2015, http://www.fox13news.com/news/local-news/hundreds-pay-it -forward-at-lakeland-mcdonalds.

114 *"Serial pay-it-forward incidents involving":* Kate Murphy, "Ma'am, Your Burger Has Been Paid For," *New York Times,* October 19, 2013, https://www.nytimes.com/2013/10/20/opinion/sunday /maam-your-burger-has-been-paid-for.html.

114 *lieutenant colonel on leave from Fort Benning:* Vanessa Wilkins, "Video of Soldier Buying Meals for Two Hungry Kids Goes Viral," ABC, January 29, 2016, https://abcnews.go.com/Lifestyle/video -soldier-buying-meals-hungry-kids-viral/story?id=36579816.

114 *Marshawn Lynch . . . who handed $500:* Claire McNear, "Marshawn Lynch Gives McDonald's Employee $500 to Go Buy Some Sneakers," SBNation, November 12, 2015, https://www.sbnation .com/lookit/2015/11/12/9723592/marshawn-lynch-mcdonalds -sneakers.

CHAPTER 10: GLASNOST

117 *January of 1990 . . . Russia's first McDonald's:* Adam Taylor, "How McDonald's Went from Hero to Zero in Russia," *Washington Post,* April 16, 2014, https://www.washingtonpost.com/news /worldviews/wp/2014/04/16/how-mcdonalds-went-from-hero-to -zero-in-russia/.

117 *Nine hundred seats. Twenty-seven cash registers:* Masha Hamilton, "1st 'Beeg Mak' Attack Leaves Moscow Agog," *Los Angeles Times,* February 1, 1990, http://articles.latimes.com/1990-02-01/news /mn-1561_1_soviet-union.

177 *"The McDonald's Golden Arches will be appearing":* David Remnick, "Moscow's Big Mac Attack," *Washington Post,* April 30, 1988, https:/www.washingtonpost.com/archive/lifestyle/1988/04/30

/moscows-big-mac-attack/b9613133-4b3b-4084-a7c4
-cbd4b943963e/.

118 *over five thousand customers queued up:* Nick Keppler, "January 31,
1990: McDonald's Opens in the Soviet Union," *Mental Floss,*
January 31, 1990, http://mentalfloss.com/article/74609/january
-31-1990-mcdonalds-opens-soviet-union.

118 *"If you can't go to America":* Michael Dobbs, "Moscow Plays Ketch-
Up," *Washington Post,* January 31, 1990, https://www
.washingtonpost.com/archive/politics/1990/02/01/moscow-plays
-ketch-up/2addbab1-da1c-4101-a2f3-313123a97035/.

118 *"Connoisseurs of fast food and human behavior":* Francis X. Clines,
"Upheaval in the East; Moscow McDonald's Opens: Milkshakes
and Human Kindness," *New York Times,* January 31, 1990,
https://www.nytimes.com/1990/02/01/world/upheaval-east
-moscow-mcdonald-s-opens-milkshakes-human-kindness-reuters
.html.

119 *The final figure of customers served:* Thomas Grove, "In Russia,
McDonald's Serves Local Fries and a Side of Realpolitik," *Wall
Street Journal,* November 8, 2018, https://www.wsj.com/articles
/in-russia-mcdonalds-serves-local-fries-and-a-side-of-realpolitik
-1541678402.

120 *from a pool of the 27,000 applicants:* Janet Adamy, "As Burgers Boom
in Russia, McDonald's Touts Discipline," *Wall Street Journal,*
October 16, 2007, https://www.wsj.com/articles
/SB119248482397359814.

120 *foreign-seeming palette of polite phrases:* Alix Spiegel, "Invisibilia,"
NPR, June 17, 2016, https://www.npr.org/2016/06/17/482443233
/listen-to-the-episode.

120 *"In the Soviet Union, when you walked into a restaurant":* Ibid.

120 *"There is a lesson to be drawn from this for the country":* Clines,
"Upheaval in the East."

121 *"A lot of Russian people walking into that McDonald's":* Spiegel,
"Invisibilia."

121 *the Pushkin Square store has vied for:* Adamy, "As Burgers Boom."

121 *By 2007, the average Russian McDonald's was annually serving:* Ibid.

121 *"In a country where there was nothing available":* Ibid.

121 *After it opened over a hundred franchises:* Adamy, "As Burgers
Boom."

122 *the tally of customers to the Pushkin Square store:* "McDonald's Still Thriving in Russia After 20 Years," Voice of America, February 1, 2010, https://www.voanews.com/a/mcdonalds-still-thriving-in-russia-after-20-years-83327327/111887.html.

122 *"McDonald's was not so much a fast-food chain":* "McDonald's in Russia: 20 Years of 'Loving It,'" Russia Today, February 1, 2010, https://www.rt.com/news/mcdonalds-russia-20-years/.

122 *McDonald's was required to build the McComplex:* Dobbs, "Ketch-Up."

122 *reportedly known to locals as the McGulag:* Dobbs, "Ketch-Up."

123 *85 percent of the products served:* David M. Herszenhorn, "A Fast-Food Symbol of America Falls in Moscow," *New York Times*, August 21, 2014, https://www.nytimes.com/2014/08/22/world/europe/mcdonalds-a-fast-food-symbol-of-america-falls-in-moscow.html.

123 *The last items to be produced at the McComplex:* Andrew E. Kramer, "Russia's Evolution, Seen Through Golden Arches," *New York Times*, February 1, 2010, https://www.nytimes.com/2010/02/02/business/global/02mcdonalds.html.

123 *"numerous violations of the sanitary code":* Herszenhorn, "Fast-Food Symbol."

123 *In 2011, McDonald's had been honored:* Herszenhorn, "Fast-Food Symbol."

123 *"Everything about this particular branch":* Mitya Kushelevich, "Taste of Freedom: What the Closure of the First Moscow McDonald's Means for Russia Today," Calvert Journal, September 1, 2014, http://www.calvertjournal.com/articles/show/3046/mcdonalds-moscow-closure-russia-martin-parr.

123 *McDonald's enjoyed paying a symbolic yearly rent of one ruble:* Ibid.

124 *about 10 percent of the four hundred:* Clint Rainey, "Burger King Is Encroaching on France's Halal Market," *Grub Street*, December 16, 2015, http://www.grubstreet.com/2015/12/burger-king-france-halal.html.

124 *accusing Burger King of bowing to sharia law:* Thomas, "Burger King Announced They Will Follow Sharia Law," Political Insider, December 17, 2015, https://thepoliticalinsider.com/burger-king-just-announced-they-will-follow-islamic-sharia-law-stop-them/.

125 *the company unveiled a specialty menu:* Deena Shanker, "Burger King Might Take Its Indian Vegetarian Menu Global," Quartz,

June 30, 2015, https://qz.com/440660/burger-king-might-take-its
-indian-vegetarian-menu-global/.

125 *Burger King is called Hungry Jack's:* Benedict Brook, "How a Random
US Brand Became the Household Name Hungry Jack's in
Australia," News.com.au, September 9, 2017, https://www.news
.com.au/lifestyle/food/restaurants-bars/how-a-random-us-brand
-became-the-household-name-hungry-jacks-in-australia/news
-story/cef292929099d8dd2a9ff6ob8deaf93e.

125 *Texas Chicken . . . what the company calls its stores:* "Dine with Us
Around the World," Church's Chicken, http://www.churchs.com
/international.php.

125 *religious authorities have compelled chains:* Victoria Ho, "Why Auntie
Anne's Was Forced to Rename Its Pretzel Dogs in Malaysia,"
Mashable, October 20, 2016, https://mashable.com/2016/10/20
/auntie-annes-malaysia-hot-dogs/#YSMiDirR8qqm.

125 *the rise of the "hot dog":* Boze Hadleigh, *Holy Cow!: Doggerel, Catnaps,
Scapegoats, Foxtrots, and Horse Feathers* (New York: Skyhorse
Publishing, 2015), 7.

125 *root beer . . . is referred to as RB:* Ibid.

127 glocalization . . . *is more than adapting a menu:* Roland Robertson,
"Glocalization," in *The Post-Colonial Studies Reader*, ed. Bill
Ashcroft, Gareth Griffiths, and Helen Tiffin (London: Routledge,
2006), 477–78.

128 *another steady contender for the title:* Ladka Bauerova, "McDonald's
Sues to Avoid Being Priced off the Champs-Élysées," *New York
Times*, May 22, 2008, https://www.nytimes.com/2008/05/22
/business/worldbusiness/22iht-mcdo.4.13138077.html.

128 *A recent redesign of the store was conceived:* Lilit Marcus, "The World's
Most Popular McDonald's Is Now Also the Most Stylish," *Condé
Nast Traveler*, March 14, 2016, https://www.cntraveler.com/stories
/2016-03-14/the-worlds-most-popular-mcdonalds-is-now-also-the-
-most-stylish.

128 *Burger King Japan ran a promotion:* Raphael Brion, "Burger King
Japan Will Put 15 Bacon Strips on a Burger for 100 Yen ($1.23),"
Eater, April 17, 2012, https://www.eater.com/2012/4/17/6595295
/burger-king-japan-will-put-15-bacon-strips-on-a-burger-for-100
-yen-1.

128 *$16 burger topped with foie gras and truffles:* Paula Forbes, "Wendy's

in Japan Serves Hamburgers with Foie Gras," Eater, December 27, 2011, https://www.eater.com/2011/12/27/6627129/wendys -in-japan-serves-hamburgers-with-foie-gras.

129 *After a successful spring trial at the 1970 World Expo:* Nina Li Coomes, "The True Meaning of KFC Christmas," Eater, December 21, 2017, https://www.eater.com/2017/12/21/16805576/kfc-christmas-japan -life-in-chains.

129 *a national marketing campaign:* K. Annabelle Smith, "Why Japan Is Obsessed with Kentucky Fried Chicken on Christmas," *Smithsonian,* December 14, 2012, https://www.smithsonianmag.com/arts -culture/why-japan-is-obsessed-with-kentucky-fried-chicken-on -christmas-1-161666960/.

130 *an estimated 3.6 million families seek out:* Author interview with Yuko Nakajima at KFC Japan headquarters, December 24, 2015.

130 *The standard set is a $40 spread:* Author interview with Nakajima.

131 *the country's Christian population is thought:* Michael Hoffman, "Christian Missionaries Find Japan a Tough Nut to Crack," *Japan Times,* December 20, 2014, https://www.japantimes.co.jp/news /2014/12/20/national/history/christian-missionaries-find-japan -tough-nut-crack/.

131 *And since 1985, KFC has produced specialty collector:* Ibid.

CHAPTER 11: THE CULINARY CONSCIOUSNESS

133 *"The student maintained good health":* Hogan, *Selling 'Em,* 13.

135 *"It was the first time we almost ran out":* Author interview with Richardson.

136 *Anything less, as Alice Waters":* Kate Cox, "Making Lunch with Alice Waters," New Food Economy, July 14, 2017, https:// newfoodeconomy.org/making-lunch-with-alice-waters/.

136 *"make a sacrifice on the cell phone":* Kim Severson, "Some Good News on Food Prices," *New York Times,* April 2, 2008, https://archive .nytimes.com/www.nytimes.com/learning/teachers/featured _articles/20080403thursday.html.

136 *Between 2006 and 2016, the number of listed farmers' markets:* Tim Carman, "For Some Growers, Farmers' Markets Just Aren't What They Used to Be," *Washington Post,* June 21, 2016, https://www .washingtonpost.com/lifestyle/food/for-some-growers-farmers

-markets-just-arent-what-they-used-to-be/2016/06/21/c5d93644
-3271-11e6-8758-d58e76e11b12_story.html.

137 *the sunny patio was filled with diners:* Author visit, August 19, 2015.

137 *"The clean lines and fresh colors of Northstar reflect":* "Philosophy,"
Northstar Café, https://www.thenorthstarcafe.com/about/.

139 *"Eat food. Not too much. Mostly plants":* Author interview with
Michael Pollan, March 15, 2016.

140 *In 2015, Whole Foods, a pioneer in the organic game:* Lauren Katz,
"Costco Sells More Organic Food Than Whole Foods," Vox,
June 4, 2015, https://www.vox.com/2015/6/4/8724641/costco
-organic-food.

140 *Whole Foods responded by creating "Responsibility Grown":* Dan
Charles, "Organic Farmers Call Foul on Whole Foods' Produce
Rating System," NPR, June 12, 2015, https://www.npr.org
/sections/thesalt/2015/06/12/411779324/organic-farmers-call-foul
-on-whole-foods-produce-rating-system.

140 *"Clean eating—whether it is called that or not":* Bee Wilson, "Why We
Fell for Clean Eating," *Guardian*, August 11, 2017, https://www
.theguardian.com/lifeandstyle/2017/aug/11/why-we-fell-for-clean
-eating.

141 *Pop-Tarts and Frosted Flakes would qualify as healthy:* Annie
Gasparro, "FDA Seeks to Redefine 'Healthy,'" *Wall Street Journal*,
May 10, 2016, https://www.foxbusiness.com/features/fda-seeks-to
-redefine-healthy.

141 *an episode in the public health wars of 2006:* Martin Wainwright, "The
Battle of Rawmarsh," *Guardian*, September 20, 2006, https://
www.theguardian.com/education/2006/sep/20/schoolmeals
.schools.

143 *Fan food, not fast food:* Mark Brandau, "Dairy Queen to Debut New
Ad Campaign," *Nation's Restaurant News*, May 21, 2013, https://
www.nrn.com/advertising/dairy-queen-debut-new-ad-campaign.

143 *It's waaaay better than fast food:* "Wendy's Puts Honest Quality
Front and Center," Wendy's, January 28, 2008, http://ir.wendys
.com/phoenix.zhtml?c=67548&p=irol-newsArticle_pf&ID
=1201672.

143 *Fast crafted:* "Who We Are and What We Do," Arby's, https://arbys
.com/about.

143 *Jason Alexander and major league slugger Barry Bonds:* "2002

Jason Alexander Barry Bonds KFC Popcorn Chicken Commercial," TheRetroTimeMachine, YouTube, https://www.youtube.com/watch?v=9mWUNe6L8dc/.

143 *"There's fast food. . . . Then there's KFC"*: Ibid.

143 *"modern, progressive burger company"*: Bill Chappell, "McDonald's CEO Promises 'Modern, Progressive Burger Company,'" NPR, May 4, 2015, https://www.npr.org/sections/thetwo-way/2015/05/04/404166605/mcdonald-s-ceo-promises-modern-progressive-burger-company.

143 *"At McDonald's, we're making changes"*: "Our Food Philosophy," McDonald's, https://www.mcdonalds.com/us/en-us/about-our-food/our-food-philosophy.html.

144 *or about 5 percent of all the eggs*: Roberto A. Ferdman, "McDonald's Is Changing the Eggs We Eat," *Washington Post*, September 9, 2015, https://www.washingtonpost.com/news/wonk/wp/2015/09/09/mcdonalds-is-changing-the-eggs-we-eat/.

144 *moved from using margarine to butter*: "McDonald's Is Now Using Real Butter," Eater, September 1, 2015, https://www.eater.com/2015/9/1/9239019/mcdonalds-uses-real-butter-axes-margarine-shocker.

144 *it unveiled plans to eschew palm oil*: Elliott Negin, "McDonald's Pledges to Eliminate Deforestation from Its Entire Supply Chain," *Huffington Post*, April 21, 2015, https://www.huffingtonpost.com/elliott-negin/mcdonalds-palm-oil-pledge_b_7104982.html.

144 *the company announced that it would stop*: Allison Aubrey, "McDonald's Now Serving Chicken Raised Without Antibiotics—Mostly," NPR, August 2, 2016, https://www.npr.org/sections/thesalt/2016/08/02/488285374/mcdonalds-now-serving-chicken-raised-without-antibiotics-mostly.

145 *In 1985, Wendy's spent $10 million*: Anthony Ramirez, "Fast Food Lightens Up but Sales Are Often Thin," *New York Times*, March 19, 1991, https://www.nytimes.com/1991/03/19/business/fast-food-lightens-up-but-sales-are-often-thin.html.

145 *Dairy Queen introduced the Breeze*: Schuyler Velasco, "10 Fast Foods That Have Disappeared," *Christian Science Monitor*, August 21, 2013, https://www.csmonitor.com/Business/2013/0821/10-fast-foods-that-have-disappeared/Breeze.

145 *In 1990, McDonald's, Burger King, and Wendy's*: Nancy Rivera

Brooks, "Fast-Food Firms to Cook Fries in Vegetable Oil," *Los Angeles Times*, July 24, 1990, http://articles.latimes.com/1990-07 -24/business/fi-782_1_vegetable-oil/.

145 *Burger King introduced the B.K. Broiler:* Ramirez, "Fast Food Lightens Up."

145 *Pizza Hut also introduced and scrapped:* Ibid.

145 *General Mills had to resume its use:* Stacey Yuen, "Trix Cereal Is Bringing Back Artificial Colors Because Customers Complained," CNBC, September 21, 2017, https://www.cnbc.com/2017/09/21 /trix-bringing-back-to-artificial-colors-after-customers -complained.html.

146 *his company . . . briefly started selling a skinless chicken:* Alan Gerstein, "Kentucky Fried Chicken Plans Lighter Menu," UPI, January 23, 1991, https://www.upi.com/Archives/1991/01/23/Kentucky-Fried -Chicken-plans-lighter-menu/3669664606800/.

146 *the company even took the extreme step:* Ozersky, *Colonel Sanders*, 118.

146 *McDonald's released the fabled McLean Deluxe:* Anthony Ramirez, "Low-Fat McDonald's Burger Is Planned to Answer Critics," *New York Times*, March 13, 1991, https://www.nytimes.com/1991/03/13 /business/low-fat-mcdonald-s-burger-is-planned-to-answer-critics .html.

146 *the 91 percent fat-free burger:* Ibid.

146 *"Securities analysts doubted whether the new sandwich":* Ibid.

146 *Once word got out that McDonald's was using:* Richard Gibson, "McDonald's Skinny Burger Is a Hard Sell," *Wall Street Journal*, April 21, 1993, http://community.seattletimes.nwsource.com /archive/?date=19930421&slug=1696983.

146 *Hardee's poked fun at the seaweed:* Associated Press, "Lower-Fat Burger from Hardee's," July 16, 1991, https://www.nytimes.com /1991/07/16/business/company-news-lower-fat-burger-from -hardee-s.html.

147 *"Consumers have had their fill of healthier fare":* Ibid.

147 *White Castle has introduced veggie and vegan sliders:* Clint Rainey, "Get Ready for 'Bleeding' Veggie Sliders at White Castle," *Grub Street*, April 11, 2018, http://www.grubstreet.com/2018/04/white -castle-unveils-impossible-burger-vegan-sliders.html.

147 *Taco Bell has touted meatless items:* Kushbu Shah, "Taco Bell Launches Certified Vegetarian Menu," Eater, October 1, 2015,

https://www.eater.com/2015/10/1/9431775/taco-bell-vegetarian
-menu.

147 *promoting new burgers made with ground turkey and grass-fed beef:*
Bruce Horovitz, "Carl's Jr. to Roll Out 'Natural' Burger," *USA
Today,* December 9, 2014, https://www.usatoday.com/story
/money/business/2014/12/09/carls-jr-hardees-fast-food
-restaurants-all-natural-burger/20139287/.

147 *Sonic . . . saw its sales boom:* Roberto A. Ferdman, "What Sonic Gets
That McDonald's Doesn't," *Washington Post,* January 9, 2015,
https://www.washingtonpost.com/news/wonk/wp/2015/01/09
/what-sonic-gets-that-mcdonalds-doesnt/.

147 *it started a strategy of healthful incrementalism:* Bret Thorn, "Sonic
Drive-In Rolls Out Mushroom-Blended Burger Nationwide,"
Nation's Restaurant News, March 1, 2018, https://www.nrn.com
/whats-hot/sonic-drive-rolls-out-mushroom-blended-burger
-nationwide.

147 *Arby's reversed a years-long sales slump:* Katie Richards, "How Arby's
Broke Its Marketing Slump and Became One of Today's Beefiest
Brands,"*Adweek,* October 16, 2015, https://www.adweek.com
/brand-marketing/how-arbys-broke-its-marketing-slump-and
-became-one-todays-beefiest-brands-167625/.

149 *"We'd invite you to try it":* Martha C. White, "Kraft Reveals Revamped
Mac and Cheese, 50 Million Boxes Later," *New York Times,*
March 20, 2016, https://www.nytimes.com/2016/03/21/business
/media/kraft-reveals-revamped-mac-and-cheese-50-million-boxes
-later.html.

149 *"We call it stealth health":* Rick A. Munarriz, "The Crazy Thing
Chick-fil-A Is Afraid to Tell You About Its Menu," AOL, December 17, 2013, https://www.aol.com/article/finance/2013/12/17
/chick-fil-a-stealth-health-menu-changes/20787443/.

149 *the craft coffee craze might seem ubiquitous:* Roberto A. Ferdman, "It's
True: Americans Like to Drink Bad Coffee," *Washington Post,*
February 24, 2015, https://www.washingtonpost.com/news/wonk
/wp/2015/02/24/its-true-americans-like-to-drink-bad-coffee/.

149 *as recently as 2015, eleven brewers:* "These 11 Brewers Make Over 90%
of All U.S. Beer," Fox Business, July 28, 2015, https://www
.marketwatch.com/story/these-11-brewers-make-over-90-of-all-us
-beer-2015-07-27.

150 *The average age of first-time homeowners:* Gillian B. White, "What Will It Take for Millennials to Become Homeowners?," *Atlantic*, October 22, 2014, https://www.theatlantic.com/business/archive/2014/10/what-will-it-take-for-millennials-to-become-homeowners/381730/.

150 *"The important factor contributing to what parents choose":* Author interview with Professor Shashi Matta, August 19, 2015.

150 *Only about 40 percent of US citizens:* Niall McCarthy, "The Share of Americans Holding a Passport Has Increased Dramatically in Recent Years," *Forbes*, January 11, 2018, https://www.forbes.com/sites/niallmccarthy/2018/01/11/the-share-of-americans-holding-a-passport-has-increased-dramatically-in-recent-years-infographic/.

150 *average American only lives eighteen miles:* Quoctrung Bui and Claire Cain Miller, "The Typical American Lives Only 18 Miles from Mom," *New York Times*, December 23, 2015, https://www.nytimes.com/interactive/2015/12/24/upshot/24up-family.html.

150 *the average age that Americans become grandparents:* Peter Francese, "The Grandparent Economy," Considerable, April 20, 2009, https://considerable.com/the-power-of-the-grandparent-economy/.

CHAPTER 12: CRISP DIGITAL NUGGETS

153 *"Yo @Wendys," he asked in 2017, "how many retweets":* @carterjwm, April 5, 2017.

153 *Wendy's account, which has become one of the truer sages:* @Wendys, April 5, 2017.

153 *after all, only one tweet had even reached:* Victor Luckerson, "These Are the 10 Most Popular Tweets of All Time," *Time*, March 21, 2016, http://time.com/4263227/most-popular-tweets/.

153 *"HELP ME PLEASE. A MAN NEEDS HIS NUGGS":* @carterjwm, April 5, 2017.

153 *an unlikely coalition including social media influencers:* Twitter, "#NuggsForCarter is now the most Retweeted Tweet of all time," May 9, 2017, https://blog.twitter.com/official/en_us/topics/events/2017/-nuggsforcarter-is-now-the-most-retweeted-tweet-of-all-time.html.

154 *"It's good to have dreams":* Jeff Beer, "Carter Got His Wendy's Nuggs and a Twitter World Record," *Fast Company*, May 9, 2017,

https://www.fastcompany.com/40419538/carter-got-his-wendys
-nuggs-and-a-twitter-world-record.

154 *Even the automatons joined in:* Twitter, "#NuggsForCarter."

154 *Wendy's gave the plea new life:* @Wendys, April 7, 2017.

154 *a selfie taken live in the middle:* Ryan Faughnder, "Oscars 2014 Draws
43 Million Viewers, Biggest Audience in 10 Years," *Los Angeles
Times,* March 3, 2014, https://www.latimes.com/entertainment
/envelope/cotown/la-et-ct-oscars-ratings-ellen-degeneres
-20140303-story.html.

155 *Mentioning Wilkerson's tweet on her talk show:* Randee Dawn, "Ellen,
Bradley Cooper Take on 'Nugget Boy' over Twitter Record," *Today,*
April 14, 2017, https://www.today.com/popculture/ellen-bradley
-cooper-take-nugget-boy-over-twitter-record-t110387.

155 *"Not today nugget boy":* @TheEllenShow, April 13, 2017.

155 *"sabotage my selfie":* Shane Lou, "Ellen DeGeneres Gives 'Nugget Boy'
a TV, Underwear to Keep Her Twitter Record," *Today,* April 18,
2017, https://www.today.com/popculture/ellen-degeneres-gives
-nugget-boy-tv-underwear-keep-her-twitter-t110528.

155 *"If somehow you pass me":* Ibid.

155 *Wilkerson's tweet surpassed Ellen's with over 3.4 million retweets:*
Twitter, "#NuggsForCarter."

156 *Taco Bell coordinated a massive publicity stunt:* Haniya Rae, "Taco
Bell's Burner Phone Breakfast Campaign," Digiday, March 21,
2014, https://digiday.com/marketing/taco-bells-burner-phone
-breakfast-campaign/.

156 *The phones were sent out via UPS:* The author received one of these
magical phones.

157 *The company's social insights team:* Author interview with Taco Bell
social insights team, Taco Bell headquarters, Irvine, California,
January 21, 2016.

159 *Nearly as popular is the parody account Nihilist Arby's:* Richard Feloni,
"Arby's Sent Sandwiches and a Puppy to Its Biggest Troll, and It
Shows Why Its Transformation Has Been So Successful," *Business
Insider,* November 21, 2017, https://www.businessinsider.com
/how-arbys-made-peace-with-nihilist-arbys-2017-7.

159 *KFC's Twitter follows exactly eleven accounts:* Six random guys named
Herb and all five of the Spice Girls: KFC Twitter, https://twitter
.com/kfc.

162 *"We'd all been waiting an entire month":* Ted Berg, "Army Vet Miraculously Wakes from 48-Day Coma and Demands Taco Bell," *USA Today*, May 12, 2016, https://ftw.usatoday.com/2016/05/this -week-in-taco-bell-army-vet-miraculously-wakes-from-48-day -coma-and-demands-taco-bell.

162 *over one hundred shell-shocked mourners:* David Moye, "Heartbroken Locals Hold Candlelight Vigil for Taco Bell That Burned Down," *Huffington Post*, January 22, 2018, https://www.huffingtonpost .com/entry/taco-bell-candlelight-vigil_us _5a6679e1e4b0e5630072d2be/.

163 *"in an effort to help the national debt":* John Kopp, "Two Decades Ago, Taco Bell Convinced America That It Had Bought the Liberty Bell," PhillyVoice, March 30, 2018, https://www.phillyvoice.com /two-decades-ago-taco-bell-convinced-america-it-had-bought -liberty-bell/.

163 *"We will be doing a series of these":* Paul Farhi, "A Joke That Rang True," *Washington Post*, April 2, 1996, https://www .washingtonpost.com/archive/business/1996/04/02/a-joke-that -rang-true/748a6749-53d7-4952-ba23-e3a5f8daceca/.

163 *Burger King used April Fools' Day:* Scott Mayerowitz, "The Eight Best April Fools' Day Pranks Ever," ABC News, April 1, 2010, https:// abcnews.go.com/Travel/best-april-fools-day-pranks-left-handed -whoppers/story?id=10233031.

164 *the company's bizarro promotions have included:* Bridgett Weaver, "KFC's Plan to Have Your House Smelling like Fried Chicken for the Holidays," *Louisville Business First*, December 13, 2018, https://www.bizjournals.com/louisville/news/2018/12/13/kfcs -plan-to-have-your-house-smelling-like-fried.html; Tim Nudd, "KFC Just Made Edible 'Finger Lickin' Good' Nail Polish That, Yeah, Tastes like Chicken," *Adweek*, May 4, 2016, https://www .adweek.com/creativity/kfc-just-made-edible-finger-lickin-good -nail-polish-yeah-tastes-chicken-171245/; Joe Pinsker, "The Most Dystopian Marketing Stunt Ever?," *Atlantic*, August 29, 2018, https://www.theatlantic.com/family/archive/2018/08/kfc-baby -name-harland/568915/.

164 *the company announced it would release Whopper-flavored toothpaste:* Kristina Monllos, "Burger King Just Made Toothpaste That Tastes like a Whopper," *Adweek*, March 29, 2017, http://www.adweek

.com/creativity/burger-king-just-made-toothpaste-that-tastes-like
-a-whopper/.

164 *"We did not anticipate the overnight crowds"*: Taylor Rock, "'Rick and
Morty' Szechuan Sauce Is Finally Coming Back to McDonald's,"
Daily Meal, February 22, 2018, https://www.sun-sentinel.com
/features/food/sns-dailymeal-1888474-eat-rick-and-morty
-szechuan-sauce-mcdonalds-022218-20180222-story.html.

CHAPTER 13: BELONGING

168 *"I just got caught up in the moment"*: Scott M. Gleeson, "Joakim
Noah Chewed Out for Trying to Win Big Macs," *USA Today*,
November 7, 2012, https://www.usatoday.com/story/gameon/2012
/11/07/joakim-noah-chewed-out-for-trying-to-win-big-macs
/1690387/.

168 *Sixers coach Doug Collins had the public address announcer*: Isaac
Rauch, "Doug Collins Bought 18,000 Big Macs Last Night,"
Deadspin, December 22, 2012, https://deadspin.com/5970749
/doug-collins-bought-18000-big-macs-last-night.

168 *"The 'We want tacos!' chant"*: Author interview with Ben Smith,
April 20, 2017.

168 *Lakers fans have had pretty good luck*: Los Angeles Twitter, https://
twitter.com/Lakers/status/78339624983151208.

168 *the 1984 Olympics in Los Angeles*: Tim Loc, "Let's Remember
McDonald's Marketing Disaster in the 1984 Olympics," LAist,
October 11, 2016, https://laist.com/2016/10/11/mcdonalds
_olympics.php.

169 *"It's a trick"*: T. J. Simers, "Phil Jackson Thinks About the Whole
Enchilada Instead of Free Tacos," *Los Angeles Times*, April 22,
2009, http://articles.latimes.com/2009/apr/22/sports/sp-simers
-lakers22.

169 *The corn shells are produced at plants*: Russell Adams, "Americans Eat
554 Million Jack in the Box Tacos a Year, and No One Knows
Why," *Wall Street Journal*, January 3, 2017, https://www.wsj.com
/articles/americans-eat-554-million-jack-in-the-box-tacos-a-year
-and-no-one-knows-why-1483465285.

170 *"Wet envelope of cat food"*: Ibid.

170 *Jack in the Box sells over 550 million tacos every year*: Ibid.

000 *In spite of referring to*: James Oseland, 5@5—*Eatocracy*,

CNN, August 4, 2010, https://cnneatocracy.wordpress.com/2010 /08/04/55-saveur-editor-in-chief-james-oseland/.

171 *"On Fridays, we only took in about"*: Paul Clark, "No Fish Story: Sandwich Saved His McDonald's," *Cincinnati Enquirer*, February 20, 2007, https://usatoday30.usatoday.com/money/industries /food/2007-02-20-fish2-usat_x.htm.

172 *"Hell no! I don't care if the pope himself"*: Kroc, *Grinding It Out*, 140.

172 *"Friday came and the word came out"*: Paul Clark, "Filet-O-Fish Inventor Brought Patrons Back to McDonald's," *Cincinnati Enquirer*, February 26, 2016, https://www.usatoday.com/story /money/nation-now/2016/02/26/mcdonalds-filet-o-fish-sandwich -lent-catholics/80926146/.

172 *Kroc . . . later claimed that the odd half slice*: Ibid.

172 *"fish that catches people"*: Kroc, *Grinding It Out*, 141.

172 *"For a surprisingly good taste"*: K. Annabelle Smith, "The Fishy History of the McDonald's Filet-O-Fish Sandwich, *Smithsonian*, March 1, 2013, https://www.smithsonianmag.com/arts-culture /the-fishy-history-of-the-mcdonalds-filet-o-fish-sandwich-2912/.

173 *A recent company estimate put the annual sales*: Ibid.

173 *Several fast-food chains now have specialty items*: Danny Klein, "Fast Food Preps for Seafood Boom During Lent," *QSR*, March 3, 2017, https://www.qsrmagazine.com/news/fast-food-preps-seafood -boom-during-lent.

173 *a blue polystyrene clamshell package*: "McDonald's Clam Shell Container," National Museum of American History exhibition *Food: Transforming the American Table, 1950–2000*.

174 *"You fellows just watch"*: Kroc, *Grinding It Out*, 141.

174 *McDonald's declared that it would phase out*: Paul Farhi, "McDonald's Trashing Its Styrofoam Containers," *Washington Post*, November 2, 1990, https://www.washingtonpost.com/archive/politics /1990/11/02/mcdonalds-trashing-its-foam-containers/e1ac982a -8058-4308-8d6f-fff1bef20ec5/.

174 *Filet-O-Fish would appear*: "McDonald's Obesity Suit Thrown Out," CNN, September 4, 2003, http://www.cnn.com/2003/LAW/09 /04/mcdonalds.suit/.

174 *the sandwich became a popular tool*: Heather MacDonald, "How to Interrogate Terrorists," in *The Torture Debate in America*, ed.

Karen J. Greenberg (New York: Cambridge University Press, 2006), 91.

174 *Filets-O-Fish would only feature wild Alaskan pollack:* Tiffany Hsu, "McDonald's Filet-O-Fish, Fish McBites Going All-Sustainable," *Los Angeles Times*, January 24, 2013, https://www.latimes.com /business/la-fi-mo-mcdonalds-sustainable-fish-20130124-story .html.

176 *"We're in the temptation business":* Author interview with Arby's senior vice president of product development and innovation, Jim Taylor, August 2, 2016.

176 *"You're not just coming up with the flavor of the day":* Author interview with Popeyes vice president for culinary innovation, Amy Alarcón, January 11, 2016.

177 *a poster that featured corned beef:* Sarah Halzack, "The $10 'Meat Mountain' from Arby's: It's Exactly What It Sounds Like," *Washington Post*, August 25, 2014, https://www.washingtonpost .com/news/business/wp/2014/08/25/the-10-meat-mountain-from -arbys-its-exactly-what-it-sounds-like/.

177 *secret menu items, which are often schemed up by customers:* For an extremely comprehensive list of secret menu items, see Jon Hein, *Fast Food Maniac* (New York: Three Rivers Press, 2016).

178 *the story of Todd Mills and the Doritos Locos Taco:* Unless otherwise noted, the following information is from author interviews with Ginger Mills and Jimmy Looney in August 2015.

179 *"Imagine this . . . taco shells made from Doritos":* Stephen Miller, "RIP: Todd Mills, the Man Who Dreamed of the Doritos Taco," *Wall Street Journal*, December 3, 2013, https://blogs.wsj.com/corporate -intelligence/2013/12/03/in-memoriam-todd-mills-the-man-who -dreamed-of-the-doritos-taco/.

181 *"the idea of taco, tostada and taco salad shells":* Letter by David Peterman in Alexis Madrigal, "We Could Have Had Doritos Locos Tacos in the '90s," *Atlantic*, June 24, 2014.

182 *Taco Bell sold a staggering 100 million Doritos Locos Tacos:* Ibid.

182 *"The shell is paper-thin, with a delicate crunch":* William Grimes, "Looks like a Taco, Tastes like a Chip," *New York Times*, June 19, 2012, https://www.nytimes.com/2012/06/20/dining/looks-like-a -taco-tastes-like-a-chip.html.

182 *Doritos Locos Taco sales had surpassed the $1 billion mark:* Madrigal, "Doritos Locos Tacos."

CHAPTER 14: THE FAST-CASUAL FRONTIER

185 *there's a Wendy's that served as a test prototype:* Author visit, Columbus, Ohio, August 18, 2015.

186 *92 percent of respondents cited "treating employees well":* Bethany Wall, "Fast Casual Restaurants—US—October 2013," Mintel, 2013, https://store.mintel.com/fast-casual-restaurants-us-october -2013.

186 *In Louisville, one of KFC's new model stores:* Author visit, Louisville, Ky., August 17, 2015.

187 *The first, full-scale Chick-fil-A store in New York City:* Stephanie Strom, "Chick-fil-A Brings Its Sandwich, and Its Values, to New York," *New York Times,* September 30, 2015.

187 *"Overall, we had a strategy to bring Arby's":* Author interview with Arby's CEO Paul Brown, December 3, 2015.

188 *"The fact that we do sixtyish percent of our business":* Ibid.

189 *In 2014, White Castle raised some eyebrows:* "White Castle Unveils Veggie Slider," White Castle, December 30, 2014, https://www .whitecastle.com/about/company/news/white-castle-unveils -veggie-slider.

189 *Burger King has also offered a Morningstar Farms–produced:* Victoria Zunitch, "Burger King Serves Up Veggie Burger," CNN, March 14, 2002, https://money.cnn.com/2002/03/14/news /companies/burgerking_veggie/.

190 *Wendy's expanded the test market:* Melinda McKee, "Wendy's Expands Vegan Options," PETA, 2016, https://www.peta.org /living/food/wendys-vegan-black-bean-burger/.

191 *disgraced former Illinois governor Rod Blagojevich:* "After Stop at Burger Place, Blagojevich Enters Prison," *Chicago Tribune,* March 15, 2012, https://www.chicagotribune.com/news/local /breaking/chi-blago-leaves-home-for-colorado-prison-20120315 -story.html.

191 *24 percent of death-row inmates have burgers:* "Study: Death Row Inmates Pick Comfort Foods for Last Meals," Associated Press, August 29, 2012, https://www.cbsnews.com/news/study-death -row-inmates-pick-comfort-foods-for-last-meals/.

191 *At a store in Wichita, the booths were squeezed:* Author visit, Wichita, Kans., August 4, 2015.

192 *the 150-unit company had launched:* Freddy's, "Freddy's Opens 21 Stores in 21 Weeks," *QSR*, June 3, 2015, https://www.qsrmagazine .com/news/freddys-opens-21-stores-21-weeks.

192 *"We opened our first Freddy's":* Author interview with Freddy's cofounder Randy Simon, August 4, 2015.

192 *Gus would wait until the restaurant was full:* "History," Steak 'n Shake, http://www.steaknshake.com/history.asp.

192 *Shake Shack founder and restaurant mogul Danny Meyer:* Florence Fabricant, "Steak 'n Shake Comes to New York," *New York Times*, January 9, 2012, https://dinersjournal.blogs.nytimes.com/2012 /01/09/steak-n-shake-comes-to-new-york/.

194 *Chipotle . . . suffered through one of the more astonishing:* "Timeline: Tracking Chipotle's Food Safety Crisis," January 22, 2016, http://www.nrn.com/stub-1616/.

194 *their co-CEOs had their 2015 salaries cut in half:* Hayley Peterson, "Chipotle CEOs' Insanely High Pay Was Just Cut in Half," *Business Insider*, March 13, 2016, https://www.businessinsider .com/chipotle-ceos-pay-cut-in-half-2016-3.

194 *one outbreak happened in the midst of the company's:* Mike Benner, "Chipotles Close in Ore., Wash., After 22 Sick from *E. coli*," *USA Today*, October 31, 2015, https://www.usatoday.com/story/news /nation/2015/10/31/e-coli-chipotle/74944642/.

194 *it poached Brian Niccol:* Danny Klein, "Chipotle Names Taco Bell's Brian Niccol CEO," *QSR*, February 2018, https://www .qsrmagazine.com/fast-casual/chipotle-names-taco-bells-brian -niccol-ceo.

195 *main items at fast-casual restaurants averaged:* Shereen Lehman, "'Fast Casual' Restaurant Dishes Have More Calories Than Fast Food," Reuters, June 1, 2016, https://www.reuters.com/article/us -health-calories-fast-casual-idUSKCN0YN5QT.

195 *"While being aware of calories and sodium can be helpful":* Ibid.

195 *"Most orders at Chipotle give you close":* Kevin Quealy, Amanda Cox, and Josh Katz, "At Chipotle, How Many Calories Do People Really Eat?," *New York Times*, February 17, 2015, https://www.nytimes .com/interactive/2015/02/17/upshot/what-do-people-actually -order-at-chipotle.html.

196 *consumers aged forty-five or older:* Darren Tristano, "This Is Why All the Top Burger Chains Are Launching Value Menus," *Forbes*, January 18, 2016, https://www.forbes.com/sites/darrentristano /2016/01/18/this-is-why-all-the-top-burger-chains-are-launching -value-menus/#11e74fb528f6.

CHAPTER 15: THE LONESOME HOURS

197 *She explained that she'd grown up:* Unless otherwise noted, all information comes from an author interview with Sara Dappen in Story City, Iowa, August 7, 2015.

198 *Between 1977 and 2007, the employment rate of workers:* "Are There More Older People in the Workplace?," Bureau of Labor Statistics, US Department of Labor, July 2008, https://www.bls.gov /spotlight/2008/older_workers/.

199 *By the second quarter of 2017:* Ben Steverman, "Working Past 70: Americans Can't Seem to Retire," Bloomberg, July 10, 2017, https://www.bloomberg.com/news/articles/2017-07-10/working -past-70-americans-can-t-seem-to-retire.

199 *In the 1980s, as more and more American teenagers:* Ben Steverman, "Why Aren't American Teenagers Working Anymore?," Bloomberg, June 5, 2017, https://www.bloomberg.com/news/articles /2017-06-05/why-aren-t-american-teenagers-working-anymore.

199 *a number of lower-wage businesses and retailers:* Kerry Segrave, *Age Discrimination by Employers* (Jefferson, N.C.: McFarland, 2001), 167–68.

200 *Between 2000 and 2018, the number of American teens:* Rachel Abrams and Robert Gebeloff, "A Fast-Food Problem: Where Have All the Teenagers Gone?," *New York Times*, May 3, 2018, https:// www.nytimes.com/2018/05/03/upshot/fast-food-jobs-teenagers -shortage.html.

200 *The median age of a fast-food worker:* Alan Feuer, "Life on $7.25 an Hour," *New York Times*, November 28, 2013, https://www.nytimes .com/2013/12/01/nyregion/older-workers-are-increasingly -entering-fast-food-industry.html.

200 *seven of the ten lowest-paying jobs in the United States:* Danielle Kurtzleben, "The 10 Lowest-Paid Jobs in America," *U.S. News & World Report*, March 29, 2013, https://www.usnews.com/news /articles/2013/03/29/the-10-lowest-paid-jobs-in-america.

200 *lists of anointed luminaries for whom the fast-food industry:* Sharon Feiereisen, "27 Celebrities Who Worked at Fast Food Places," Yahoo, December 12, 2016, https://www.yahoo.com/news/27 -celebrities-worked-fast-food-220259385.html.

201 *he lost part of his middle finger:* Greg Morabito, "The Time Rahm Emanuel Sliced Off His Finger at Arby's," Eater, March 22, 2010, https://www.eater.com/2010/3/22/6739591/the-time-rahm -emanuel-sliced-off-his-finger-at-arbys.

201 *In 1996, McDonald's estimated that one of out every eight:* Schlosser, *Fast Food Nation*, 4.

201 *Jeff Bezos once gloated that he can still:* Charles Fishman, "Face Time with Jeff Bezos," *Fast Company*, January 1, 2001, https://www .fastcompany.com/42412/face-time-jeff-bezos.

201 *"Time is very important":* "McDonald's New TV Ad Fights 'McJob' Image," Reuters, September 21, 2005, https://www.foxnews.com /story/mcdonalds-new-tv-ad-fights-mcjob-image.

201 *Usain Bolt, who infamously ate one thousand:* Laura Stampler, "Usain Bolt Ate 100 Chicken McNuggets a Day in Beijing and Somehow Won Three Gold Medals," *Time*, November 4, 2013, http://time .com/3912896/usain-bolt-chicken-mcnuggets-olympics/.

201 *"I remember thinking that McDonald's":* Bloomberg, "McDonald's Famous Former Burger Flippers," August 17, 2012, https://www .bloomberg.com/news/photo-essays/2012-08-17/mcdonalds -famous-former-burger-flippers.

202 *"I don't know about you":* Ibid.

202 *Her story inspired such headlines as:* Heather Schwedel, "A 94-Year-Old Woman Who's Worked at McDonald's for 44 Years Is Making the Rest of Us Look Bad," Slate, March 27, 2017, http:// www.slate.com/blogs/xx_factor/2017/03/27_94_year_old_loraine _maurer_has_worked_at_mcdonald_s_in_indiana_for_44_years .html.

203 *"Evansville Woman, 94":* McCabe Brown, "Evansville Woman, 94, Still Going Strong 44 Years into Mcdonald's Job": *Evansville (Ind.) Courier & Press*, March 23, 2017, https://www.courierpress.com /story/life/2017/03/23/evansville-woman-94-still-going-strong-44 -years-into-mcdonalds-job/99529688/.

203 *"sunshine of this place":* Joi-Marie McKenzie, "94-Year-Old Woman Celebrates 44 Years Working at McDonald's," ABC, March 26,

2017, https://abcnews.go.com/Lifestyle/94-year-woman-celebrates -44-years-working-mcdonalds/story?id=46386408.

203 she "would never be a manager": Brown, "Evansville Woman."

203 "I'd been in the food business all my life": Eric Robinette, "93-Year-Old Wendy's Employee Going Strong," *Dayton (Ohio) Daily News*, July 13, 2014, https://www.daytondailynews.com/news/year-old -wendy-employee-going-strong/OUOaZruzpIzD54z90dmgfN/.

204 local retirees at a Burger King in Oahu: Carla Herreria, "Every Friday, These Senior Citizens Turn Burger King into a Hawaiian Music Fest," *Huffington Post*, March 6, 2015, https://www .huffingtonpost.com/2015/03/06/hawaiian-singers-burger-king _n_6805518.html.

204 "We are sort of like a family": Julia Bayly, "Fort Kent McDonald's Becomes Unofficial Senior Club as Retirees Gather to Socialize, Play Cards," *Bangor (Maine) Daily News*, December 23, 2012, https://bangordailynews.com/2012/12/23/news/aroostook/fort -kent-mcdonalds-becomes-unofficial-senior-club-as-retirees -gather-to-socialize-play-cards/.

205 "It's how we keep track of each other now": Michael Kimmelman, "The Urban Home Away from Home," *New York Times*, January 28, 2014, https://www.nytimes.com/2014/01/29/arts/design/lessons -from-mcdonalds-clash-with-older-koreans.html.

205 Service with the Speed of Sound: Ronald Nykiel, *Handbook of Marketing Research Methodologies for Hospitality and Tourism* (Binghamton, N.Y.: Haworth Press, 2007), 166.

205 a 2008 study published in the Journal of the American Dietetic Association: Sarah A. Rydell, Lisa J. Harnack, J. Michael Oakes, Mary Story, Robert W. Jeffery, and Simone A. French, "Why Eat at Fast-Food Restaurants: Reported Reasons Among Frequent Consumers," *Journal of the American Dietetic Association*, December 2008, https://www.sciencedirect.com/science/article /pii/S0002822308017288.

206 A full third responded that fast-food restaurants offer: Ibid.

206 "On Tuesdays, there is a bingo game": Chris Arnade, "McDonald's: You Can Sneer, but It's the Glue That Holds Communities Together," *Guardian*, June 8, 2016, https://www.theguardian.com /business/2016/jun/08/mcdonalds-community-centers-us -physical-social-networks.

206 *"If you give people a world of sterile fast-food places":* Author interview with Chris Arnade, November 9, 2016.

207 *The McDonald's on West Florissant:* Author visit to Ferguson, Mo., August 8, 2015.

208 *"When a protestor blasted with tear gas":* Matt Pearce, "Ferguson McDonald's a Haven amid Protests and Tear Gas," *Los Angeles Times*, August 21, 2014, https://www.latimes.com/nation/la-na -nn-ferguson-mcdonalds-20140821-story.html.

209 *Coffee with a Cop, a national initiative:* "About," Coffee with a Cop, https://coffeewithacop.com/about/.

209 *A Whataburger in northwest Florida:* Ibid.

209 *"no speeches or agendas, just a chance":* "Coffee with a Cop," City of Dayton, June 29, 2017, https://www.daytonohio.gov/Calendar .aspx?EID=373.

209 *"When our officers engage people in different ways":* "Coffee with a Cop," https://www.facebook.com/DutchBrosAlbanyOR/.

210 *"My husband and I want to make sure":* John Dykstra, "Manteno Police: 'We Are Just Like Everybody Else,'" *Kankakee (Ill.) Daily Journal*, August 21, 2017, https://coffeewithacop.com/media-news /manteno-police-we-are-just-like-everybody-else/.

EPILOGUE

213 *"If you want an example of how":* Yoav Gonen, "De Blasio Lends a Hand to Fast-Food Workers with New Proposal," *New York Post*, September 16, 2016, https://nypost.com/2016/09/16/de-blasio -lends-a-hand-to-fast-food-workers-with-new-proposal/.

213 *"the nation's fast-food president":* Ashley Parker, "He'll Have Fries with That," *New York Times*, August 8, 2016, https://www .nytimes.com/2016/08/09/us/politics/donald-trump-diet.html.

213 *Mike Pence also posted a picture of himself:* Catherine Garcia, "The Trump/Pence Ticket Really, Really Likes Kentucky Fried Chicken," *Week*, August 22, 2016, https://theweek.com /speedreads/644453/trumppence-ticket-really-really-likes -kentucky-fried-chicken.

215 *"the perfect example of classic American fast food":* Jackson Connor and Zachary Harris, "14 Quotes About In-N-Out Burger from Chefs, Rappers, and Other Celebrities," First We Feast, November 28, 2016, https://firstwefeast.com/eat/2016/11/famous-quotes

-about-in-n-out-burger/jaden-smith; "The Best Fast Food in America: *Esquire*'s Chef Survey," *Esquire*, August 10, 2009, https://www.esquire.com/food-drink/restaurants/g289/top-fast-food-restaurants-0909/.

215 *Laurent Tourondel . . . is partial to the Burger King Whopper*: "*Esquire*'s Chef Survey."

215 *"the jewel in the King crown"*: Ruby Tandoh, "Eating Dirty with Ruby Tandoh #5: Burger King," *Vice*, April 21, 2016, https://www.vice.com/en_uk/article/ex9qqm/eating-dirty-with-ruby-tandoh-5-burger-king.

215 *Celebrity fusionist Dale Talde carries the McRib*: Rachel Freeman, "Famous Chefs Reveal Their Favorite Fast-Food Chains and What They Order," Thrillist, July 27, 2014, https://www.thrillist.com/eat/nation/famous-chefs-share-their-favorite-fast-food-chains.

215 *"Who doesn't like spicy, delicious, perfectly greasy"*: "*Esquire*'s Chef Survey."

215 *Craig Hopson . . . favors Jack in the Box*: Ibid.

INDEX